# ASTONISHING C[...]

Second editio[n]

*To Tony Constable*

*Best wishes*

*Mike*

Michael Lawrence 2011

Notori

**Front cover by Hannah Lawrence**

SECOND EDITION

Astonishing credulity
Michael Lawrence

Printed and bound in the UK by the MPG Group
Bodmin and King's Lynn
2011
: +44 (0)1553 764 728
enquiries@mpg-biddles.co.uk
www.biddles.co.uk

Published by
Notori 2011
www.notori.co.uk
mike.lawrence100@ntlworld.com
07790 034362

ISBN- 978-0-9568166-0-3

## Acknowledgments

I wish to acknowledge the following groups, and people, for their help in forming the content of this book, by way of feed back - both adverse and favourable - to the 'Just Suppose' presentations.

North London Humanist Group
Humanist Society of West Yorkshire
Essex Humanists
Bedford Humanists
South Place Ethical Society
Milton Keynes Humanists
Sutton Humanist Group
Lewisham Humanist Group
Suffolk Humanists and Secularists
Chiltern Humanists
Watford Area Humanists
Guildford Humanist Group
Coventry & Warwickshire Humanists

Special gratitude goes to Hannah Lawrence for the front cover illustration, and to John Dowdle, President of the Watford Area Humanists, for his help with the editing of this second edition.

# Contents

To

My wife and my girls


Thank you for your support

# --Introduction--

The subject matter of this book evolved out of a personal interest in mythology and theology. However, I am secular, and have always been secular, coming from a non religious family background. I have never considered the religious stories to be anything but stories. In point of fact, I see no real distinction between mythology and theology; save one is considered past defunct beliefs, and the other presently held beliefs.

With this book I aim to create an argument that could be used to convince the powers that be in our country today that we, as a society, should not allow the theological world access to developing young minds through the school curriculum; particularly when such access is used to promote the acceptance of personally held theological beliefs. I formed the view that: if it could be demonstrated that the main figurehead of Christianity is not a character from history, it would be sufficient to use as the opening for a wider debate on the role of religion within the school curriculum and its inclusion in political issues. From this standpoint I believe the book successfully confronts head on the claim from the Church that we cannot use an argument from silence to claim the character 'Jesus of Nazareth' did not exist in history. That is: the Church claim that just because there is no contemporary corroborative writing about the character, of which there is not, does not prove he did not exist. It is interesting though to consider that, if the character did not exist, there would, by default, be no contemporary corroborative writing about him.

The Church as an organisation therefore feels impregnable behind this 'you cannot use an argument from silence' wall. I take the reverse approach. I claim, and demonstrate, that literature does exist which reveals Jesus, as in 'Jesus Christ', existed as an allegorical character long before the dates attributed to the Jesus character from the books of Matthew, Mark, Luke, John and Acts in the New Testament; thereby proving the five books to be updated fictional stories of an ancient allegorical myth, as opposed to factual biographies.

To put the reader into the mindset of this concept: Suppose that today we have been unwittingly duped by the events of history. Suppose that the idea of a Christ figure is centuries older than the literal figure we now know; that he was originally an allegorical figure and today's literal figure is in fact plagiarised from this earlier allegorical version. We might imagine that the allegorical Christ is in effect a myriad of different Christ figures followed by many diverse Christian groups. Further suppose that these allegorical Christ characters have been efficiently eradicated from history by the founders and successors of the Catholic Church over a 900 year period between the years of 325 to 1230 CE. This surmised plagiarism of a literal Christ would be the current version of a Christ figure from the four post-70 CE Bible gospels of Matthew, Mark, Luke and John; The Christ figure taught to us while we are children via religious education in our schools, preached to us by the clergy from the pulpit, and the subject of blockbuster Hollywood movies from the last 80 years. In short, the original allegorical Christ figures are effectively extinct via the burning of literature and the historic silencing of adherents, while the subsequent evolution of the literal Christ figure we identify with is a post-325 CE marketing success story. The two key marker dates to this hypothesis are: the destruction of Jerusalem and its second temple in 70 CE, and the birth of Catholic Christianity under the rule of Constantine in 325 CE. For this hypothesis to stand scrutiny we would have to illustrate that literature does still survive which demonstrates the 'death and resurrection' of a Jesus Christ character did exist as a concept prior to the governorship of Pontius Pilate in Judah. Something which should, of course, be impossible to do if the New Testament gospels of Matthew, Mark, Luke and John are indeed biographical, but not if they are plagiarised fiction.

Having presented the case for a mythical, as opposed to a historic Jesus the book then demonstrates how theological belief evolved from ancient astrology. I present many parallels with naked eye astronomy and mythology. I also demonstrate how these links have found their way from ancient mythology, to form the base line stories in present day theology. The book then tackles the issue of how these newly created theologies came to be entrenched into the psyche of mankind.

So, that being the main content of the book, what is the rationale behind the book? I wish to promote the idea that 'religious theology' is quite simply just 'Iron Age ignorance'. Primitive man of the earliest civilisations did not understand the natural causes of anything. Out of this ignorance religion was born; then came theology, which is essentially the art of verbally expressing the ignorance of religion (adapted slightly from Draper). That is, it was an acceptable description of how the world works, given the knowledge available at the time that description was fashioned. But it was a theology formed in all ignorance of what we now know today. Just as we should also accept that our current scientific view of how the universe works is acceptable today, given the knowledge we have amassed to date. But this view will undoubtedly be seen as ignorant by the people of the fifth millennium, given what humans will find out about the universe over the next two thousand years; things that we today, do not yet know. If we can accept this argument, then it follows that we simply should not be teaching 'Iron Age ignorance' to our children in our schools as stated fact. Moreover, we should promote the view that Christianity is: a massive literal misinterpretation of ancient allegorical stories, on a global scale.

# --Chapter 1: Clement and Barnabas--

Is the Earth the centre of the universe, or just a tiny insignificant part of the universe? Does the Sun travel around the Earth, or does the Earth travel around the Sun? Is the Earth a young recent creation, or is it ancient beyond belief? Could all the stars be very distant suns that might have their own planets? Was Jesus a historic character, or is he a character from an ancient mythical story? Every one of these questions have been put forward in the past and people who dared to voice them have been tortured in the most hideous of fashions; and then executed by the founders of the Christian faith. They were executed for daring to voice such heretic and blasphemous suppositions, every one of these suppositions, including the last one. The irony is: we now know the Christian Church was unequivocally wrong to oppose the first four and they have since adjusted their position. The assumption that Jesus was not a real person, but rather a character in an ancient allegorical story is still opposed to this day; but just suppose they are wrong about that too, all this book requires you to do is just suppose.

Having a keen interest in archaeology, I love to watch the television programme 'Time Team'; it is both entertaining and educational. It helps one understand the more simplistic high level concepts of archaeology and it enables the viewer to gain more from reading archaeological books, and from watching archaeological programmes. One such concept is the understanding of strata. Strata are the sequential layers of sediment in which fossils and artefacts can be found. Knowledge of strata is of vital importance when attempting to date finds. Of equal importance, is answering the question: does an object sit in the correct strata? If this is not ascertained, an object could be allocated an incorrect date. This can occur via the disturbance of the ground and the archaeological objects it contains; my back garden provides a good example. When I dig in my garden I find old white clay smoking pipes and small animal bones in abundance; what does this tell me about the historic location of my house? Well, absolutely nothing, since my house is built into the side of a hill and the ground at the back of my house, my back garden, has been raised in order to create a level plane. At some time in the past, lorry loads of earth have been transported in to affect the levelling; the earth could have come from anywhere.

Another excellent example of the need to understand strata comes from a particular episode of Time Team. In this episode the team were asked to investigate an area of land in an extensive garden which produced interesting geophysical results. After selecting an area, opening a small trench and digging down, the team discovered the rusty remains of a sword. This was greeted with some excitement at first, but then one of the team voiced concern. The team member said *"it is too shallow; it is in the wrong strata"*. The team therefore dug further down and discovered barbed wire running underneath the sword and off in both directions for some distance. This demonstrates the usefulness of understanding strata precisely. It is not possible for a pre-twentieth century sword, left lying on the ground and subsequently buried and left undisturbed for centuries, to be laying above twentieth century barbed wire. The sword must therefore have been placed in its current location long after the barbed wire had become buried in the ground. The sword therefore betrayed itself as a hoax, and it betrayed itself as a hoax because it had been placed into the wrong strata.

Over a period of time, an artefact will develop a natural coating of a certain chemical composition created from its surroundings. This coating is much like a chemical fingerprint and is known as patina. As with strata, patina can also help to determine the age of artefacts; and for those artefacts which did not originate from a recognised archaeological dig, the ones which just mysteriously appear on the antiquities market, it can be used to ascertain whether they are genuine or fake. There are some very recent examples of the use of this technique. They include an ornamental ivory pomegranate inscribed with ancient text which suggests the artefact came from Solomon's temple, and an ossuary, which is a stone box used to house the bones of dead relatives, inscribed with the words *"James son of Joseph brother of Jesus"*. The patinas from an area on the surface of each artefact and from inside the inscription grooves were tested. If the inscriptions had been placed on the artefacts at the time they were made, the patina inside the inscription grooves would be identical in chemical make up to the patina on the surface area of the rest of the artefact. The patina from the surface of these artefacts was found to be ancient, but the patina from the grooves was found to be recent in origin, very recent. Since a patina results from the area in which an artefact resides over its lifetime, the tests proved that, although the artefacts were indeed ancient, the inscriptions were not. Experts in this field have now identified both of these inscriptions as forgeries.

Can the knowledge of strata and patina have any useful application outside of archaeology; say for example with ancient literature? Well, not physically, but the concept can be transferred to literature in a conceptual capacity quite effectively. Any piece of writing might or might not give clues as to its order and possible date of authorship by elements written within in the work; for example: if work A makes reference to work B, work B clearly comes first in order of authorship. If work C makes specific reference to a historically recognised and dateable event, work C would clearly have been written after that event took place. If work D displays complete ignorance of a well known world event, work D would have been written before that event took place. Consider a work entitled 'The

Unconquered Everest', this would clearly have been written before 29<sup>th</sup> May 1953. The use of prominent historical characters in a text can also be used in this way; any work citing Adolf Hitler as Chancellor of Germany cannot have been written until after Hitler became Chancellor. On a similar vein, the use of place names can be used to locate a story; they can also date a story if archaeology already knows when that place first existed, and when it became derelict or was destroyed. The tense used when describing events also helps. Qumran by the west bank of the Dead Sea can help illustrate this: archaeology demonstrates when it was built and occupied, history and archaeology demonstrates when it was destroyed. Any text which talks of human activity within Qumran in the present tense would have been written between these dates. Text which talks of human activity at Qumran in the past tense might have been written at any time during, or after occupation.

When we take the ideas and principles above and apply them to the works inside the New Testament, the result is quite shocking. Moreover, the Christian community are not going to like the unquestionable result it produces. The results show that the Jesus story from the New Testament is in the wrong strata, it is a new patina made up and painted in to a groove. That conceptual groove in terms of dates is circa post-70 CE. Literary evidence does exist which demonstrates the concept of a dying and resurrecting character called Jesus was circulating as an allegorical belief long before 30 CE; the accepted date of the crucifixion of Jesus. The concepts of strata and patina also demonstrate that the idea of a physical Jesus being crucified and physically resurrecting, as portrayed in the Matthew, Mark, Luke, John and Acts stories from the New Testament, did not exist until after 70 CE.

In the heart of Jerusalem on the top of the second temple remains, sits the Dome of the Rock, also called the Temple Mount; it is the most contentious site of the three Abrahamic faiths of Judaism, Christianity and Islam. For the Jews it is the reputed site of the first temple to Yahweh,

Solomon's temple, and the confirmed site of the second temple to Yahweh constructed after the enforced Jewish exile to Babylon of 586 BCE. According to Jewish tradition, the natural stone platform now encompassed by the structure of the dome is the site where Abraham prepared to sacrifice his son Isaac. For Christians, it is the location of Jesus' act of defiance to the Jewish authorities inside the temple walls, where he confronts the money lenders and sellers of sacrificial animals by upending all the tables and chasing the traders out of the temple grounds; a scene the New Testament asserts he was compelled to commit in order to achieve sacrifice by execution. For Islam, the rock platform is the location from which Muhammad set out on his famous night journey whereby he ascended to heaven to meet with Allah, accompanied by the angel Gabriel.

The date for the destruction of the first temple to Yahweh by the Neo-Babylonian Empire is given as the nineteenth year of the reign of Nebuchadnezzar, which equates to 586 BCE. The date for the opening ceremony after the completion of the rebuilding of the temple, the second temple, is given as the sixth year of the reign of the Persian King Darius which is 516 BCE, exactly seventy years later. The second Jewish temple to Yahweh is destroyed by the Roman General Titus in the second year of the reign of Vespasian, which equates to 70 CE; or seventy years after the supposed birth of the Jesus character. Muhammad has to flee Mecca in order to escape persecution following the communication of his recitals from Allah. This is known as the Hijra, which is alleged to have taken place in 622 CE. The date for the construction of the Islamic Dome of the Rock, on top of the rock from which Muhammad started his night journey to Allah, is recorded to be 692 CE, exactly seventy years after the self-styled Hijra.

One of the main aims of this book is to call into question the reputed historicity of the Jesus character by the Christian faithful. Therefore the gap of seventy years between the alleged birth of a character called

9

Jesus and the date of the second temple destruction will be cross examined. But we should note that all three date pairs above comprise a specific gap between connected major religious events of exactly seventy years; coincidence or contrived? We shall see!

With the background detail covered, we will now turn our attention to the literature of the New Testament. The New Testament is made up of twenty-seven separate works; some of which are stories and some letters. In fact, five are past tense stories, one is a future tense prophecy and the remaining twenty-one are present tense correspondence commonly referred to as epistles. The four past tense stories entitled Matthew, Mark, Luke and John come first in the New Testament in order of display, which is not necessarily the order of authorship. All tell what is purported to be the life of a person known as Jesus of Nazareth. All four of these works cite certain places, events and historic characters which allow us to ascertain an earliest possible date of authorship. They also allow us to apply a date to the birth and death of the main character, being Jesus of Nazareth. Today those dates are accepted as 4 BCE to 6 CE for the birth and circa 30 CE for the death. The fifth past tense story entitled Acts then picks up the thread and tells of the creation of the Church of Jesus Christ after the death and resurrection scene. Millions of people, all over the world, consider the five works of Matthew, Mark, Luke, John and Acts to be factual accounts; biographies. No one in the world wide Christian community considers them to be fictional stories with a main character by the name of Jesus Christ. The interesting thing is, nowhere in the five books do they ever specifically claim to be historical biographies or fictitious allegorical stories. The main key is, whether allegorical stories or historic accounts, the first four works depict a death sentence imposed by a Roman governor of Judah called Pontius Pilate; this death sentence was announced in the location of Jerusalem. They then state that after the death sentence had been administered the character came back to life physically and then spiritually

10

ascended to heaven. The first four books then allude to, and the fifth book portrays, the creation of a church movement by a character named Paul, also known as Saul of Tarsus; this church being the Church of Jesus Christ who was sacrificed and resurrected on the third day.

This is where the concepts of strata and patina come in. If we are to accept the texts of Matthew, Mark, Luke, John and Acts as biographies; then, due to the specific date tags within in their literature, the Church of Jesus Christ, which celebrates the resurrection of Jesus Christ, cannot possibly have existed anywhere in the world before the governorship of Pontius Pilate in Judah. Pontius Pilate was governor in Judah from 26 CE to 36 CE. So no such church could exist before 26 CE, be it physical or allegorical. Now, suppose we could find ancient literature, which when dated via similar means reveals that it was in existence before Pontius Pilate became governor of Judah, and, that literature made positive reference to the concept of a crucifixion of Jesus Christ. Can you see the problem? It would be like the sword in the episode of Time Team; something would be in the wrong strata. It would demonstrate that the five books of Matthew, Mark, Luke, John and Acts are in fact plagiarised fictitious stories and not biographies. It would further demonstrate that there could not possibly have been a crucifixion of a man named Jesus of Nazareth, in Jerusalem, by a governor named Pontius Pilate, circa 30 CE. It could not have happened, because the concept of a character named Jesus Christ being crucified and returning to life already existed before that date. Matthew, Mark, Luke, John and Acts would then all be contemporary reworked versions from the first century CE, of an already ancient mythical story. Well, literature does exist which identifies the concept of Jesus' crucifixion being in existence before 26 CE, and it does prove that the almost identical plots of Matthew, Mark, Luke and John, along with the story from Acts, are expanded and enhanced rewordings of a fictitious mythical story. This means that today's common understanding of the Jesus character, force-fed to our ancestors by

11

the Catholic Church, is a colossal, global and longstanding misinterpretation of the original content of a story which started life as mythical, not factual.

Before revealing the literature concerned, we first need to look at the twenty-seven works in the New Testament and use the tags within the texts to find earliest and latest possible authorship dates. To do this I will split the work in to two groups. Group one I will call 'literal', not because I believe them to be literal, but because the Church tell us they are literal. They are the four gospels of Matthew, Mark, Luke and John, which tell the story of Jesus from birth to death and resurrection, and Acts, which tells the story of the creation of the Church after resurrection. Group two I will call 'allegorical', because none of their content references the life of Jesus. They are letters written to a church, or a person within a church. The first thirteen letters being: 'Romans', 'One Corinthians', 'Two Corinthians', 'Galatians', 'Ephesians', 'Philippians', 'Colossians', 'One Thessalonians', 'Two Thessalonians', 'One Timothy', 'Two Timothy', 'Titus', and 'Philemon' are purported to have been written by a character called Paul or Saul of Tarsus. The next eight being: 'Hebrews', 'James', 'One Peter', 'Two Peter', 'One John', 'Two John', 'Three John' and 'Jude' are of unknown authorship. Also in this group is a prophecy called 'Revelation' which foretells man's last days on earth before its impending destruction. It is important to note that group one are past tense stories; the letters in group two are present tense correspondence and Revelation is a future tense prophecy. It is also important to note that while the letters make endless reference to "*the gospel*" or "*scripture*", the four Bible gospels are not the only gospels to talk of a character called Jesus. There are countless gospels of a character called Jesus, and they all conflict in their portrayal of the character, and they all come from a different time frame. So to assume that the letters of group two are referencing the gospels of Matthew, Mark, Luke and John from group one whenever they mention "*the gospel*" is an unfounded assumption.

If we place all twenty-seven works in chronological order, we not only see that the works are displayed in the New Testament in almost reverse order, we also see why. They are in reverse order so as to plant the story of Jesus as per Matthew, Mark, Luke, John and Acts into the reader's mind before the reader encounters the letters of the apostles. The reader will then read the letters with the full story from Matthew, Mark, Luke, John and Acts already implanted into his/her psyche. So when the letters claim "*the Lord Jesus Christ raised from the dead*", which they frequently do, the reader then subconsciously overlays the rest of the story from Matthew, Mark, Luke, John and Acts. However, as we shall see, the letters actually came first by a significant time frame, and they contain none of the account of the story found in Matthew, Mark, Luke, John and Acts.

We will now date the works I have classed as literal from group one. Matthew chapter twenty-four, Mark chapter thirteen and Luke chapter twenty-one all narrate a prophecy of the destruction of Jerusalem, and the temple of Jerusalem. The New Testament gospels also make reference to Caesar, which puts the Roman rule of Palestine into the back drop of the stories, so we can assume the second temple here and disregard the first temple because the first temple was destroyed some 500 years before the Roman rule of Palestine began. We do know that Jerusalem and its temple were destroyed during the climax of the Roman/Jewish war of 66 to 70 CE. Now, you cannot write about an event until after it has happened, so we can therefore place an earliest possible date of authorship for Matthew, Mark, and Luke as 70 CE. Acts is believed to have been written by the same author as Luke and to be a continuation of Luke. John does not make specific mention of the temple destruction, but scholars from the theological and atheist world alike seem to agree that John was written after Matthew, Mark and Luke, and in the last decade of the first century CE. This dates Matthew, Mark, Luke, John and Acts to a date after 70 CE. How long after is still a matter of fierce debate but does not concern the main hypothesis of this book. It is sufficient to establish that all five works were written after 70 CE.

We will now move on to the works of group two; being the twenty-one letters and the Book of Revelation. The first thirteen letters are attributed to Paul or Saul of Tarsus, and in three separate places the author talks in the present tense of worshiping and making sacrifice in the temple of Jerusalem. In the letter called Two Corinthians, which is attributed to Paul, Paul talks of being whipped by Romans and whipped by Jews and being in danger while in Damascus during the reign of King Aretas. This would indicate King Aretas IV, who reigned as King of the Nabataeans from around 9 BCE to 40 CE. From the remaining eight letters, two others, Hebrews and One Peter also talk in the present tense of worshipping and making sacrifice at the temple. Revelation talks in the future tense of offering sacrifice at the temple. This dates the bulk of the letters, and with a little intuition all of them, along with the Book of Revelation to a date prior to 70 CE; this being the case, the letters, and the Book of Revelation, all predate Matthew, Mark, Luke, John and Acts. But none of the letters, nor the Book of Revelation, display any knowledge of the version of the Jesus story related in Matthew, Mark, Luke, John and Acts.

I must add one small caveat to that last statement: One Timothy makes one reference to Pontius Pilate, when the author, who identifies himself as Paul, talks of Jesus standing before Pontius Pilate; and this is the only direct reference to a specific piece of data from the Jesus story in Matthew, Mark, Luke, John and Acts from all of the letters, and definitely the only reference to Pilate. But One Timothy, and Two Timothy, are composed as present tense correspondence from Paul to Timothy while Paul is in prison, awaiting execution; Two Timothy ends just prior to the implied execution. It is highly doubtful that a prisoner incarcerated by the Roman authorities and awaiting execution is going to be given the privilege of writing materials, much less access to a personal delivery service. For this reason (and other compelling reasons) One, and Two Timothy, are widely accepted by scholars to be forgeries and cannot therefore be properly dated. in fact the scholarly consensus is that One and Two Timothy are both post-90 CE and contemporary with the first appearances of the Matthew, Mark, Luke, and John stories. It is, at the time of writing, undeniably correct to say that we do not possess any Christian literature, which dates to 70 CE or before, which displays any knowledge of the Matthew, Mark, Luke, John and Acts versions of the Jesus story.

While the letters from the New Testament and the Book of Revelation can definitely be dated to sometime before 70 CE, the only other workable date tag is a reference to King Aretas who reigned from 9 BCE onwards; therefore the letters could have been written anywhere between post-9 BCE and pre-70 CE. We only assume the New Testament letters were written between 30 CE (reputed date of Jesus' crucifixion) and 70 CE (destruction of the temple) because that is what the Church tell us to believe; and this mindset is reinforced by placing Matthew, Mark, Luke, John and Acts before the letters within the structure of the New Testament. In harsh reality the Church has to insist that the letters are written after 30 CE, despite there being no solid evidence to prove the claim, because if any one of the letters were believed to have been written before 26 CE, they would have been written before Pontius Pilate became governor of Judah. This would in turn prove that Matthew, Mark, Luke, John and Acts are mythical stories about a fictitious character and not biographical; clearly an idea which the Church cannot possibly promote. It is true that there is a mention of Paul being imprisoned by Gallio while in Corinth, and Gallio did not become Pro Consul of Achaia until 51 CE to 53 CE, but this excerpt comes from Acts, not Paul's letters. Paul did not write Acts, and Paul himself does not make this claim about Gallio within his letters.

We can now prove that the New Testament letters were written before the Jesus story of Matthew, Mark, Luke, John and Acts. But when we read these letters and the Book of Revelation without the tainted prior knowledge of the story in Matthew, Mark, Luke, John and Acts one strong fact comes through. The resurrection of the Jesus in these works is purely spiritual. None of the letters quote a physical reappearance of the character. Also, many of the letters allude to the whole process as being spiritual, in that the character never existed on earth, and the remainder place a physical being on earth, who is physically crucified, and then spiritually resurrects. The letters go no further than stating 'Jesus Christ was crucified and resurrected for our sins'. That is it; that is all they say! None of the letters contain any account of: the nativity scene with the virgin birth and Mary and Joseph, John the Baptist, Herod, the slaughter of the innocents, the miracles, the teachings, the last supper, the betrayal, the trial, any of the locations (Nazareth, Bethlehem, Jerusalem) within the context of the Jesus story, or the physical resurrection and reappearances. There is no way to construct any of the Jesus story according to Matthew, Mark, Luke, John and Acts by reading any of the letters or the Book of Revelation; and we have seen, the letters were written first.

Having dated the works in group one (literal) and group two (allegorical), it is entirely reasonable to assume that the letters were written first and have no knowledge of the Jesus story in Matthew, Mark, Luke, John and Acts; and that Matthew, Mark, Luke, John and Acts came much later, very much later, and adapt and enhance certain elements from the letters; in doing so they create a story! We can therefore say, whether true or false, it is a legitimate possibility that the story simply did not exist at the time the letters were written. So did the full story exist or not? How much earlier than 70 CE were the letters written? Did a Gnostic allegorical version of a Jesus being crucified and resurrecting on the third day exist before Pilate's governorship in 26 CE?

It is now time to reveal the ancient literature referred to earlier in this chapter. There is a work, of which only one reproduction remains in

existence, which has been given the title of the 'First Epistle of Clement'. Its content was unknown to us until it was found in a book now called the Alexandrian Codex which was discovered in 1628. The book is believed to have been written during the fifth century CE, and contains the Greek Septuagint (Old Testament), the New Testament epistles and gospels, plus two other epistles referred to as one and two Clement. Therefore, the work we are interested in - the one called the First Epistle of Clement - used to be included in the New Testament canon, but has long since been removed.

The letter itself does not state who the author was, or when it was written, but the Church have seen fit to allocate the letter to the Bishop Clement of Rome, dated it to circa 96 CE and claim it is the earliest non-biblical text in existence which makes reference to Jesus. The First Epistle of Clement is a letter from the 'Church of God' at Rome to the 'Church of God' at Corinth in Achaia. Eusebius, the early fourth century CE Church historian, tells us the following in his 'History of the Church' Book 3 chapter 34: *"In the bishopric of Rome, in the third year of Trajan's reign, Clement departed this life, yielding his office to Evarestus. He had been in charge of the teaching of the divine message for nine years in all."* This places Clement as Bishop of Rome firmly between 91 and 100 CE. The Church argues that the letter was written towards the end of Clement's office due to a mention of persecutions within the letter. The Church appoints the alleged persecutions to the Emperor Domitian. Domitian was assassinated in 96 CE, so the Church therefore postulates that the letter must have been written by Clement in 96 CE. In the letter, written in the present tense, we find the following caption: Chapter XXIII *"...as the scripture also bears witness, saying, speedily will He come, and will not tarry; and, The Lord shall suddenly come to His temple, even the Holy One, for whom ye look."* Here, the author is quoting existing scripture (past tense) as a present tense message. We could then assume that the Lords temple has not yet been destroyed and still stands. Then, in Chapter XLI we find: *"...Not in*

*every place, brethren, are the daily sacrifices offered, or the peace offerings, or the sin-offerings and the trespass-offerings, but in Jerusalem only. And even there they are not offered in any place, but only at the altar before the temple, that which is offered being first carefully examined by the high priest and the ministers already mentioned."* If the first caption left us in any doubt as to the state of the temple in Jerusalem, this second caption expels all doubt. At the time this letter was written the temple had not yet been destroyed.

By 96 CE the temple in Jerusalem had been destroyed and disused for a full twenty-six years. It is not possible, or at least highly improbable, that members of the church in Rome circa 96 CE would have been unaware of the temple destruction of 70 CE, particularly since the vestments of the temple, and the Jewish slaves from the war, were paraded through the streets of Rome in Titus' victory parade in 71 CE; also, the scene of the destruction is depicted on the Arch of Titus in the forum in the centre of Rome, a structure which was completed in 82 CE. It seems therefore logical to conclude that a Christian resident of Rome in 96 CE would be fully aware that the temple had been destroyed and would not have written about the temple, and temple activities, in a manner which suggests the temple still stands and still functions. However, a Christian resident of Rome writing pre-70 CE is not in possession of such information since at this time in history, the temple still stands and still operates, and this is exactly the thought process displayed in this letter. So the letter must have originally been written before 70 CE. Furthermore, unless the Church dates for a Bishop Clement of Rome are incorrect, it could not have been written by Clement. Another problem with the Church interpretation of the letter is that the persecutions can no longer be attributed to the Emperor Domitian. However, the part which the Church claims alludes to Christian persecution is the following: Chapter I. *"...Owing, dear brethren, to the sudden and successive calamitous events which have happened to ourselves, we feel that we have been somewhat tardy in turning our attention to the points respecting which you consulted us"*, In what fashion does this caption make specific reference to a state organised Christian persecution? This is just one interpretation of hundreds of possible interpretations of this caption. It could refer to the sad loss of dear friends or relatives, or an earth tremor that caused loss of life, or any number of such events. The idea of a persecution is not stated, let alone a specific state organised persecution of Christians. The concept of interpreting chapter one as referencing the persecutions of Domitian is simply beneficial to the date the Church wish to stamp on the letter; a date we have already established as incorrect. We shall also see later in this chapter that the Church have good underhand reasons for wanting to pervert the authorship date of this letter.

The remainder of the letter is comparable to all of the letters in the New Testament in that it displays a complete absence of knowledge of the story of Jesus Christ as per Matthew, Mark, Luke, John and Acts. In fact, in chapter V the author cites examples of Christian heroism from his "...*own generation*". Given that this letter was written before 70 CE, we might expect to find the crucifixion of the leader of the Christian movement in 30 CE to have pride of place in such a list. Chapter V: *"But not to dwell upon ancient examples, let us come to the most recent spiritual heroes. Let us take the noble examples furnished in our own generation. Through envy and jealousy, the greatest and most righteous pillars [of the Church] have been persecuted and put to death. Let us set before our eyes the illustrious apostles. Peter, through unrighteous envy, endured not one or two, but numerous labours and when he had at length suffered martyrdom, departed to the place of glory due to him. Owing to envy, Paul also obtained the reward of patient endurance, after being seven times thrown into captivity, compelled to flee, and stoned. After preaching both in the east and west, he gained the illustrious reputation due to his faith, having taught righteousness to the whole world, and come to the extreme limit of the west, and suffered martyrdom under the prefects. Thus was he removed from the world, and went into the holy place, having proved himself a striking example of patience.*" Incredibly, not only is Jesus not at the top of this list, as we would expect if Matthew, Mark, Luke and John are to be biographies, he does not even make the list. The absence of the martyrdom of Jesus himself in this chapter is astonishing if we are to consider the author to be a literalist Christian; a man who fervently believed a flesh and blood Jesus gave himself up to be crucified, in order to save the souls of all mankind, a mere forty years (or less) ago; a sacrifice which kick-started the Christian faith, the ultimate sacrifice! However, its absence is not entirely remarkable if the crucifixion of Christ is considered by the author to be an ancient allegorical concept, and therefore not a recent example of physical martyrdom.

Whilst this letter displays no knowledge of the story of Jesus Christ as per Matthew, Mark, Luke, John and Acts, It is coincidentally full of Gnostic Christian references and it quotes Old Testament scripture relentlessly; while at every opportunity regurgitating the general phrase 'The Christ Jesus who died for our sins and resurrected on the third day'. The key problem for the Church with this letter is to be found in its historic strata; the statement which makes this letter a smoking gun appears in chapter XLVII, which states: *"It is disgraceful, beloved, yea, highly disgraceful, and unworthy of your Christian profession, that such a thing should be heard of as that the most steadfast and ancient church of the Corinthians should, on account of one or two persons, engage in sedition against its presbyters."*

Take serious note of the adjective *"ancient"* here; it is being used to enhance the noun *"church"*. From the content of the letter, the noun *"church"* is positively indicated to be the Christian church of Corinth in Achaia; according to Acts, the Christian church of Corinth is established after the crucifixion scene of circa 30 CE. In order to ascertain how accurately this text had been translated, prior to drawing any conclusions, I have purchased a reprint of the 1869 translation by J B Lightfoot (Elibron Classics 2007), which contains the Koine Greek script of the last surviving copy of the letter, followed by a general English translation. The section we are concerned with in Greek is as follows: **καί ἀρχαίαν Κορινθίων εκκλησίαν**, the exact English translation is given below:

In Greek:      {**καί ἀρχαίαν Κορινθίων εκκλησίαν**}

In English:      {and ancient  Corinthian  church}

In his 1869 translation, J B Lightfoot (Bishop of Durham) does not translate the word '*ancient*' and I have to wonder why! A note for the critics: some internet versions of J B Lightfoot's translation do translate the word '*ancient*'; however, J B Lightfoot's original text does not and reads as follows: *"It is said indeed that two or three ringleaders should sully the fair fame of the Corinthian church and bring dishonour on the name of Christ."* In his footnotes, J B Lightfoot evades the issue with the following dismissive comment: *"Ἀρχαίαν] this epithet seems hardly consistent with the very early date which some critics would assign to Clements epistle"*. Notice, he does not actually translate the word in the footnote either, so the reader would have to be able to read Greek in order to understand his comment; and if a person could read Greek, why would they need to refer to a translation? Therefore, by not translating the word in the footnotes, J B Lightfoot does not draw undue attention to the use of word. It would appear then that I am not the first person to notice the problem caused by this letters reference to an 'ancient Corinthian church'. J B Lightfoot was also very aware of the problem caused by the use of this adjective. The early date J B Lightfoot refers to is 96 CE, but as the letter must have been written sometime before 70 CE, this further compounds the problem J B Lightfoot is trying to hide.

So to recapitulate, there is no ambiguity here; the text refers to the Christian church of Corinth in Achaia as being *"ancient"*. That is: ancient at the time the letter was written. We have already seen that the letter must have been written before 70 CE because it makes positive present tense reference to the temple in Jerusalem. If Matthew, Mark, Luke, John and Acts are to be factual accounts, no Christian church could exist, anywhere in the world, before 30 CE. This means that the Christian church of Corinth in Achaia can only be a maximum of forty years old at the time the letter called the First Epistle of Clement was written. A maximum - note - so it will have been less than forty years old, because the letter would have been written before the temple was destroyed and the church would have been created after the alleged crucifixion of 30 CE. Less than forty years old is hardly ancient, but the adjective 'ancient' has been used in this letter to describe the church in Achaia. Now, the crucifixion scene is set at around 30 CE, and the church grows up after that date. If the accounts relayed in Acts are to be believed, it will have taken time to establish churches around the known world; starting first in Jerusalem, then spreading to the rest of Palestine and Asia, while moving along the Mediterranean to Italy and Greece at the same time. In fact, Eusebius suggests that nothing happened with reference to leaving Jerusalem for the first twelve years! But for a more accurate Church dating, courtesy of Acts in the New Testament, we can look at Paul's reputed second journey (remember though, this was not written by Paul, and probably without Paul's knowledge or input). Acts 18.1 states: *"After this, Paul left Athens and went to Corinth. There he met a Jew named Aquila, a native of Pontus, who had recently come from Italy with his wife Priscilla, because Claudius had ordered all the Jews to leave Rome"*. In Acts, this is the first visit by an apostle to Corinth and the church in Corinth does not start until after this visit; but, at the time of the visit Claudius is already the Emperor and Claudius did not become Emperor until 41 CE. Then, in Acts 18.12 we have: *"When Gallio was made the Roman governor of Achaia, the Jews got together, seized Paul and took him into court"* Gallio was made Pro Council of Achaia around 51 to 53 CE.

Consul

22

Therefore, according to Acts, and according to official Church dating, Paul's visit to Corinth takes place in 51 CE, and the church in Corinth does not form until after this visit. So, if Matthew, Mark, Luke, John and Acts are to be factual biographies it would mean that the Christian church of Corinth is now only a maximum of nineteen years old at the time the letter called the First Epistle of Clement was written. Moreover, according to Acts it is one of the last churches to be established and therefore would have been very much the 'junior church' at the time the letter was written. So *'fledgling'* would have been a more accurate description than *'ancient'*; and these two words are poles apart in meaning. We must also bear in mind that we still do not know how early the letter was written, only that it was written before 70 CE.

If we take what has been written in this letter at face value, and there is no reason not to, we have to say that ancient implies, at the very least, more than one lifetime; say forty years minimum. in fact the age at the time of writing of an idea concerning the resurrection of a specific Christ known as 'Jesus', is further stated in chapter XXII where we find a plea to the church to be faithful in their belief in Jesus: *"Wretched are they who are of a double mind, and of a doubting heart; who say, 'These things we have heard even in the times of our fathers; but, behold, we have grown old, and none of them has happened unto us'."* This strongly suggests that the concept of the 'crucifixion of Jesus' had already been in existence for at least two generations at the time of the letter's construction. In a translation by Maxwell Stainforth, circa 1944, we have an epilogue to the letter which does not appear in J B Lightfoot's translation. This epilogue reveals who the church of Rome have entrusted to deliver the letter and describes them thus: *"We have sent envoys to you of trustworthiness and discretion, whose lives here among us have been irreproachable from youth to age."* Again we must be mindful that this letter is dispatched from a group identifying themselves as the 'Church of God' which sojourns in Rome to a group known as the 'Church of God' which sojourns in Corinth, and it was written before 70 CE. The envoys of the letter are of "*age*" and have been with the 'Church of God' in Rome since birth. If "*age*" represents a mere forty years old, it would make the 'Church of God' in Rome more than forty years old at the time the letter was dispatched; this would mean that the 'Church of God' in Rome, who worship the crucifixion of Jesus Christ, existed before 30 CE, before the Matthew, Mark, Luke, John and Acts crucifixion scene, and before the apostles are reputed to have left Jerusalem in order to create and spread the 'Church of Jesus Christ'. This would of course be impossible; however, the letter does exist and it does contain the above captions. It would not be impossible if the concept of Jesus existed prior to the Matthew, Mark, Luke, John and Acts literalist version of Jesus; and if the Jesus character identified in this letter had nothing whatsoever to do with the Matthew, Mark, Luke, John and Acts version of the Jesus character. We now have a letter which makes endless references to the 'death and resurrection of Jesus Christ', written some time before 70 CE, which states the concept is already ancient at the time of writing; a concept which stretches back at least one lifetime, at least forty years. This takes the existence of the concept of Jesus being crucified for our sins and resurrecting on the third day, back to a date before 26 CE; the date Pontius Pilate became governor of Judah; and well before 30 CE, the accepted date of the crucifixion. Therefore, Matthew, Mark, Luke, John and Acts cannot possibly be factual accounts; they can only be a circa post-70 CE contemporary fictional take on an already ancient allegorical story; they cannot possibly be true!

We also have to bear in mind, the letter was written before 70 CE; but how long before? The author states in chapter V that Paul and Peter are of his generation and are already martyred. Given Paul's reference to King Aretas, which can be assumed to be King Aretas IV because King Aretas III would be far too early in history, Paul's activities would range from somewhere between 9 BCE for the start of the reign of King Aretas IV, up to a time prior to the publication of the letter called the 'First Epistle of Clement'; which is in turn written before the temple was destroyed in 70 CE. So the letter called the 'First Epistle of Clement' could have been written up to seventy-nine years before the temple was destroyed. Therefore, the letter itself might have been written long before Pontius Pilate became governor of Judah. in fact a mere forty-four years is all that is required for this to be the case. Small wonder then that the letter is no longer included as part of the New Testament. Small wonder also that the Church wish to push the date of authorship as far as possible in the opposite direction by claiming that Clement wrote the letter and that he makes reference to the persecutions of Domitian. The motive for the later dating of this letter to 96 CE by the Church is now explicitly clear. It increases the gap between the 30 CE crucifixion scene and the letter date less a nominal amount of years to represent the historic existence of the churches in Rome and Corinth; thus leaving a presentable and feasible amount of time to spread the Christian faith from Jerusalem to Rome and Corinth. We also have to wonder why: the only surviving copy, a copy found inside the Alexandrian Codex, has one page removed towards the end of the letter. In J B Lightfoot's own translation notes he writes: *"Here a leaf of the manuscript is torn out"*. We will never know what was written on that page, but whatever it said, it clearly presented a problem to the Church. The three captions presented above are very slight indicators to the age of the groups referred to within the letter. I would conjecture that the missing page might have contained rather more direct indicators; also, the missing page comes exactly between the end of the subject matter of the letter, and the start of the spiritual sign off. The very place where the actual author is most likely to have inserted his name! I would not hesitate to guess that if a name was present on the removed page, that the name was not Clement, and hence the reason the page no longer exists. If the early Church wished to falsely re-date this letter by allocating its authorship to a later Bishop in history, this page would then have to be removed in order to conceal the deceit. Since the burning of people, in order to silence alternate debate, proved to be no issue of conscience to the early Church, removing a page from a letter in a book becomes a simple task.

Why does the letter refer to one of the most junior churches of the Christian world, a church that is less then nineteen years old, as ancient? Because it was ancient at the time the letter was written, it is the age of nineteen years or less according to Matthew, Mark, Luke, John and Acts which is incorrect. It is incorrect because Matthew, Mark, Luke, John and Acts are all stories, not factual accounts; stories that turn the nucleus of an ancient allegorical idea into a full blown literal narrative with all the trappings and trimmings of a novel.

The second piece of ancient literature which demonstrates the antiquity of the Jesus story has been allocated the title the 'Epistle of Barnabas', and currently given a date of origin of between 70 and 130 CE; it is not to be confused with the 'Gospel of Barnabas' which is a separate work. Our first modern-day glimpse of the full text came with the discovery in 1859 of the Codex Sinaiticus; a book believed to have been compiled circa 360 CE; the first translated publication of partial texts from the epistle date to 1645.

The letter itself contains no New Testament content at all, epistles or gospels. Moreover the backdrop of a Roman Empire is also entirely absent, suggesting the Romans do not yet feature as a world power. Nor does this author write about times of oppression in the Jewish world, but rather writes in a manner which suggests freedom of expression and belief. He is relaying an argument to a Jewish population and cajoling them to reject attachment to the temple of Yahweh, and Mosaic laws, and to become followers of the new message from the messiah Jesus. His intended audience would not therefore be present in history between the years of 70

26

and 130 CE, since the temple and Jerusalem itself simply did not exist between these dates. Therefore, the currently attributed date range is clearly in error.

The suggested author, Barnabas, is claimed to be the apostle Barnabas who preached with Paul. However, once again the name allocated to the letter by the Church cannot be used as confirmation of the author, since the author does not include his name within the work. The name given as Barnabas is simply beneficial to Church dogma and allows the Church to apply an incorrect date of authorship to the work; a date which fits within the framework of the literalist Jesus story. We are about to see that the Church are compelled to do this, or admit Christianity has absolutely no substance.

This epistle was removed from the canonical list of works accepted as genuine by Eusebius of Caesarea when the accepted Catholic view of Christianity was formed by Eusebius and the Emperor Constantine following the council of Nicaea in 325 CE. So, as with the First Epistle of Clement, this work did once form part of the early New Testament canon but has long since been removed and classed as 'disputed' by the founders of the Catholic faith.

Before examining the content of the letter we need a brief appreciation of the history of the temple to Yahweh in Jerusalem. We do not actually know when the first temple began construction or where it was sited, as this is largely portrayed in myth within the Old Testament. We do know: that by the time the chronology of the Old Testament reaches the closing decades of the sixth century BCE the book enters the realm of politically motivated spin on actual events. In 586 BCE the first temple was destroyed by King Nebuchadnezzar of Babylon and the population of Jerusalem were taken into slavery, an event portrayed as the Babylonian exile. Within one hundred years, the captives of Babylon, which included the Jews, were allowed to return and govern their own lands as vassals to the Persian King Cyrus. The Jews returned to Jerusalem and rebuilt their temple, now commonly referred to as the second temple, under the rule of their new masters from afar and completed its construction in the reign of King Darius. As the centuries progress the second temple falls into a ruinous state; in 19 BCE Herod the Great took the opportunity to repair the temple in order to gain acceptance from the Jewish people as their King. Herod was appointed King by order of the Romans, but was not himself a Jew and the appointment was not popular with the Jewish people. The renovated second temple was then destroyed, along with Jerusalem, by the Roman General Titus in 70 CE; the second temple was never rebuilt after its destruction. In 130 CE Hadrian erected a pagan temple to Jupiter on top of the second temple ruins. Around 670 CE Palestine fell in to the hands of the Umayyad Caliphate and became part of a Muslim empire which saw the construction of the first of several mosques on the site; al-Aqsa and the Dome of the Rock, being the mosques which still stand there today, collectively termed the Temple Mount.

We will now look at an excerpt from the Epistle of Barnabas as translated by Maxwell Stainforth circa 1944. The excerpt contains the anonymous author's thoughts on the Jewish temple in Jerusalem.

*"He also says, 'Behold, those who pulled the temple down shall rebuild it', the very thing which is actually in process of fulfilment now; for after their armed rebellion it was demolished by their enemies, and now they themselves are about to build it up again, as subjects of their foemen. All the same, it has been revealed that the city, temple and Jewish people are all alike doomed to perish one-day."* Other translations give *"the very thing which is actually in the process of fulfilment now"* as *"it is happening".*

The Church attribute the temple destruction depicted in this letter as the destruction by Titus in 70 CE, and of course, they have no choice but to do this; to attribute the caption to the earlier destruction of Nebuchadnezzar in 586 BCE would completely destroy their entire theology; it would effectively bring down the Vatican itself. But the letter cannot possibly be referring to the destruction of 70 CE. This caption talks of a temple having been recently destroyed, and in the process of being rebuilt, in a Jerusalem which exists at the time of writing; it further states that the city, and the temple being built, will both be destroyed in the future, in an as yet unfulfilled prophecy. This demonstrates that Jerusalem itself, and the reconstruction of the temple, exist intact in the authors present. We should also consider that: between the dates of the destruction by Titus in 70 CE and the decision of Hadrian in 130 CE to build a temple to Jupiter on top of the second temple remnants, Jerusalem had lain in ruins and had been uninhabited. Hadrian built his pagan temple and constructed a new city which he named 'Aelia Capitolina' and duly populated with Roman citizens. He barred the practice of circumcision in the Roman Empire and exiled all Jews from the lands of Judah; he then renamed Judah to 'Palaestina'. The concept of 'Jerusalem' ceased to exist after 70 CE and it does not reappear in history until the post-324 CE section of Constantine's rule. The second temple was never rebuilt after it was destroyed in 70 CE. The first temple was however rebuilt, within 100 years of its 586 BCE destruction by Nebuchadnezzar and became the second temple; the author is clearly depicting the destruction of the first temple and the construction of the second. In addition, while displaying knowledge of the general death and resurrection concept of Jesus, the letter displays no knowledge of the content of the literal Jesus story as per Matthew, Mark, Luke and John; in fact, the author of this letter is also ignorant of the New Testament epistles, most of which date to circa 50 CE and therefore prior to the event of the second temple destruction. This author knows none of the starring roles in the early days of the New Testament style of Christianity such as Paul and Peter; He is completely unaware of all New Testament content and is only able to quote passages from the Old Testament. Passages dated to the sixth century BCE, passages which originate from, and talk specifically of, the first temple destruction era. Why then, when the author speaks of a 'temple destruction', would we jump 656 years into the future and claim he is speaking of the 70 CE destruction? This is not logical!

When talking of the death and resurrection, the author uses the prophecy of the messiah from Isaiah in the Old Testament as opposed to the theoretical 'eye witness', would be, past tense accounts from the New Testament; the author would only do this if the New Testament content was not available to him to quote from. That is: the New Testament version did not exist at the time this epistle was written. Furthermore, the Book of Isaiah is considered to have had three authors, and to have been written in three specific time frames, being: Just before the first temple destruction, the exile period following the first temple destruction and the period just after the exile, the period when the second temple was actually constructed; and recall the author writes *"the very thing which is actually in the process of fulfilment now";* referring to the temple being rebuilt!

The prophecy used from Isaiah in the Old Testament is in point of fact, the basic Jesus passion scene and the concept of offering death to absorb sin on our behalf, without actually giving a name to the messiah, or a date when he is due; the Epistle of Barnabas simply regurgitates this prophecy and adds the name 'Jesus' to the character within the prophecy, and eludes to the fact that the events have already taken place in the past. That is: Isaiah's prophecy of a coming messiah has already been fulfilled; but the author does not state when.

The Church forward a proposed date of origin for the letter of between 70 and 130 CE in order to place it conveniently between the years after the 70 CE second temple destruction by Titus and before the 132 CE uprising of Simon Bar Kochba which was quelled by Hadrian in 134 CE. They justify these dates with the following two arguments: the letter mentions the destruction of the temple and must therefore be post-70 CE (inferring that the letter is making reference to the second temple destruction, without offering any explanation as to why they arrive at this assumption), and, the letter speaks of the 'desire and aspirations' of the Jewish populace to rebuild the temple, a desire that would have been completely quelled after Hadrian had successfully subdued the 132 revolt. We can also note with suspicion the fact that the Church cleverly turn, what is clearly a description of an activity *"the very thing which is in the process of fulfilment now"*, and in other translations *"it is happening"*, to a statement of 'desire and intent', in order to divert the letters clear portrayal of the second temple construction, and allow the allocation of the text to the second temple destruction. Since the epistles of the New Testament date to circa 50 CE and the author of this epistle is not aware of their content, this author is then by deduction also writing prior to 50 CE, and therefore prior to the 70 CE second temple destruction. We can make this claim with confidence because, if we consider the author to have written within the currently claimed date range of 70 to 130 CE, the author should be extremely familiar with the content of the New Testament. Recall that, the claim is made that the author 'Barnabas' believed to have written this letter is the Barnabas who travelled and preached with Paul; It is therefore somewhat strange to find that he knows nothing of Paul, or Paul's writings or Paul's works.

We find then, that the author can only be making reference to the 586 BCE first temple destruction and the circa post-516 BCE second temple construction; because the above logic dictates that he writes before the 70 CE second temple destruction event had actually taken place. This means that the origin of this epistle, if not the written content itself, is effectively some 586 years older than the date attributed to it from the Church. Its origin actually dates from around post circa 516 BCE and it does make positive reference to the concept of Jesus and the crucifixion. There are no other tags within the letter to allow a later dating; but recall, the letter speaks in the present tense of the rebuilding process of the temple, in that the second temple is being built at the time the letter is being written. This ties the origin of the letter down to a specific era, being the beginning of the second temple age circa post-516 BCE, rather than to a date between the second temple destruction of 70 CE and the defeat of Simon Bar Kochba's revolt in 134 CE. Equally important, is the fact that this author's Jesus, rose from the dead, revealed himself, but not to any specific characters, and ascended to heaven all on the same day. *"and we too rejoice in celebrating the eighth day; because that was when Jesus rose from the dead, and showed himself again, and ascended into heaven"*, also note the eighth day, not the third; this passage does not reconcile with the Matthew, Mark, Luke and John versions, or Paul's epistles, which state Jesus rose on the third day and also claim a forty day gap between resurrection and ascension! So, is this author the Barnabas who accompanied Paul on his missionary journeys; the journeys alluded to by the 'Epistles of Paul' in the New Testament written pre-60 CE, and the supposed biography of Paul's journeys depicted in Acts from the New Testament, written post-70 CE? If this author is travelling and preaching with Paul, why does Paul's Christ rise on the third day, while the Christ of this author rises on the eighth day? And why does the Christ of this author achieve resurrection, presentation and ascension all on the same day, whereas Paul clearly indicates a period of forty days between resurrection and ascension? If the author of this letter did write between 70 and 130 CE, as the Church postulates, these conflicts would not exist; the account of the death, resurrection and ascension in this letter would be identical to the accounts found in the post-70 CE New Testament scriptures. But it is not! It is not, because this letter was written before the Matthew, Mark, Luke and John versions of a literal Jesus were published; before 70 CE, before the second temple destruction!

This letter betrays the fact that the core basis of the Jesus crucifixion concept predates Pontius Pilate's governorship of Judah by some 550 years; therefore my concept on the authorship date predates the

Church point of view by some 586 to 646 years. To challenge the orthodox and accepted view of a letter date by such a margin would be considered a theory from the lunatic fringe by many, particularly by devout Christians and the Church; but their reason for taking this opposition to the revelation would rest solely on the fact that my date is considered preposterous because it predates the Jesus character by 550 years. This argument makes the incorrect presupposition that the Jesus character did actually exist in history circa 30 CE, and as we shall see in chapter six, Matthew, Mark, Luke and John aside, there is no such evidence in existence to substantiate this claim. If we take away this objection, then, suggesting that the Epistle of Barnabas is referencing the first temple destruction of Nebuchadnezzar in 586 BCE is perfectly feasible, and perfectly logical. The only possible argument left for theology is that the letter is indeed making reference to the first temple destruction and was indeed written before the second temple was destroyed in 70 CE; but since, in the Christian view, Jesus did exist and was crucified in 30 CE, the letter would therefore need to have been written between 30 and 70 CE. The contention being that: the letter simply 'tells the story' of the first temple destruction. But this too would be a null hypothesis, since if this was the case the author would not need to use the prophecy from Isaiah in the Old Testament, in order to describe the death and resurrection scene. Coming from Jerusalem circa 30 CE, and particularly at Passover, the author could have been an eye witness to the whole event and would be writing from personal experience. At the very least, if he did not witness the events he would have been reporting hearsay and/or the base material for the Matthew, Mark, Luke and John stories. But he does not! He relies solely on Old Testament prophecy.

We will now return to the twenty-one letters that are included in the New Testament, and analyse the Jesus character they speak of. Recall - with the exception of One Timothy and Two Timothy - all of the letters are written pre-70 CE and therefore predate the literal Jesus character from the story in Matthew, Mark, Luke and John. We will compare the Jesus captions from the twenty-one letters with the idea of a Gnostic version of a Jesus, a mythical Jesus that did not exist in reality but in the ether, and the thoughts of those who worshipped this particular God. We will see that all of the references to the Jesus character in these letters actually conflict with the statements in, or demonstrate a lack of knowledge of, the Matthew, Mark, Luke and John Jesus character; this is as we would expect, if the letter authors were not promoting the idea of the post-70 CE Matthew, Mark, Luke and John physical Jesus, but rather an earlier allegorical version of a Jesus figure.

**Romans 1.3:** *"regarding his Son, who as to his human nature was a descendant of David, and who through the Spirit of holiness was declared with power to be the son of God by his resurrection from the dead: Jesus Christ our Lord"* Why does the author of this letter not allude to the virgin Mary as mother, or Joseph being the father who is a descendant of David?

**Romans 6.6:** *"For we know that our old self was crucified with him so that the body of sin might be done away with, that we should no longer be slaves to sin, because anyone who has died has been freed from sin."* This does not refer to actual death; it refers to the death of the old self. The new self (still living) has been freed of sin when Jesus is accepted. This can be more comfortably viewed as a reference to the Gnostic allegorical version of Christianity which will be more fully explored in later chapters.

**1 Corinthians 2.8:** *"None of the rulers of this age understood it, for if they had, they would not have crucified the Lord of glory".* There is a clear opportunity here to state who those rulers were, and when and where the crucifixion took place. The absence of such information suggests that the crucifixion is still metaphorical at the time this letter was written; also, the word translated here as *'age'* appears in the Greek New Testament as 'αἰῶνοςν' which actually means eon and is therefore more likely to be referring to an astrological age, the age of Pisces. This comment will be become clearer in the next chapter.

**1 Corinthians 5.7:** *"Get rid of the old yeast that you may be a new batch without yeast, as you really are. For Christ, our Passover lamb, has been sacrificed"* This again displays only a Gnostic allegorical understanding of the passion of Christ. Many ancient mystery religions involved, or seem to require, a sacrificial deity of some description.

**1 Corinthians 10.16:** *"Is not the cup of thanksgiving for which we give thanks a participation in the blood of Christ? And is not the bread that we break a participation in the body of Christ? Because there is one loaf, we, who are many, are one body, for we all partake of the one loaf. Consider the people of Israel: Do not those who eat the sacrifices participate in the altar?"*

**1 Corinthians 11.23:** *"For I received from the Lord what I also passed on to you: The Lord Jesus, on the night he was betrayed, took bread, and when he had given thanks, he broke it and said, 'This is my body, which is for you; do this in remembrance of me.' In the same way, after supper he took the cup, saying, 'This cup is the new covenant in my blood; do this, whenever you drink it, in remembrance of me.' For whenever you eat this bread and drink this cup, you proclaim the Lord's death until he comes."*

There is no mention of the extremely detailed story of the last supper with the twelve disciples from the New Testament here; although it could easily be a portrayal of an ancient Gnostic ritual which has been used as the baseline idea for the last supper story. We must also take into account the fact that the idea of 'sacred banquet' can be found in the cave art of Stone Age man, and other Bronze and Iron Age religious cults also practiced a Eucharist ritual with symbolic wine and bread, such as the Roman soldiers who worshipped Mithras; so this is not a new idea conceived by the Catholic Church, it is religious plagiarism.

**1 Corinthians 15.3:** *"For what I received I passed on to you as of first importance: that Christ died for our sins according to the Scriptures, that he was buried, that he was raised on the third day according to the Scriptures, and that he appeared to Peter, and then to the Twelve. After that, he appeared to more than five hundred of the brothers at the same time, most of whom are still living, though some have fallen asleep. Then he appeared to James, then to all the apostles, and last of all he appeared to me also, as to one abnormally born."* Although this letter is written in the present tense and claims a resurrection occurred on the third day and that the appearances happened in living memory, we need to be careful not to automatically apply the Matthew, Mark, Luke, John and Acts stories when interpreting this paragraph. The letter does not confirm any time gap between the claimed resurrection and the appearances; so to assume a same day appearance, or appearances within forty days of resurrection, is simply to overlay the story from Matthew, Mark, Luke, John and Acts. We could equally assume that the resurrection stated is a mythical occurrence from antiquity and the 'appearances' were recent. It is Acts, written post-70 CE, which claims that Paul said the gap between resurrection and ascension (the time frame of the appearances) was forty days. But Paul did not write Acts, and Acts is most certainly a fictitious 'biography of Paul'. Also, the letter does not allude to physical appearances, only appearances. The allegorical Gnostic view of a Christ figure fits this paragraph as well as, if not more than, the Matthew, Mark, Luke, John and Acts version of a physical Christ. Finally, the author of this letter, written before 70 CE, has no knowledge of the endings in Matthew, Mark, Luke and John. In Matthew, Mark and John, Mary is the first person the Jesus character appears to, in Luke, The Jesus character first appears to two previously un-stated characters who are termed followers; one called Cleopas and the other unnamed. None of Matthew, Mark, Luke or John mentions an appearance to the five hundred, or any such large number of people prior to the ascension, as alluded to in this letter.

**2 Corinthians 11.4:** *"For if someone comes to you and preaches a Jesus other than the Jesus we preached, or if you receive a different spirit from the one you received, or a different gospel from the one you accepted, you put up with it easily enough. But I do not think I am in the least inferior to those 'super-apostles.' I may not be a trained speaker, but I do have knowledge. We have made this perfectly clear to you in every way."*

**Galatians 1.6:** *"I am astonished that you are so quickly deserting the one who called you by the grace of Christ and are turning to a different gospel which is really no gospel at all. Evidently some people are throwing you into confusion and are trying to pervert the gospel of Christ. But even if we or an angel from heaven should preach a gospel other than the one we preached to you, let him be eternally condemned! As we have already said, so now I say again: If anybody is preaching to you a gospel other than what you accepted, let him be eternally condemned!"* These passages clearly identify that at the time these letters were written, pre-70 CE; there were many versions of the Jesus story being told and many gospels. To reiterate: whenever we see a reference to the gospel which does not specify which gospel, we are completely in error if we automatically attribute the reference to Matthew, Mark, Luke, John or Acts.

**Galatians 2.19:** *"For through the law I died to the law so that I might live for God. I have been crucified with Christ and I no longer live, but Christ lives in me. The life I live in the body, I live by faith in the son of God, who loved me and gave himself for me. I do not set aside the grace of God, for if righteousness could be gained through the law, Christ died for nothing!"* This is a clear Gnostic reference to the old self dying, and the new self resurrecting when faith in Christ has been accepted.

**Galatians 4.4:** *"But when the time had fully come, God sent his son, born of a woman, born under law".* This passage does not state when the time was, who the mother was, or make any reference to the current state of her virginity; all of which it should have been able to do if Matthew, Mark, Luke, John and Acts are to be accepted as biographical. However, in pagan and Gnostic folklore, numerous sons of gods are written as being born of a mortal woman, this is nothing new and extremely old-hat at the time this letter was composed. This implies that this caption makes reference to an 'allegorical' god child.

**Philippians 2.5:** *"Your attitude should be the same as that of Christ Jesus: Who, being in very nature God, did not consider equality with God something to be grasped, but made himself nothing, taking the very nature of a servant, being made in human likeness. And being found in appearance as a man, he humbled himself and became obedient to death even death on a cross! Therefore God exalted him to the highest place and gave him the name that is above every name, that at the name of Jesus every knee should bow, in heaven and on earth and under the earth, and every tongue confesses that Jesus Christ is Lord, to the glory of God the father."* This is identical to most Gnostic versions of Christianity in that a god assumed the guise of man of his own free will. This leaves no room for, and is completely opposed to, the literalist view that encompasses a virgin birth. There is therefore no scope for the virgin birth contained in Matthew and Luke in the above passage from Paul and no way to conceive of one. The writer of this letter clearly identifies himself as a Gnostic Christian.

**1 Thessalonians 2.14:** *"You suffered from your own countrymen the same things those churches suffered from the Jews, who killed the Lord Jesus and the prophets"*. This is a general statement, and in isolation of the knowledge of Matthew, Mark, Luke, John and Acts should only be read as such. Despite the opportunity, there is no mention of Herod, Caiaphas or Pontius Pilate in the text; moreover, the Old Testament book of Daniel, circa 600 to 500 BCE, does prophesise that the Jews will reject the Messiah when he arrives. The author is simply referring to this ancient prophecy.

**Hebrews 7.3:** *"This Melchizedek was King of Salem and priest of God Most High. He met Abraham returning from the defeat of the kings and blessed him, and Abraham gave him a tenth of everything. First, his name means "king of righteousness"; then also, "king of Salem" means "king of peace." Without father or mother, without genealogy, without beginning of days or end of life, like the son of God he remains a priest forever."* Here is a character being compared with Jesus because he is without father or mother and without genealogy. Even the most fundamentalist Christian believers have to admit that this is completely contrary to the Jesus in Matthew, Mark, Luke, John and Acts.

**Hebrews 8.4:** *"If he were on earth, he would not be a priest."*
This statement clearly refers to a Jesus in the allegorical and spiritual sense, not the physical sense and once again alludes to the existence of Gnostic Christianity.

**Hebrews 13.12:** *"And so Jesus also suffered outside the city gate to make the people holy through his own blood. Let us, then, go to him outside the camp, bearing the disgrace he bore. For here we do not have an enduring city, but we are looking for the city that is to come."* The author only alludes to a city, and an area outside the city. The author should have been able to cite 'Jerusalem' and 'Golgotha' but does not!

**Revelation 11.1:** *"Go and measure the temple of God and the altar, and count the worshipers there. But exclude the outer court; do not measure it, because it has been given to the Gentiles."*

**Revelation 11.8:** *"Their bodies will lie in the street of the great city, which is figuratively called Sodom and Egypt, where also their Lord was crucified".* The first verse clearly dates the authorship of Revelation to a date before 70 CE due to its future tense reference to the temple. The second verse does not associate the crucifixion with Jerusalem; it only alludes to a nameless *"Great City"* which is then symbolically associated with Sodom and Egypt. The author of this work, who was clearly writing before 70 CE, displays no knowledge of Matthew, Mark, Luke, John or Acts.

The above list is not a selection of references from the letters in the New Testament which mention Jesus; they are the comprehensive list of all such unique references. Not many are there? All other references are just repeats of the above or copious mentions of Jesus Christ who was crucified and resurrected for our sins. The remaining ninety-nine percent of the writings in these works simply refer back to elements of the Old Testament.

Earlier I asked: *"So did the full story exist or not"*, referring to the full Matthew, Mark, Luke, John and Acts versions of the Jesus story existing in 70 CE, a date we now know the letters in the New Testament were written before. Clearly, I am asserting that it did not and that the story surfaced post-70 CE.

There is a group of writers known as the early Church fathers. These are Christian writers from the first two centuries; 90 CE through 200 CE and beyond. The comprehensive list of such writers from the first and second centuries CE, cited by the Church is as follows: Clement of Rome, Mathetes, Polycarp, Ignatius, Barnabas, Papias, Justin Martyr, Irenaeus, Hermas, Tatian, Theophilus, Athenagoras, Clement of Alexandria and Tertullian. The first six writers all wrote pre-150 CE; the remainder all wrote post-150 CE. With the exception of Ignatius, who I will discuss in a short while, all the writers writing pre-150 CE know nothing of the Jesus story as per Matthew, Mark, Luke, John and Acts; whereas, all the writers who write after 150 CE do, and are able to cite the four Bible gospels and the content of these gospels at will. Ignatius is more of a challenge: he was executed in the Colosseum in Rome around 110 CE and his works do contain New Testament gospel subject matter. However, his works are letters which, from their content, purport to be written while under arrest and escort from Syria to Rome by the Roman Army, in order to face execution. As with the letters from Paul to Timothy, it is highly doubtful that Ignatius would have been able to write and dispatch these letters himself, given his predicament. The letters would have been written by an unknown author purporting to be Ignatius and could therefore have been written after 150 CE. Given that the synoptic gospels of Matthew, Mark and Luke all mention the temple destruction, that Acts follows Luke, and John is believed to have been written after Matthew, Mark and Luke; coupled with the fact that the Christian writers of post-150 CE do seem to be aware of the existence of Matthew, Mark, Luke, John and Acts; whereas the Christian writers of pre-150 CE are unaware; we can conclude that the literal version of the Jesus story surfaced between 70 and 150 CE. Therefore, the literal story from Matthew, Mark, Luke and John takes an already ancient allegorical story and expands, enhances and evolves it into a supposed biography post-70CE. In the early fourth century CE, the literal story got a serious boost to its credibility as factual when it was adopted by the despotic rule of the Emperor Constantine I.

In this book, the First Epistle of Clement and the Epistle of Barnabas are the only works being offered to support the view that the Jesus crucifixion idea existed prior to the governorship of Pontius Pilate; in terms of logic, only one is needed to disprove the validity of the Matthew, Mark, Luke, John and Acts stories. But why is such literature so hard to find? Why can we not find volumes of such work? We do know that the Catholic Church burnt volumes of pagan and Gnostic literature, because the Church tells us so in their own polemics against pagan and Gnostic beliefs. The laws passed by the Emperor Theodosius II who reigned between 408 and 450 CE bear witness to this book burning process:

**Edict 268**: *Eunomians and Montanists are to be expelled from the cities, and if they reside in the country and should hold assemblies, they are to be deported and the owners of the land they inhabited punished. Heretical books are to be destroyed. Those who refuse to surrender such books are to suffer capital punishment on the charge of sorcery.*

**Edict 313**: *All astrologers are to be expelled and exiled, unless they burn their books in the presence of a Bishop and convert to Christianity.*

**Edict 422:** *Nestorianism is condemned. Those who follow Nestorius's teaching are to be called Simonians in the same way that Constantine ordered Arians to be called Porphyrians. Their books are banned and shall be burned. Furthermore, their assemblies are forbidden; violators will have their property confiscated.*

The Church also burnt copies of the Bible written in the vernacular; mostly along with their owners, because the Catholic Church did not want serfs forming their own personal views of God; and the Catholic Church is not the only despotic regime from history to try to eliminate a culture by burning literature:

**Suetonius; Life of the Twelve Caesars (Augustus):** *"He assumed the office of Pontifex Maximus as soon as Lepidus was dead, for he could not bring himself to deprive him of it during his lifetime. All prophetical books, both in Latin and Greek, the authors of which were either unknown or of no great reputation, he caused to be called in from all places. They reached the number of 2000 and above: and of these he burnt all except the Sibylline Oracles, which he subjected to a strict examination to determine their authenticity."*

**Suetonius; Life of the Twelve Caesars (Tiberius):** *"All foreign religions, including the Egyptian and Jewish rights, he prohibited: compelling those who practiced that kind of superstition to burn their vestments and all their sacred utensils."*

**'Tyndale Bible' by William Tyndale:** William Tyndale completed his English translation of the New Testament in 1524; the work was condemned by the English Church in 1526 and banned from England. All existing copies of Tyndale's Bible that had made their way to England were to be burnt by order of the Church and King. In 1536 the Catholic Church burnt Tyndale at the stake for heresy.

We can also witness other book burning episodes from our recent history when we study the Protestant reformation of 1547, the Catholic restoration of 1553 and most recently the rise of Nazi Germany post-1933.

This list is by no means comprehensive; indeed it is merely a small sample of how despotic regimes from history found the burning of literature and people, in order to silence and eradicate ideas which competed against their totalitarian rule, a very useful tool. We have to class Christianity from 400 CE onwards, and all resulting streams of Christianity up to the late 1600's, quite firmly into this despotic totalitarian class of rulers. The result of the book burning and competing theology eradication process up to the late 1600's has meant all literature which came to light during this period, which proved problematic for the literal view of Jesus contained in the Matthew, Mark, Luke, John and Acts stories, has been destroyed. All links with Christianity and former pagan and Gnostic religions, along with all links with Christianity and Astrology have been eradicated. It is up to us to use our intuition and process of rational interrogation and investigation to recreate and rediscover those links.

The letters called 'First Epistle of Clement' and 'Epistle of Barnabas' give us solid grounds for supposing that Matthew, Mark, Luke, John and Acts are much later adaptations of the New Testament Letters; adaptations which enhanced certain elements of the letters in order to create a fictitious story of a physically resurrected Jesus. If we are to make this supposition we then have to answer two questions: Why is Christianity a worldwide religion, and how did it get that way? The rest of this book is dedicated to giving a commonsense, rational answer as to how the Christian religion managed to entrench itself in to the psyche of millions of people around the globe; and, why it is still entrenched into our psyche today. But first, we have to be able to suppose; we have to be able to suppose that the stories in the Christian Holy Bible are all allegorical. Just suppose!

## --Chapter 2: Astro-Maths--

The first thing we have to consider when attempting to understand how religion became ingrained into the consciousness of mankind is the many similarities between religions. There is one similarity which is prevalent in nearly all world religions, which manifests itself with monotonous regularity in the verbal traditions, artefacts, scripture and supporting literature of: Babylonian and Egyptian Mythology, Greek and Roman pagan beliefs, Gnosticism, Judaism, ancient Indian texts 'Rig-Veda', Christianity and Islam. That similarity is the unceasing infatuation with the numbers seven and twelve. There are other numbers too; five and two appear together in some of the literature as a sub split of seven, four is quite common, and so is thirty and 360. Forty and seventy also make frequent appearances being special extensions of four and seven. Seventy also has special significance beyond the simple extension of seven and is often used in conjunction with, and interchangeably with, seventy-two.

We could hypothesise that the three Abrahamic religions of today are just an evolution/adaptation of original ideas created from star gazing. Ideas nurtured when man first formed civilisations in Sumer, modern-day Iraq, followed closely by Egypt, Turkey and Greece; if we did, how would we set about finding evidence to support this hypothesis? Moreover, if the hypothesis could be supported, it would demonstrate that there is absolutely no substance at all behind Judaism, Christianity and Islam.

To assist in imparting the basis behind the above hypothesis, and to illustrate how major theological ideas become entrenched into the psyche of society, consider the following two words and their meaning as given in the Penguin Concise English Dictionary:

**Gene**: *A unit of inheritance that is carried on a chromosome, controls transmission of hereditary characteristics and contains DNA or, in some viruses, RNA.*

**Meme**: *A behavioural or cultural trait that is passed on by other than genetic means. e.g. by imitation.*

In short, religious theology is not a tangible thing; it is merely a highly efficient thought virus which is passed from parent to child, teacher to student and priest to parishioner. Stark as it might sound, it is a thought virus which is capable of infecting brains; it can be considered highly infectious given the correct conditions for infection to take place. The ideal time for the brain to be infected is while it is still very young.

To support the hypothesis that modern-day theologies all have their origins firmly grounded in simplistic star gazing, origins that have travelled distance and time as an evolving meme, we can try to imagine the forming and evolution of such thoughts when man first starts to ponder. We could set ourselves the task of recreating such first thoughts on the heavens. We can then cross reference the ideas we surmise with the three Abrahamic faiths of today and compare similarities. We can also look at religious literature and art in existence today which is reliably date stamped, along with the absence in some cases of such literature and art, to follow links and establish time frames of evolving ideas. Finally, we can recall recorded history and make a decision on whether or not we feel the dominance of the three Abrahamic faiths of today is due to the presence of any real substance in their message, or simply the chance outcome of past battles. It is important to note that memes can survive and thrive or struggle and die out quite naturally; and this is not dependant on how useful the meme is. Good memes can and do die out, and harmful memes can and do survive. But this natural process can be greatly assisted, in both directions, by despotic regimes. Memes can be both forcefully eradicated, and forcefully promoted.

I believe this book supplies the meat behind the above statements and presents a convincing view. This view will demonstrate that the three Abrahamic faiths of today are based on stories plagiarised from pre-Israelite Kingdom times. Stories that were themselves created from simple star gazing. This book will also reveal that the New Testament version of Jesus was created by artistic interpretation of the most basic astrological events; particularly the resurrection and the virgin birth scenes. This is achieved by collating and presenting material recently discovered and published by a host of scholars, alongside some of my own findings. After reading the assertions that follow, I invite the reader to research the Ancient Sumerian and Akkadian stories of King Gilgamesh; particularly the stories of the flood caused by Enlil, and of Mami creating men from clay on the seventh day of each month. These stories will reveal that the Jewish Torah (Old Testament) is full of plagiarism. Please also research Dionysus, Attis, Mithra/Mithras and Bacchus. I should warn deeply devout Christians at this stage that you will need to research these mythical characters with an open mind; you will uncover information which directly challenges the existence of a literal Christ and provides damning evidence that the concept of Jesus is simply a perennially regurgitated myth. Also recommended for research is the I-kher-nefert stele. This stone stele reveals the mythical characters of Osiris, Isis, and Horus, an Egyptian trinity consisting of the father, virgin mother and saviour son. Horus is not only the saviour son, he is also Osiris reborn and he fought an eternal fight with Set who embodied evil, giving a parallel with Jesus and Satan. The stele has chiselled into it the passion play of Osiris and depicts his death and resurrection. You will discover that he died and resurrected as a god after three days at the spring equinox. He then impregnated his virgin sister, and wife, Isis without physical intercourse.

The 'saviour son' of the immaculate conception was Horus who was born at the winter solstice, around Dec 25$^{th}$ by ancient calendars. Horus also suffers a death and resurrection scene as a young child.

For an appreciation of the astrology discussed in the assertions that follow, I need to give a quick description of an astrological age and an astrological year. They are derived from a phenomenon known as 'the precession of the equinox'. This is the name given to the fact that the Earth not only spins on its axis once a day, but that the axis also wobbles like a spinning top over time, an immense amount of time: roughly 25,800 years per wobble. This 25,800 year period is known as an astrological year, or a great year. There are twelve astrological ages per astrological year, so an astrological age, or 'epoch', is roughly 2,150 years long. The phenomenon is termed the precession of the equinox because we use the spring equinox, currently around 21$^{st}$ March, as a marker for the start and end of an astrological age, or each 2,150 year period. On the spring equinox the Sun rises exactly due east viewed from anywhere in the populated world. On that day the Sun will rise into one of the zodiac signs, currently Pisces, hence the term the 'Age of Pisces'. During the course of the next 365 days, as we orbit the Sun, the sunrise will move through all twelve zodiac signs and back to Pisces again on the next spring equinox. However, it does not end up in exactly the same position within that star sign each year; each year the constellations shift a minute amount on the horizon. The amount moved is so small it is barely noticeable in one lifetime, let alone one year, but move they do. in fact they move one of the 360 divisions (degrees) of the horizon every 71.6 years; this is a best approximation as the actual time taken constantly fluctuates both sides of this figure. We shall see later how this figure became significant in spiritual thought and was simplified to both seventy and seventy-two for its inclusion in allegorical stories. Over a period of roughly 2,150 years the constellations will have moved enough on the horizon for the spring equinox sunrise to be in the next star sign. This then, is an astrological age; therefore an astrological age is linked to a particular star sign and lasts for 2,150 years. A second phenomenon occurs here too: the direction of the rotation of the wobble is in the opposite direction to the rotation of the Earth on its axis. This causes the visual effect of the spring equinox sunrise precessing backwards through the zodiac signs. We will move out of the 'Age of Pisces' and into the 'Age of Aquarius' in about 2100 CE.

I now need to progress the aims of this chapter and the rest of the book; but before embarking on the issues explored in the book, I wish to paint a picture in this chapter which needs to be in everyone's mind while reading the book. The picture painted will lay the foundation for the main hypothesis of the book; being that: modern-day theology has no basis in fact and actually evolved from simplistic ancient stargazing. Acceptance or rejection of the picture about to be painted is largely up to each individual reader, but it is important that the book is read with an appreciation of the concept being put forward.

To tackle the issue of recreating humankind's first thoughts on the heavens, I will condense the hypothetical events of a great many years into a few years; while at the same time placing three constraints on the experiment:

**1:** I will assume that human beings are realising these thoughts for the first time.

**2:** That the thoughts are inspired by the most obvious things that can be observed with the naked eye and are, in themselves, worth wondering about.

**3:** Human beings try to understand and communicate the conclusion of these first thoughts by creating stories around them.

Imagine beginning to wonder about existence for the first time and looking up into the sky during the day; that large bright disc in the sky, is it this that rules the heavens? As I began to study the large bright disc moving across the sky each day, warming up the surface of the earth, I wonder: why does it appear at different locations on the horizon each morning, and why is it present for different lengths of time each day? I am so intrigued, that I conduct an experiment. I drive a large stake into the ground, and ten paces from this stake, in a line with the stake and where the bright disc rises in the morning I put in another smaller stake to act as a marker. A few mornings later I repeat the process and drive in another smaller stake. As the mornings progress I continue to place small marker stakes ten paces from the main stake and in line with the main stake and the morning sunrise position. The small marker stakes therefore track the movement of the sunrise position on the horizon as the days' progress. Before long I have a sizable arc of small marker stakes and I notice a pattern; I notice a link with the sunrise position in the arc of small stakes and the length of the day. After many days (in fact many years) I notice that the sunrise position on the horizon moves continually from left to right and back again; but it always stops and changes direction at the same two extremities; these two extremities are now located and identified by the extreme left hand and extreme right hand marker stakes. I also notice that when the Sun rises exactly in the middle of these two extremities, effectively the midpoint stake, the days and nights are equal in length; today we know this to be the spring and autumn equinox and it is, by default, exactly due east. As I ponder further, I notice other patterns. When the Sun rises at the left extremity (the left hand marker stake); the day is the longest day, the night is the shortest night and the weather is fine. Whereas, when the Sun rises at the right extremity the day is the shortest day, the night is the longest night and the weather is cold. More interest is found by noticing that when the sunrise position passes through the midpoint travelling towards the right extremity, all plant life fails and the earth seems to die. However, when the sunrise position passes through the midpoint travelling towards the left extremity, the calves and lambs are born, the crops begin to grow, and the flowers begin to show; the earth seems to come back to life. Although I am not aware of what it is my experiment, and my resulting arc of stakes, has done, in today's terms: I have just discovered the winter and summer solstice, the spring and autumn equinox, identified the seasons, located east and created a calendar; but to me it is just watching, recording movement and pondering.

My thoughts now turn to how long this process takes. I notice that the sunrise position seems to hang at each extremity as it moves into the point, stops there for a few mornings, and then moves back out again. This pause in position seems to take between two to three days at both ends of the arc. So I observe that the sunrise hangs at the left extremity for two to three days, then spends 180 days moving over to the right extremity, hangs at the right extremity for two to three days, and then spends 180 days moving back to the left extremity. This means that the sunrise position on the horizon is on the move for one cycle across the horizon and back again for 360 days; ignoring of course the time the sunrise position spends static at each extremity. As a human first pondering this phenomenon I nurture the view that the number 360 is very significant. I have no idea that I have just made an estimate for the length of a solar year.

I now turn my thoughts to the bright disc which appears at night. This holds many more mysteries in its behaviour. Sometimes it is a full disc, sometimes half and sometimes it disappears completely. What can be determined is that it appears as a full disc twelve times per full sun cycle of 360 days. As a man first pondering the influence of the heavens on existence, I now view the Sun and Moon as very significant, along with the numbers 360 and 12.

The only logical astrological elements left to ponder are the stars. There are so many stars, and they all seem to be grouped in to individual shapes. These shapes all move in unison across the sky each night in the same direction and at the same speed. However, after many nights of observation a quirk in the patterns appears. Five of the stars appear to have

51

moved each night with regard to their position relative to all of the other stars. Although they still move across the sky each night with all of the others stars, and at the same speed, they appear to move their position over time and sometimes disappear from view altogether. I refer to them as the five wandering stars to distinguish them from the multitude of ordinary fixed stars. We now know these five 'wandering stars' to be the five visible planets Mercury, Venus, Mars, Saturn and Jupiter; not stars at all. The origin of the Greek word 'planet' is 'wanderer'.

I think of these five wandering stars, along with the Sun and the Moon, as heavenly bodies which all have influence on life; they are viewed as living entities in the ether because they appear to have the ability to move their position in the sky relative to the backdrop of fixed points of light, being the billions of fixed stars. This is a logical first conclusion; they have the ability to move, therefore they must be living entities. This gives me seven heavenly bodies. I therefore extend the list of special numbers to 360, twelve and seven. It is no coincidence that today we have 360 degrees in a circle, twelve months in a year and seven days in a week; also some of the earliest calendars only recorded a 360 day year.

Here then, are the core ingredients for all future mythology and religious theology. They are all in one place, in the minds of one group and at one particular time in history. This place and time is the area of the world's first civilisation, Sumer in Mesopotamia pre-3500 BCE. With my fellow Sumerians I take these core ingredients and make up stories with them, creating characters to represent the objects and the elements as gods. We also create characters for most of the natural things we do not quite understand which results in a plethora of demi-gods. We give form and names to the groups of fixed stars in the sky and relate these images to the demi-gods we have created. The stories we create are parables and allegories which all contain constant reference to the magical numbers; particularly seven and twelve. The constant use of these two special numbers in the stories created represents the seven heavenly bodies and the twelve moon phases per year. Three and four also feature heavily in the stories either as themselves or as multiples of themselves; three being the three solar events of the winter solstice, summer solstice and the spring (vernal) equinox, all of which are now considered very significant spiritual events, and four being the four seasons.

With civilisation forming in Sumer, people begin to move and new civilisations spring up; but, our core ingredients move with them. Over centuries, civilisations start to appear in Egypt closely followed by Greece and then Turkey. These civilisations also create their own parables and allegories using the core ingredients as the start point; their stories are also laden with reference to the magical numbers, again with lashings of seven and twelve. Because these stories evolve in isolation to each other in each civilisation, we see today a host of different ancient beliefs which all have the core ingredients at their heart. Skipping forward in history; people move, trade is born and wars take place; slaves are taken and whole communities are upended and displaced/relocated. This causes the stories to merge, morph and evolve into many overlapping, recurring and divergent mythological beliefs. The end result is: we now have different versions of the same stories appearing in different regions on the planet. But these stories still all contain constant references to the magical numbers; mostly, what are now considered to be the foremost magical numbers of seven and twelve.

The number seven is used frequently in the epics of King Gilgamesh from around 3500 BCE, and particularly in the flood scene from these stories. The Gilgamesh stories predate the Noah flood story by some 1,000 years, and the Noah flood story also makes copious use of the number seven. The first Sumerian temples known as ziggurats were constructed to worship the Babylonian moon god Nanna (Sumerian name) or Sin (Akkadian name); they had four sides and seven ever decreasing platforms.

The Egyptian 'Book of the Dead' contains instructions for twelve 'transformations' designed to aid the deceased to pass twelve trials in his journey to meet Osiris in the afterlife; this book also includes the 'seven Arits', the 'forty-two negative confessions' and lists the names of the twelve gods in attendance at the great hall. The ancient Rig-Veda texts from the Indus Valley indicate that: knowledge was delivered to man from the 'Saptarshi' (seven sages) who appeared from the sea. The 'Greek Theogony' lists twelve gods of Olympia; a list which originally comprised of six gods and six goddesses. Zeus expels Hestia, one of the goddesses and replaces her with Dionysus a god, thus achieving male dominance of Olympia with seven gods and five goddesses. The demi-god Heracles (Roman Hercules) is sentenced by the Olympians to complete twelve labours. From an Oedipus-themed trilogy produced by Aeschylus we can read about the 'Seven against Thebes'. As with the twelve Olympian gods, the Torah has twelve major prophets and twelve minor prophets. In the Jewish Torah (Old Testament) we find that God made the world in six days and on the seventh he did rest; this being just the first of what will be hundreds of references to the number seven within the Torah. Joshua conquered Canaan in seven years with twelve tribes and there were thirty battles; and twelve times thirty is 360. Roman history, largely mythical, records its beginnings with an age of seven kings prior to the creation of the republic; Rome is also cited as being located in area between seven hills, despite the fact that there actually more than seven. The Dii Consentes is the pantheon of the twelve major Roman gods, and is lifted directly from the Greek concept of the twelve gods of Olympus. The Persian religion of Mithra, which also morphed into the Roman religion of Mithras, took its adherents through seven stages of initiation. The New Testament tells us someone called Jesus is splitting up five loaves (wandering stars) and two fishes (Sun & Moon) to feed 5,000 men (multiple of five). When the feast is over there are twelve bowls of scraps (twelve full moons). This man then repeats the feat to feed 4,000 men and this time there are seven bowls of scraps. Jesus had twelve disciples, just as Muhammad selected twelve leaders and the Jews had twelve tribes. Muhammad receives a first recital from Allah while in Mecca in 610 CE; the people of Mecca then reject his teachings and he is forced to flee, this is known as the Hijra and it takes place in 622 CE, twelve years later. Muhammad conducts three battles, with *'twelve leaders'*, becomes strong and returns to subjugate Mecca seven years after the Hijra. The Mother of Books is an early Islamic Text which contains the following recitals:

- 'The seven and twelve light our form and body'
- 'The seven and twelve as Muhammad and his family'
- 'The seven and twelve as heavenly features'
- 'The seventh sphere'
- 'The seven ranks of spiritual beings'

A particular scene from Islamic literature tells of Allah instructing the prophet Ibrahim to leave his wife and child (Hajir and Ishmael) alone in the desert. During his absence the child becomes thirsty and Hajir runs to find water and back the child seven times. Ishmael, in his anger, stamped the ground with his foot and water miraculously gushed from the ground. Such is the story behind the origins of the 'Well of Zamzam'. All able bodied Muslims are expected to conduct a pilgrimage to Mecca at least once in their lifetime which is referred to as the Hajj. On arrival at Mecca, their task is to walk around the Ka'bah seven times. The Islamic denomination known as Shia is also known as 'The Twelvers', because its adherents believe that there have been only twelve divinely ordained leaders throughout history.

The above is a very small sample of the addiction to the numbers seven and twelve within mythology and theology; a full listing would be an impossible task. Is this all coincidence? Not likely; it's just pure fantasy fiction written around the core ingredients derived from ancient star gazing. The numbers seven and twelve appear with monotonous regularity in

Mesopotamian and Egyptian mythology, ancient Indian texts, Greek and Roman pagan beliefs, Gnosticism, the Old Testament, New Testament and the Koran along with other Islamic literature.

**Enter the god child idea:**

During these early stages of upheaval, the concept of the god child makes its first appearance in Egypt as Osiris; and the theme is an instant hit. Each civilisation likes the new, must have, religious fashion fad so much, that over time they all create their own mystery god child. Osiris then becomes: Horus, Dionysus, Bacchus, Attis, Mithra etc. etc. and eventually Jesus. The most common base concept is a man born to a god and a virgin. This man dies and then resurrects after a variety of very short periods of between three to five days. God childs appear all over the Mediterranean and the Middle East, all with different names and slightly different takes on the same basic story. They are woven into a new religious concept of 'The Mysteries' and the base roots of Gnostic theology are born. These pagan mystery cults had superficial outer stories and esoteric inner mysteries. The outer stories were revealed to followers by way of passion plays. The inner mysteries were revealed to a convert via staged initiations; they became very popular.

The passion plays enacted the death and resurrection scenes of the allegorical god child; as for the content of the initiations into the esoteric mysteries, we can turn to Plato. Plato records in his book 'The Republic' that the initiations were conducted by priests ordained by the gods themselves. The process of initiation was used to give divine absolution for all sins committed in life by the initiate. This ensured the gods would allow the soul access to the heavens, and thereby avoid the agony of eternity with the gods of the underworld. Everyone wanted to be initiated; everyone wanted to find the enlightenment which came hand in hand with full initiation.

56

A search of the pagan mysteries from antiquity reveals many resurrecting god childs, all of which predate the New Testament version of Jesus by centuries; in the case of Osiris, circa 2400 BCE, millennia. So, Jesus is a perennial myth figure who appears time and time again throughout history all over Asia and Europe. This figure was, at its conception, a Gnostic figure, and a dying and resurrecting god child born of a god and a virgin. He dies and resurrects after various short delays, usually two to three days in length. His parables and allegories are also laden with the core ingredients from astro-maths and the numbers seven and twelve occur constantly in his stories and deeds.

We will now delve much deeper into these mystery resurrecting god childs with many different names in so many stories and relate their common elements back to the Sumerian concepts of astro-maths. In nearly all cases the character is born on the winter solstice and dies and resurrects at the spring equinox. This is reasonable; he is the salvation allegory for our life. He is therefore born when the year starts at the winter solstice, about the 25th December, which is the right hand stake in the sunrise position experiment. The precise dates of the solstice and the equinox have shifted by a few days over the last 2,000 years due to the fact that the Earth slowly wobbles as it spins; added to this is the fact that there have been many different calendars in use throughout the world over the last 2,000 years. He is killed and comes back to life at the spring equinox around March 25th; just when the planet seems to be reborn with flowers appearing and calves and lambs being born. This is the midpoint stake in the experiment, due east. Ancient Egypt also celebrated this day. This is signified by the fact that the Great Sphinx faces the spring equinox sunrise. In fact almost all ancient monuments are aligned to the compass points, but this is just a consequence of them actually being aligned to face the spring equinox sunrise; mans devotion to the two solar events of the winter solstice sunrise and the spring equinox sunrise predate the Christian Christmas and Easter celebrations by thousands of years. The god child resurrection allegory is as follows: the figure is our salvation, just as the planet dies and is reborn so is he, just as we shall die, like him we will be reborn.

Given that the stories in the theological books all make constant use of the numbers seven and twelve, for the seven visible planets and the twelve moon phases each year, why do most of the dying and resurrecting god childs come back to life after two to three days? Where in astro-maths does this concept come from? Look at the Moon and think outside of the box! There are twelve full moons each full sun cycle from left to right and back again; but there are also twelve dark moons (new moons). Every month, without fail, for about two nights the Moon literally and visibly dies and then comes back to life three nights later. The Moon is the symbolic mystery god child who dies and comes back to life on the third day! To give the reader some confidence in this assertion: clay tablets which contain Sumerian cuneiform writing have been found and translated; most of which originate from the area of modern-day Baghdad. Some of these tablets reveal a religious ceremony concerned with mourning the death of Nanna, the moon god. This ritual involved covering oneself in fire ash or river mud and lamenting until Nanna returned, or resurrected from death; which of course it always did, some three nights after it disappeared. One can imagine the priest of ancient Uruk standing on the topmost platform, being the seventh platform, of their ziggurat to witness the god Nanna disappearing in the east just before sunrise. Three days of lamenting would follow until Nanna reappeared again in the west just after sunset. Indeed, the first appearance of the new moon in the west, just after sunset, is still used today as the marker for the start of the Islamic lunar months. In addition, Herodotus circa 450 BCE tells us that the people who live in the cultivated parts of Egypt purged themselves for three consecutive days every month; although Herodotus does not speculate as to why, there is only one cosmic event which lasts for three days, and occurs every month.

We will now explore the concept of being born to a virgin; this is common to many of the god child myths. An astrological age is roughly 2,150 years. This is the time it takes the vernal equinox (Latin for spring) to travel through one of the zodiac signs. Since it takes about 2,150 years, moving into a new star sign is a big event, the dawning of a new age. The current age, Pisces, began about 100 BCE to 10 BCE when the vernal equinox moved into Pisces, which in zodiac terms is the sign of the fish; or, if we like, in religious terms, the sign of the fish. Visually, this means that Pisces is rising on the horizon exactly due east just before daybreak on the vernal equinox; the midpoint stake in our earlier experiment. The Sun also rises exactly due east on this day and therefore rises into Pisces, hence the 'Age of Pisces'. At the same time, Virgo, the virgin, is setting on the horizon due west, exactly in line with the stakes viewed in the opposite direction. Is this a coincidence? No; it is where the idea for the story of a god born of a virgin comes from. So, many of the new resurrecting god child characters, created after 100 BCE, not only died and came back to life at the spring equinox, they were also born of a virgin. The emerging idea of a virgin birth could then easily have been retrospectively overlaid onto previous god child characters from history. One of these emerging god child myths I believe is called 'a fisher of men' and his first two of twelve disciples were two fishermen, or fish, (vernal equinox, eastern horizon Pisces); and his mother was a virgin, (vernal equinox, western horizon Virgo). This visual astrological event can still be viewed today just before daybreak on the spring equinox and will continue until we move into the 'Age of Aquarius' sometime around 2100 CE.

Since the precession of the equinox moves backwards through the zodiac signs, the last three astrological ages were: Taurus, then Aries, then Pisces (the current age). When we were in the 'Age of Taurus' the bull, a god by the name of Moloch Baal was the main deity all over the Middle East. The Canaanites from this period represented Moloch Baal with graven images of a bull and images of a god in human form with a bulls head. Then we entered the 'Age of Aries' the ram, and the Israelite Kingdoms reigned in the Levant; consequently we find the Old Testament is awash with passages which reject the worship of graven images of bulls, particularly golden calves, and the god called Moloch Baal; rams horns and sacrificing sheep became the symbolism of Judaism. Then we entered the 'Age of Pisces' the fish, and the Jesus story was born; Christian tradition is awash with references to fish, the very first Christian symbol was an image of a fish! This is not coincidental, it is by design. It is why all religion is conceptually derived from astronomy and astrology.

In a passage from the Gnostic gospel of Thomas, which is basically a list of the parable sayings of Jesus, the Jesus characters claims: *"People may think I have come to impose peace upon the world. They do not know that I have come to impose conflicts upon the earth: fire, sword, war. For there will be five in a house. There will be three against two and two against three."* This passage is not referring to five people gathering in a dwelling, it refers to the visual alignment of the five visible planets all appearing within the area of one of the zodiac signs (*"in a house"*). The strange split between two and three replicates the fact that two of the wandering stars are positioned between the Earth and the Sun (Mercury and Venus), while the remaining three are positioned on the outer side of the Earth (Mars, Jupiter and Saturn). However, the writers of this text would not have known this; what they would have realised is: although all five might be in alignment with a particular zodiac sign, only three would be visible at night, not all five. Some Gnostic astrological Jesus quotes have found their way into the New Testament canon. In Luke 22.10 the disciples are preparing for the final pass over meal, the meal that the main character, the current god child, knows is the last meal before leaving this life, or this astrological age. The disciples ask Jesus *"where should they prepare the meal?"* Jesus replies: *"As you enter the city a man carrying a jar of water will meet you, follow him into the house that he enters"*. A house is a very common reference to the areas of night sky occupied by the signs of the zodiac, a man carrying a jar of water is a reference to Aquarius; and when we move out of the 'Age of Pisces', we will move into, the 'Age of Aquarius'. In Matthew 28:20 the Character Jesus assures doubters among his followers with the following caption: *"And surely I am with you always to the very end of the age"*. The actual word was not 'Age' but 'Eon' which means epoch and refers specifically to an astrological age. So the character was really saying: *"I will be with you until the end of the Age of Pisces"*. This is because Jesus, as in allegorical Jesus as opposed to literal Jesus, was a specific God, for a specific astrological age. He even appears in history at the start of the 'Age of Pisces' with stories which contain references to fish, fishing and fishermen; this is not, and cannot be, coincidental.

To expand the main hypothesis of this chapter further, I now wish to include two concepts currently being circulated on the internet of unknown authorship under the heading of 'zeitgeist'. These concepts put forward two other ideas which demonstrate the same hypothesis as astro-maths; namely, that the theological ideas of a god child are purely conceived from simple astrological observation. The work of Robert Bauval and Graham Hancock has made us aware of the following relationship between the three stars of Orion's Belt and the three pyramids of Giza: if we lay a scaled up photo of the three stars over the top of an aerial photo of the three pyramids, we find that the star centres match the pyramid apexes exactly. Since the three stars do not form a perfect line and the three pyramids follow the same dogleg precisely, we can conclude, without doubt, that these three stars are the plan for the layout of the three pyramids and consequently that these three stars were highly venerated.

The brightest star in the sky bar the Sun is called Sirius. Sirius was also venerated by the Egyptians because they used its reappearance after a long absence from the night sky, its heliacal rising, to mark the start of the Nile floods. For the Egyptians it was literally 'the star in the east'.

On the winter solstice, the sunrise has moved as far south along the horizon as it is ever going to get; the right hand stake in our experiment. After the solstice, the sunrise starts to move back to the north. This marks the start of a return to longer warmer days and a move towards spring. The ancient Egyptians did celebrate this astrological event; for them it was literally, 'the birth of the Sun'.

The three stars of Orion's Belt line up and point in the general direction of Sirius. Every night, the three stars of Orion's Belt break the eastern skyline about one hour before Sirius. Once Sirius is in view, all four then generally line up, and at the moment when Sirius is just above the eastern horizon, all four stars align with a particular spot on the eastern horizon. They point to the same particular spot every single day of the year. However, the line up can obviously only be viewed when the stars rise in darkness as opposed to daylight. This particular spot also happens to be where the Sun rises on one particular day of the year, being the winter solstice (give or take a few degrees). This is December $21^{st}$ today, but in antiquity, when the allegorical stories were created, it was December $25^{th}$ (by their calendar). The commonality regardless of time line is that the spot on the horizon identified by the alignment of these four highly venerated stars is always the sunrise point of the winter solstice; the farthest south the sunrise ever gets, the day on which the ancient Egyptians celebrated the 'birth of the Sun'. So: 'The three kings follow the eastern star which leads them to where the Sun is born on the winter solstice', ($25^{th}$ December). Now, notwithstanding the fact that 'solar sun' and 'father of son' sound similar in the English language, because this is coincidental and does not form part of the assertion here; we can see how an original story with a solar deity, has been transformed some way down the line to a story with an allegorical deity, and then further transformed further down the line to a story with a literal person as the deity; which gives us the nativity scene of today. The nativity therefore, was not a factual event; it is a fictional allegorical interpretation of the daily movement of some very specific and highly venerated stars in relation to the yearly movement of the Sun. The Gnostic allegorical interpretation of this ancient astrological myth was turned into a supposed factual interpretation circa post-70 CE by the literalist Christians of the Roman Empire.

Once the concept of Orion's Belt and Sirius pointing to the winter solstice sunrise formulated to explain the original 'three kings, star of the east and birth of the god child' story, web site posters sought immediately to discredit it. The detractors have turned towards 'star tracking software' to forward their objections. In this, they look for a level of accuracy which is neither required nor justified, and they make incorrect assumptions when deciding on their parameters. The detractors point out that the alignment of the four stars and the sunrise point is not perfect; but perfect results are not really required, the point being made is that the distance between the two extremities of the summer solstice sunrise and the winter solstice sunrise is visibly immense on the horizon. The winter solstice sunrise was the event the ancients interpreted as the Sun being reborn. It was to this point that the ancients concluded Orion's Belt and Sirius, the brightest star in the sky, were pointing to; a conclusion drawn using line of sight, not with the use of modern-day theodolites and computer software programs. This perceived alignment gave rise to the veneration of these four particular stars and the origin of an allegorical myth: that myth being 'the three kings followed the star of the east which indicated where the Sun will be born on the winter solstice', namely the winter solstice sunrise. Sirius today, rises on the horizon to the left of the winter solstice sunrise position as we view it; the rise of Sirius is drifting further to the left by a rate of 1 degree every seventy years. However, two thousand years ago Sirius rose to the right of the winter solstice sunrise; therefore, with its slow leftward drift it has drifted past the winter solstice sunrise and over to its present day position. Sirius has therefore been in the general vicinity of the winter solstice sunrise for the last two thousand years at least.

To give a modern-day analogy, in order to demonstrate why we do not have to be so precise before we accept the above explanation: no one today would have a problem with the statement 'the two end stars of the Plough, aka the Great Bear and Ursa Major, point to the north star, Polaris'. This statement is widely accepted today, and has been for centuries. The two end stars of the Plough do not however point directly at the north star, Polaris; they only point in the general direction of Polaris. Moreover, Polaris is called the north star because it indicates the direction of north to us, but it is not exactly above north, only in the general direction of north. Just as we have no problem with the generality of this concept, we should also accept the generality of the three stars of Orion's Belt lining up with Sirius and pointing to the winter solstice sunrise. It is so close, that it is close enough to give rise to the myth it has created.

When we move to the date for the winter solstice event (25$^{th}$ Dec), detractors commonly use computer programs to calculate the date of the winter solstice in ancient times in order to discredit the idea of the theory. This does not create the correct answer for many reasons. Let's say for example, we wish to know the exact date allocated to the winter solstice 3,000 years ago, and we use a modern-day astrological computer program to find it. The answer produced would be the date attached to that particular day according to the calendar algorithm in use today, the Gregorian calendar. But that calendar is a very recent calendar. The calendars in use over history have changed many times, and even today we have different calendars in use at the same time; this was even more prevalent in ancient times. There used to be only 360 days in a calendar year consisting of twelve months of thirty days each, there were then five extra days added at the end of each year which were given over to the veneration of the five main Egyptian deities; there was not always a leap year. The first Roman calendar, circa 750 BCE, had only ten months; it was revised circa 700 BCE to twelve months. This is why September, October, November and December which originally represented the $7^{th}$ $8^{th}$ $9^{th}$ and $10^{th}$ months of Romulus (as their names suggest), actually now represent the $9^{th}$ $10^{th}$ $11^{th}$ and $12^{th}$ months. So, no computer algorithm could calculate what date a given people in a given area would have allocated to a given day at a given time. It could only display what it would have been called if the Gregorian calendar had been in use from that time to this in that area.

We can make very good guesses as to what the date attributed to a winter solstice was for a particular culture, from the original god child myths of that culture. This is because the winter solstice is the day used to denote the deities birthday. For the Mithra religion of Persia and later Mithras of pagan Rome it is the $25^{th}$ Dec. Mithra is an excellent example to use for many reasons, one of which is very significant. Mithra is often depicted in art as master of the Sun, 'Sol Invictus'. This is because Mithra was Sol Invictus. Sol Invictus means invincible sun, so Mithra's miracle virgin birth was linked with the birth of the Sun. The birth of the Sun was the event of the winter solstice sunrise. We know from historical literature that Mithra's birthday was allocated as $25^{th}$ Dec. We can conclude from this that, at the time the Mithra myth emerged, whenever and wherever that was, the winter solstice was on the $25^{th}$ Dec. by their calendar, not ours.

Now for the politics: Roman literalist Christians circa 70 to 300 CE decided on the date of birth for the new Jesus character. They selected a winter solstice from antiquity, indirectly, and in all ignorance. They had no concern with star alignment and winter solstice dates. They had no idea this ever had anything to do with the birthdates applied to the many deities. They were simply trying to kill off the old Roman pagan Mithras religion in order to replace it with their new Christian religion. That is why they chose the $25^{th}$ Dec as the date of birth, and for that matter the spring equinox for the resurrection scene. It was to overlay and drown out Mithraism; it was purely political. It is also why Constantine I, who initiated the enforcement of literalist Christianity onto the world, built his Basilica of St Peter over the top of the main temple to Mithras in Rome. This building was in turn demolished and rebuilt. It was completed in the 1590's during the reign of Pope Sixtus V. The building is now known as St Peters in Vatican City. Excavations under the Vatican revealed some old mausoleums; one of these mausoleums, named 'mausoleum M' contains a mosaic of a solar deity. This deity has a sun image emanating from behind his head which is comprised of seven rays of light. It is an image of Sol Invictus, also known as Mithras.

I accept people will seek to discredit theories, indeed this entire book was written for that very purpose. It does however seem extraordinary that such a perfectly reasonable, rational and logical explanation for the existence of all the god child myths and their miracle virgin birth stories, would be rejected in favour of a physically impossible theory; such as: that of a human, conceived in a womb, without the presence of human sperm.

To explain the second 'zeitgeist' concept mentioned earlier: The star constellation 'Crux', (Latin 'Cross') was also known as the Southern Cross. This is because its stem points to celestial south in the same way the Great Bear points towards celestial north. It was therefore also highly venerated due to its usefulness in navigation. Its historic veneration is demonstrated by the fact that the constellation has been used in the design of many national flags. It is too far south today for us to see in Northern Europe. However, from the Middle East it can be seen each night very low on the southern horizon, and post-400 CE it was much higher. It is extremely bright and forms a perfect cross. That is: A perfect Roman Catholic style cross. It is not: almost a cross, or any old cross, but a perfect Roman Catholic depiction of a cross.

When we arrive at the winter solstice, the sunrise and sunset have both moved as far south as they are going to get, and the Sun's arc across the day time sky is the lowest it is ever going to be. After the winter solstice the sunrise and sunset start to move north again and the Sun's arc across the day time sky starts to rise. The Sun gets progressively higher in the sky each day at noon. When we arrive at the summer solstice the Sun's arc has risen to its upper limit and the Sun reaches its highest midday point. The Sun then spends the next six months descending back to its lowest point on the winter solstice. In the area of the Middle East pre-400 CE, during the period of the winter solstice, when the Sun reaches its lowest arc in the sky, the arc the Sun takes across the daytime sky is in the same area as the arc the constellation Crux takes across the night sky. The Sun's arc changes from its highest to lowest point in a matter of six months; this movement is therefore very perceptible to humans. The stars however, move from their highest to lowest point over a period of 12,900 years, their arc across the night sky therefore appears to be static to human perception. The Sun's arc consequently appears to move down to the area of the constellation Crux's arc at the moment of the winter solstice, and then rises again after the winter solstice. Or put another way: 'The Sun dies on the cross, and then the Sun rises again'.

If this happens at the winter solstice, why is the resurrection celebrated at the spring equinox? The answer to this conundrum is quite simple; the first three day resurrection concept probably originated from the twelve instances per year of the two night (so three days) 'dark moon' analogy discussed earlier, coupled with the apparent rebirth of the planet around the spring equinox. The spring equinox is also the time when the light symbolically defeats the dark, i.e. a return to the days being longer than the nights. The Crux constellation analogy is realised centuries later; long after the birth of the Sun had been associated with the winter solstice and the three day resurrection with the spring equinox; dates which had by then been celebrated for eons. This can be verified by the fact that: god child's existing before the Jesus character simply died and resurrected, whereas the Jesus version died 'on the cross' and resurrected. Moreover, there is conflict in literature about the Jesus character as to whether he was crucified on a tree or a cross; I would conjecture that this demonstrates the early diversity of Jesus characters, both allegorical and literal, identified in chapter one.

It hardly needs stating that the motion of these stars, (Orion's Belt, Sirius and Crux) predates the Earth, never mind the religious stories. But what has become clear from archaeology is that these particular stars were highly venerated by the civilisations in the Middle East centuries before the concept of Jesus. That is, they are not just any old stars selected at random and used to try to discredit theology; they are the most venerated stars from Egyptian and Roman antiquity, and they just happen to explain theology; they happen to explain it extremely well! The origin of these astrological allegories has been completely forgotten over the passage of time, and a reminder of the edicts of Theodosius in chapter one would be quite timely here; **Edict 313**: *All astrologers are to be expelled and exiled, unless they burn their books in the presence of a Bishop and convert to Christianity.* The early Catholic Church was indeed paranoid by astrology and its documents; so much so that the eradication of all astrological worship and literature was conducted in a ruthless and merciless manner. This was not because Christianity simply wanted to be the only belief system on the block; it was because Christianity had something to hide, and that something could be found in the books of the astrologers. With regard to the evolution path from astrology to mythology through to theology suggested above, we must bear in mind that everything, absolutely everything, evolves from very simplistic beginnings; this includes great mythical stories.

Almost every allegorical god child from 1900 BCE onwards, from the area of the Middle East: Osiris & Horus, Attis, Bacchus, Dionysus,

Mithra etc, was born on the winter solstice and died and resurrected at the spring equinox; including the latest allegorical solar god child, Jesus. This, as previously stated, is written in stone on the I-kher-nefert stele with the passion play of Osiris circa 1900 BCE. So in short, Jesus simply did not exist. There was no virgin birth, or miracle studded missionary and no crucifixion or resurrection. He is an astrological invention; his stories are all purely allegorical.

I will now pull all of the ideas from chapter one and two together into one time line. Pre-100 BCE we see the creation, over time, of several allegorical god child figures. Around 100 BCE we see the dawning of a new astrological age, the Age of Pisces. After the start of the Age of Pisces we see the various allegorical god childs being distilled down into one hybrid allegorical god child who is termed the messiah or Christ. We then experience a dividing line around 70 CE; the date of this dividing line is very significant and will be investigated further in chapter four. After 70 CE we see the emergence of the Matthew, Mark, Luke, John and Acts stories; these stories turn the oral traditions of the hybrid allegorical Christ into a supposed factual Christ. However, the dividing line does not signal a homogenous move from the acceptance and adherence to the allegorical Gnostic belief over to the literal version of the belief; moreover it signals the start of a schism, an allegorical/literal schism. This schism is very real and extremely well documented by the polemicists and apologists from both sides from the first two centuries CE. Reading the polemics and apologies from this period seems to reveal that both the Gnostic allegorical and literalist followers of a Christ figure had grown to become major belief systems in the midst of the pagan Roman Empire; and that the allegorical/literalist schism seemed also to be an east/west schism, in that the literalist view began and grew in Rome and occupied the west of the empire, while the east mainly maintained the original Gnostic allegorical versions of the story.

By 310 CE, rule of the Roman Empire was divided by four emperors: Constantine and Maxentius in the West and Maximinus Daia and Licinus in the east. All four men had desires to become the sole Emperor. By 313 CE the outcome of two civil wars left just two emperors, with Constantine ruling in the west and Licinus ruling in the east. In 324 CE the inevitable happened and civil war broke out again; however, Constantine was not blind to the massive Gnostic Christian movement in the east and Licinus' loathing of this movement in favour of the Roman pagan beliefs. Constantine swelled the ranks of his army at a stroke in courting both the literalists in the west and the Gnostics in the east by proclaiming belief in God and Christ. By the end of 324 CE Constantine was the sole ruler of the entire Roman Empire. Post civil war success Constantine decrees that Christianity is to become the state religion of the Roman Empire; unfortunately for the Gnostics in the east, he resolves to settle the allegorical/literalist schism and comes down in favour of the literalist version of Christianity; and it is the beginning of the end for the Gnostics. The concepts set out above will be expanded on and enhanced in the chapters which follow.

How then, did the people of the post-324 CE Christian world make the move from pagan worship, and the worship of many different Christ figures, to the collective worship of one Christ figure, being Constantine's favoured literal Christ figure? No theology can become unanimously accepted, or even dominant, in a given area, no matter how small or large that area, until it is forced onto the population concerned upon pain of death and torture by a despotic ruler; even more so, a succession of despotic rulers, and this is true of Judaism, Christianity and Islam. To illuminate the above statement further: Scientology will never be a dominant belief within any society, in any given geographical location, because it has missed the boat. The days of forcing people to believe, at least in the western world, are long since over; and in the societies on our globe where the population are still forced to believe their despots favoured theology, Scientology would make no ground at all, because it would be perilously dangerous to support it. In the post-324 CE Christian world, peoples very being depended on them physically demonstrating their belief in God and Jesus. Mere lip service would not suffice. Their children's survival in the world was dependent on how well they, as parents, indoctrinated their children with belief in God and Jesus. If their children did not grow into adulthood with unquestioning belief in God and Jesus, they simply would not make it to adulthood. After centuries of such despotic rule, humanity then seemed to move into a kind of universal 'Stockholm syndrome': A syndrome whereby a captive becomes sympathetic to the views of their captor. A few centuries later, the need to enforce religious belief on to the people eventually diminished and ceased to be exercised, because eventually the people actually did, believe! The process of indoctrinating our children with religious belief has continued now for nearly 1,700 years, despite the fact that the original impetus for doing so, the fear of death and torture, has now evaporated. I should point out that the above is largely true for Western Europe, The Americas and most of Eastern Europe; there are still enclaves in the remainder of the eastern world and parts of Africa where belief in the state religion is accepted, due to the fear of death and torture as a retribution for demonstrating non-belief.

In this chapter, the claim is made that the knowledge of the roots of literalist Christianity - and its link with astrology, pagan mystery religions and Gnosticism - is lost to us today because all such literature has been destroyed. Clearly, such a blanket claim cannot be made without the presentation of evidence; otherwise, it would be a simple catchall, get out of jail free card, identical in nature to the religious faith position. To justify the claim that much, if not all, problematic literature - and people for that matter - were burnt by the despotic regimes of history from post-324 CE, we can present, in addition to that already presented in chapter one, the following historic documentation: starting with a list of edicts from the earliest Roman Christian emperors:

**Constantius 341 CE:** *"Superstition shall cease and the madness of sacrifices shall be abolished. If any persons should be proved to devote their attention to sacrifices or to worship images; we command that they shall be subjected to capital punishment."*

**Constantius and Constans 346 CE:** *"The temples are to be closed everywhere so as to deny to all abandoned men the opportunity to commit sin; anyone guilty of the crime of sacrificing must be struck down with the avenging sword; and provincial governors who fail to enforce the edict are subject to execution."*

**Honorius and Theodosius II 415 CE:** *"Those who publicly assemble to practice heretical rites may have their property taken and be executed."*

**Theodosius II and Valentinian III 429 CE:** *"Anyone who converts an orthodox Christian from the Catholic Church to another religion or heretical sect will have his property confiscated and be executed."*

**Theodosius II and Valentinian III 435 CE:** *"Pagan sacrifices are forbidden. Pagan temples and shrines are to be torn down and replaced with the symbol of Christianity: the cross. Anyone who mocks this law faces execution."*

Following on from these edicts, Charlemagne was a European ruler between 786 & 814 CE. The whole of Charlemagne's reign was spent waging war. He came to power as the ruler of the largest empire in Europe; he died as the ruler of the only empire in Europe. During his wars, the defeated pagan Saxon tribes were all given an infamous choice: 'accept my god and submit to baptism now, or go and meet my god now'.

The ideas in this chapter present astro-maths as the beginnings of spiritual thought, and the evidence of how that thought process evolved into - what is considered today as - mythology and then morphed into today's religious theological offerings. These resulting theological belief systems were brutally enforced onto the populace by active and ruthless eradication of their predecessors. Astro-maths hopefully conveys a strong argument to the secular and religious people of today, that the core concepts of the three main faiths are all based on nothing more than star gazing and story creation; this concept evolved along different lines and was successfully passed on throughout history; initially by brutal force, and then later, naturally, as a meme: a religious thought virus.

We should, by now, be far enough intellectually advanced as a species to realise that Christianity did not become a successful meme because of any real substance in its story; but rather because of its despotic, ruthless enforcement upon our ancestors and the lottery of the chance outcome of historic battles. The truth behind the birth and growth of Christianity lies firmly in the anthropological evolution of the human mind and the initial thoughts of astrology; thoughts that were then mixed in with the birth and evolution of societies, which create, by default, despotic rulers. These historic despotic rulers found the enforcement of theological ideas very useful with regards to controlling their subjects.

Without doubt, Christianity, Judaism and Islam will one-day be universally regarded as mythology along with all other ancient mythical beliefs. If we can look at the religious meme from this viewpoint, then maybe we can inoculate it. Maybe we, rather than future generations, can assign these three religious theologies to the label of myth.

With specific regard to the highly infectious Christian religious meme I would say: *"But do we really believe?"* To quote comedian Mark Steel: *"Do we really believe a man was executed and then came back to life; and he did this to absorb original sin. Sin created by a woman constructed from the rib bone of a man; and after a conversation with a talking snake?"*

# --Chapter 3: Theologies R Us--

There are many works in publication today which demonstrate just how varied the theological world was between 100 BCE and 100 CE. This has been made possible because these lost gospels, mainly Gnostic, have been rediscovered, translated and published. It was not previously possible to purchase such books because the existence of these theologies, and their followers, were all but eradicated by the Catholic Church of 300 to 1600 CE; with unbelievable ruthlessness and utter disregard for the right to life and free thought. Hundreds of thousands of people were murdered in the most brutal of fashions, and competing literature destroyed, by the early Catholic Church in order to achieve this total eradication of rival theologies. Compelling evidence for the eradication process is found in the polemics written by the early Catholic Church against these theologies; amazingly, the pagan and Gnostic written documents were burnt by the Church, but their content is ironically preserved, because it is reproduced in the Church's own polemic writings against the pagan and Gnostic beliefs.

Following successful eradication, the past leaders of Christian countries, curtailing to the demands of the Church, made religious education compulsory and only taught the officially accepted Catholic and Protestant versions: the eradicated theologies were dead, and destined to stay dead. Therefore, I put the record straight here and make the reader aware of the myriad of Christian faiths they might have been able to follow, were it not for the indescribable evil perpetrated by the murderous early Catholic

Church. My main source is the 'The Gnostic Bible' edited by Willis Barnstone and Marvin Meyer. This book translates the Gnostic texts found hidden at Nag Hammadi, and which comprise what is now referred to as the Nag Hammadi library. They are a group of religious texts which have survived the Catholic book (and body) burning process by their concealment some 1,700 years ago. They were found in 1945 in Upper Egypt buried in jars in the ground. The jars contained thirteen leather bound books; of which twelve survive. The twelve books comprise some fifty-two religious texts. The thirteenth book is said to have been used as camp fire fuel by the finders because they did not initially comprehend the value of their find. However, the manuscripts passed through the hands of many religious scholars before public translation of the texts was released; the public did not get to read the translated contents of the books until 1975, thirty years after the books were first discovered. It therefore remains a possibility that the loss of the thirteenth book is again religious censorship of damning material; just like the torn out page from the back of the only surviving copy of the First Epistle of Clement. The twelve surviving books contain no material which conclusively proves that their ideas on a Jesus character predate the literalist crucifixion scene of 30 CE; the lost thirteenth book might have contained such material and was therefore destroyed. This is of course, pure conjecture, but an extremely possible concept none the less. Carbon dating of the papyrus, combined with the knowledge of when the letter styles and dialects employed in the writing was common base, dates the Nag Hammadi manuscripts to the beginning of the second century. But this only dates when the manuscripts were written. The stories contained on the manuscripts clearly have to predate their writing, how long by is not yet ascertained. It is unfounded conjecture by the Christian authorities of today to state that the stories from the Nag Hammadi texts clearly post date their version of Christianity; but of course, we must also accept that faced with these alternate Jesus character stories, this is a stance of which they have no option but to take. That the Church does make this claim, does not negate the fact that the origin of these texts could, and most likely does, predate Pontius Pilate's governorship of Judah.

The main concept in Gnostic faith is that a person finds God by knowing himself/herself and obtaining gnosis (Knowledge); this secret knowledge revealed to the believer the true purpose of life. There were many flavours of Gnostic faith encompassing polytheism, dualism and monotheism and they were all mainly allegorical belief systems. These Gnostic faiths did not therefore need a hierarchy of Bishops and therefore had no authority structure; a situation with which they were happy. Needless to say, the fledgling Catholic Church of 300 CE onwards - Under Imperial Roman direction - was not.

The Gnostic theologies evolved from earlier Greek and Persian mystery pagan cults and they created an allegorical god child which the followers all aspired to become; in doing so they became the god child (Christ), found gnosis, and were united with God in this life. This is an important issue, Gnostics believed the resurrection to be something a person achieves while alive, s/he is resurrected with gnosis. One more important issue is that Gnostic faith had many different stories and forms and did not comprise any one orthodox version; this posed no problem to the Gnostics. However, it could not be tolerated by the emerging literalist Catholic Church of 300 CE onwards.

### A selection of Gnostic ideas from Nag Hammadi

In the gospel of Thomas, a character called Yeshua (Jesus) is depicted as being sent from the light to reveal that the light is in all people if they look for it. If they find it, their light (soul), will live on through the light (God) after their body dies. Yeshua announces that the Pharisees have taken this knowledge and hidden it; his mission is to reveal it. Yeshua performs no miracles, dies for no one's sins and is not therefore resurrected.

In Herakleon's interpretation of the gospel of John he explains that Jesus is not the word made flesh as in a physical man, but rather a spiritual image of flesh.

The Songs of Solomon recite verses which communicate how to become a Christ, rather than following a Christ.

A Gnostic treatise entitled 'On the Origin of the World' includes multiple gods and heavens and depicts Eve as the virgin birth. Yaldabaoth is the creator of the world and is a lesser god to the supreme God referred to as 'The Good'. Yaldabaoth's creation is seen as unauthorised and wicked and he is referred to as the 'Demiurge'. The treatise contains a strong link to the Egyptian concept of resurrection: "The just will sprout like the phoenix..." the phoenix first appears alive, then dies, and then rises again. Jesus is present in the beginning of the creation of the world by Yaldabaoth and its wickedness, but his only role is to visit the world and spread the word (gnosis) to cure the wickedness. He does not suffer crucifixion or rise from the dead. The resurrection role is played by the phoenix. The treatise ends with a version of the modern-day rapture story.

In a work called 'The Paraphrase of Shem'. God is called Derdekeas and the first human is called Shem.

The scripture known as 'Second treatise of the great Seth' criticises the emerging idea of a literal figure being crucified and resurrected called Christ. It defends the authors existing theology of an allegorical spiritual saviour called Seth. It is a polemic of the new idea of a literal god child. In this theology we have the following passage: "*I am in you and you in me*" suggesting that all people can become Seth. We also find: "*I visited a bodily dwelling*" as opposed to a virgin birth. The story tells how the rulers, who are not identified, persecute the bodily dwelling. Seth therefore leaves the dwelling, and observes the bodily dwelling being crucified from within the crowd; thus suggesting that it was not the Christ who was crucified because he had already left the bodily dwelling. There is therefore no resurrection scene. However, it does refer to the ground shaking and the earth cracking open. It portrays the graves of the dead being breached and the dead receiving new souls with which to walk the earth. Seth watches on as all this takes place. The author of Matthew in the New Testament has clearly read this passage and included much of it in his death scene for Jesus.

The gospel of Mary is another faith which sees the Christ dwelling in the person who looks for him, rather than followers following a literal Christ. In this gospel, Levi tells a gathering to *"Put on the perfect one and go out to preach"*.

The Naassene Sermon contains a 'Song to Attis'. The words of the song reveal knowledge and acceptance of all previous god child characters from Osiris circa 1900 BCE to Jesus circa 100 BCE to 150 CE. This song reveals that the Gnostics of the first century CE were all well aware of the origins of the god child myth. The fact that we today have had to rediscover those origins, presents hard evidence of an extremely ruthless and thoroughly successful eradication process.

In Hermetic 'Greek' Literature we have Poimandres. Despite these stories not having Mesopotamian, Egyptian or Jewish authorship, they still contain constant reference to the number seven. The stories range from 50 to 300 CE. In the scripture, the purpose of life is to free the soul from the prison of the body by the acquisition of gnosis and therefore make the ascent through the seven heavens (seven planets) into the eighth heaven (the realm of the fixed stars) and become God. This is seen as a return to God since every soul on earth is, in itself, a small piece of God in the earthly world.

From the same Hermetic text we have 'The Discourse on the Eighth and Ninth'; in this theology we can see confirmation that religious belief does indeed stem directly from astrology. This scripture positively links the seven heavens to the Sun, Moon and the five wandering stars (planets), one for each. It then allocates the eighth heaven to the realm of the fixed stars and the ninth heaven to be the realm of the gods beyond the fixed stars.

The suppression of the above ideas was wickedly efficient. However, there was one last attempt to revive the Gnostic faith of dualism which contained a high god 'The Good' who was displeased with a lesser god 'The Demiurge' for creating the world which 'The Good' viewed as a wicked creation. Acquiring the word 'gnosis' was the way to lead oneself from the wicked creation and back to the light. This revival, and challenge to Catholicism, began to flourish in Europe but really took hold in southern France and Italy between the 11th and 13th centuries; the group concerned were known as Cathars. The Cathars were outspoken in their opposition to many parts of the New Testament. This simply could not be tolerated by the intolerant Roman Catholic Church, so it did the all too familiar intolerant Christian thing. Its leader, Pope Innocent III to be precise (a most inapt title), declared a crusade on the Cathars in 1209 CE. In the inquisition that followed many people suffered execution by being burnt at the stake for the heresy of 'Catharism'; it is estimated that half of the population of southern France perished. In this act the Church brutally removed the last opposition to its theology in Europe for ever. They then proceeded to preach tolerance and love, turn the other cheek, love thy neighbour and forgive your enemy!

The above represents just a small section of the belief theologies we might have been practicing given a different course of events in history. This alone must alert us to the futile and fictitious nature of all theology. If any one of the theologies above is absolutely correct, the rest are by mutual exclusion completely false. But all followers believe they are following the correct theology and it is the other theologies which are false. I must reiterate to the reader at this point, when the Church claim that the above stories post date their version of the Jesus story, it is from a position of necessity, not from a position of authority or scholarship. The Church has to make this claim to substantiate their very existence as a leading religious organisation; but they can supply no evidence to support this claim. How long will it be before the whole of humankind joins the rational world and proclaims that all the above theologies are false, including today's accepted theologies, because they are all full of ludicrous statements that are physically impossible?

## Body and soul

When Plato sets out Socrates' vision for the perfect state to his small group of gathered friends he makes reference to injuries acquired by the person and relates the concept to injuries acquired by the state. He asserts that if a person receives a serious cut to his finger, that person will feel the pain; and likewise if society receives such an injury the effect should be felt by all members that make up that society.

Plato's goal in using this analogy is completely different to mine, but the concept of receiving an injury and feeling the pain is useful to me when tackling the issue of body and soul. It is clear that theology requires its followers to view a human being to be made up of two separable parts; the body which exists for a short while, controlled by the soul which lasts forever. The non theological view is that these two entities are not separable and come into and go out of existence together. Once again the theologians have created a concept that is neither provable nor disprovable; while at the same time the non religious would claim we simply have no evidence to suggest that the soul is separable and lives on, or indeed there even is such a thing as a soul, and the reality is our perception of a soul is purely pseudo. The theological view is only as rational as views which claim ideas such as: we used to be cats and dogs and came back to life as humans, or we never actually die because we are all living in a personal universe where we never die but everyone else does. The point being made is: non disprovable statements are two a penny, and as such, worthless. Statements which stand the scrutiny of evidence on the other hand, are useful to our understanding of life, and lead us to progress our efforts of research down worthwhile paths; theologies' only goal is to protect its own indefensible position by opposing and stifling such research. In the absence of any evidence to the contrary, why would we believe that we live on after the body dies? The religious counter with, 'proof is not required, just faith'.

So we need to treat the faith argument with the contempt it deserves. We need to accept that there is no hard proof for any hypothesis on what happens when we die. Therefore, we need to apply logic and reason to the arguments in order to view which is the more likely. My first retort to the supporters of the body and soul being two separate entities would be: if the soul can exist forever without a body, why on earth would it need a body in the first place? The concept of being able to exist in the ether for eternity and beyond makes the concept of using a body for a mere seventy or so years seem rather pointless.

Now I find Plato's comment on the finger cut coming into play. The pain we experience when suffering injury is a safety device courtesy of evolution, as is fear of the unknown and fear of death. The mind, or soul, is receiving a message that needs rather urgent processing and attention, hence the reason it hurts and therefore guarantees receiving urgent attention. The message is: you are in danger, you need to take action to avoid being cut any more and attend to the bleeding, or: you need to move a certain limb from the source of heat because you are being burnt. You are put into an automatic self preservation mode, but why? In the theological model, why should the conscience or the soul be so bothered about what happens to the body; it is only using it for a short while, then it will leave the body behind and begin an eternal existence? Or is it more rational to conceive that the message of pain is so severe, and we are so compelled to rectify the situation which causes the pain and danger, because the body is one entity only. Death is final and terminal; a state that should therefore be avoided at all costs.

In reality the body is millions of cells all working in unison to create one entity, a living creature; or as Richard Dawkins suggests, a survival machine for the genes. The brain is a collection of these cells performing their particular function. This function is to operate the limbs in order to move the body about. This makes sure the body finds food and water and can avoid danger. The mind therefore controls the environment in which the body exists with a view to shelter and warmth, and helps the body strive to create the situations needed in which it can reproduce copies of itself. The lungs and heart cells busy themselves oxygenating the blood and delivering that oxygenated blood to the rest of the organs. Other cells work on repairing the body when required; quite separately from any other intervention. If you cut your skin, the flesh cells repair themselves and create a new area of skin, broken bones can fuse back together. We do not consciously sit down and mend our skin or fix our broken bones, they do it themselves. All these things point not to two separable entities of body and soul, but to millions of cells working in unison as one entity, a human. When the human dies all of the cells cease to work and start to decompose. The cells which make up the brain, which is where the theologians assume the separable soul to exist, requires oxygen to function. Without oxygen the brain cells die, they stop functioning. When they die the brain dies, and the function it performs stops. That function, which is essentially thinking, is what theologians perceive to be our soul. If the thinking stops so does the concept of a soul. The brain will decompose and rot away leaving the bone of the skull with an empty cavity where the brain used to be. It was the brain that made the concept of a soul possible, if the brain has physically gone, so has the perceived soul. In short the perceived soul can only exist, as long as there is an oxygenated, functioning brain.

The body also performs functions which are all ultimately aimed at keeping the brain oxygenated and alive. We eat and drink to obtain energy; this keeps all the organs working. Blood is produced, kept clean by the liver, oxygenated by the lungs and delivered to all parts of the body, including the brain to keep it alive. All deaths are ultimately cause by lack of oxygen to the brain. I can lose my legs and arms, but as long as I maintain enough blood and blood pressure, the body can still deliver oxygen to the brain and I will survive. If I lose too much blood and the ability to pump it to the brain I would die. If I puncture my lungs and lose the ability to place oxygen into the blood and deliver it to the brain, I will die etc. So the brain, or thought process, is totally reliant on the body and its functions for its very existence. This is not what you would expect to find if the thought process could exist without the body.

Finally, if none of us know what happens after death, which is an absolute fact which cannot be disputed, what evidence can there be for an existence after death? The rationales behind the theologies of the soul are purely conceived to combat the fear of death with a refusal to believe it is final. This concept has been used by many despotic rulers from history, who have created and endorsed the idea of the soul going to hell or heaven depending on whether you did, or did not do, what the despots instructed you to do while you were alive. A very useful tool for the tyrannical leader and the biggest most effective con trick ever perpetrated.

**Probable history of Christianity:**

Given all of the above, I will now put forward a probable history of Christianity. A new small Gnostic cult starts to form in the Levant to coincide with and celebrate the dawning of the new era; being the start of the great month of Pisces. This is estimated to be around 100 BCE to 10 BCE. An astrological month can last some 2,150 years so moving into a new age, a new dawning, is quite a remarkable event. The cult adheres to all the common traits of the existing and previous mystery cults with members being led progressively through stages of initiation; the initiations culminate in full enlightenment of the mystery's inner most secrets. Due to its conception at the start of the Piscean age, the cult has many references to fish and fishermen within its outer mysteries.

Once an initiate has reached the final stage of initiation s/he is said to have found Christ in themselves, they are redeemed and fully enlightened; hence the followers of the cult are termed Christians by the Jews and by the Romans. Their actions, beliefs and ceremonies are by no means strange to the populace, being complete mimicry of all other mystery cults. They are 'just another cult' and they are small in number; as such, they are not viewed as a threat to the status quo, just a little quirky.

There is no leading light figure called Christ, this is not where their name came from. There is no Jesus Christ, Bob Christ, Jim Christ or any other Christ. There is no hierarchical authority structure and definitely no Church with bishops and priest etc. This then, is the core root and founding base of Christianity. Make careful note, this is completely foreign to our modern-day understanding of Christianity and the activities and beliefs of a Christian group. This is for a very good reason, these Christians are Gnostics, and they follow allegories. Modern Christians are Literalist, they do not look for the Christ in themselves, they follow what they see as a historical literal figure called Jesus Christ. The change between these two polarised views is via major historical events from the early fourth century CE when the Christian Gnostics literally had their religion hijacked and transformed to suit military and political goals.

Once changed, the Roman literalist Christians set about eradicating, by force, all trace of the Christian Gnostic faiths; much like the Priest of Amun tried to erase all evidence of the Aten Cult introduced to Egypt by Akhetaten, and Henry VIII tried to eradicate the Roman Catholic Church in Britain with the dissolution of the monasteries. The literalist Christians were far more successful with their eradication program than the Priests of Amun and Henry VIII. This process of eradicating the Gnostic versions of Christianity took place over the course of about 900 years and was very successful; any final remnants of Gnosticism would have been completely eliminated by the Inquisition. The full existence and variety of the Gnostic Christians is just starting to be revealed to us; we now have translations of ancient texts and correspondences, which still survive today from the start of the Common Era, which have allowed us to unveil the concepts of the Gnostic faiths.

Jumping back in time a little, when Rome burnt in 64 CE, Nero needed a scapegoat to avert claims that he set the blaze himself. He picks on the little guy and blames a small group of people who are now commonly referred to as Christians. These are the Christians referred to by Tacitus (see chapter six); they are Gnostic Christians not literalist Christians because the literalist Christians do not yet exist.

In 66 CE, the Jews revolt against Roman rule and the Romans under Vespasian and Titus retaliate with uncompromising brutal force. Judah, and eventually Jerusalem itself in 70CE are totally crushed by the might of Rome. After the war, post-70 CE, the Romans persecute the Jews physically and financially for the uprising and they place a tax on being Jewish. In reaction to the financial burden and physical oppression, there is a mass conversion from Judaism, and Gnostic Christianity is the target. With Gnostic Christianity still being tolerated by the Romans, and some Romans practicing it themselves by now, it is considered the safer option; the ranks of Gnostic Christianity in the Middle East swell almost overnight. At this point, the New Testament and the stories it contains about Jesus have not been conceived. This is why the conversion to Gnostic Christianity is not an issue to the Jews; these Christians are not following a messiah as the Roman Catholic Church would have us believe. Hey presto, we now have a new, major, religious movement. Time moves, on and the movement spreads to the western Mediterranean centres including Rome. Spread over such a large land mass, the original ideas of the cult start to morph and over time evolve in different directions. In general the western Mediterranean

Christians start to look for a literal Christ figure to follow and create the resurrecting god child born to a virgin. Meanwhile, the eastern Mediterranean Christians hold with their Gnostic mystery view of Christianity and the schism starts to form. This concept, and the rationale behind it, will be enhanced in chapter four, where we will consider how the destruction of the temple in Jerusalem came to have a date of 70 CE, an astrological number, and therefore an astonishing coincidence!

During the time span of 70 to 150 CE the western Christians morph into full blown literalists with a Church and a hierarchical bishopric. They start writing literalist gospels with tales of fantastic miracles performed by their resurrecting god child; in actual fact, these stories are once again perennial myths regurgitated. The eastern Gnostics also write gospels in their allegorical style holding true to their vision of Christ within themselves.

Now comes the decisive pivotal moment in history which spells the end of the Gnostic Christians and the beginning of the eradication process. Constantine uses the Gnostic Christians in the east to help him conquer the eastern half of the Roman Empire; but once he has succeeded he sets himself up as the despotic leader of the Christian Church. He comes down in favour of Literalism and rejects the Gnostic versions of the faith; the die is cast and it is the beginning of the end for the Gnostics.

Constantine's sidekick Bishop is Eusebius and between them they decide what the Christian religion does and does not stand for. They form the literalist gospels into the New Testament. Needless to say, none of the Gnostic gospels made it into the book. During, or after this time, the scripts of Josephus (see chapter six) are altered to place their fictional Jesus character into historic documents and therefore confirm him as a historic figure. The Church progresses through the Dark Ages, Middle Ages and the Renaissance as a ruthless despotic power spreading its influence across the globe at the end of a sword and with bloody massacre. The religion morphs into the myriad of Christian faiths we have today; many people died horrific deaths at the hands of the Catholic Church in this period of Christianity's evolution. However, at least one division of the Christian faith is missing from today's pool on offer; that division being the original Christian Gnostic versions.

## Anti Christian polemics:

For a cross reference, we can take a good estimation of the date the New Testament gospels were created by considering the works which rebuff the New Testament gospels; the polemics against the new faith. Without doubt, you cannot criticise a theology until the theology exists and becomes public. Without doubt, all theologies do receive polemics from other faiths as soon as they become public knowledge. The earliest anti 'Literalist' Christian Polemics we seem to know of at the present time from antiquity are: Heracleon, Celsus, Porphyry, Hierocles and Julian the Apostate.

The earliest known commentary on the New Testament (at the time of writing) came from Heracleon. He wrote a polemic on John which is dated to circa 170 CE. Celsus wrote a strong polemic against the Christian faith around 175 to 180 CE which is lost to us today; but we know what Celsus wrote, because his claims were each rebuffed by Origen in several volumes of his work 'Origen against Celsus'. Next comes Porphyry who lived circa 234 to 305 CE and wrote fifteen volumes 'Against the Christians'. Hierocles of Alexandria was a Platonist active around 430 CE whose writing style seems to try and reconcile Christian ideas to the Greek religions, and was himself inspired by the philosophy of Epictetus. Then we have a Roman Emperor, Julian the Apostate, Emperor 361 to 363 CE; he tried to turn back the tide and oust Christianity in order to re introduce Roman Paganism. Julian wrote 'Against the Galileans' as an anti Christian polemic.

Well, that is it; the interesting fact that emerges from this exercise is that there are no anti 'literalist Christian' polemics known to us today that date between 30 CE, the proposed date of the crucifixion, and 70 CE, the earliest possible date of authorship for Matthew, Mark, Luke, John and Acts. I will leave the reader to interpret that issue as they wish, but for me it is simple; you simply cannot oppose something that does not yet exist. I remain open to any new evidence. If the Christian faithful could put forward an anti 'literalist Christian' polemic that can be dated to between 30 and 70 CE, it would need to be considered proof that the New Testament gospels did exist between those dates; if there are any? Bear in mind, any polemic would need to address and oppose the ideas from Matthew, Mark, Luke and John specifically to be considered anti 'literalist Christian' polemics in the sense of modern-day Christianity. If they do not specifically mention the content of Matthew, Mark, Luke or John, or talk of a physical resurrection, they would then be a polemic against Gnostic Christianity and we already know Gnosticism is grounded in Paganism and Astrology, and therefore most likely to be far older than literalist Christianity.

The life and work of Epictetus is even more damming. His work emanates from his exile by the Emperor Domitian some time during 90 CE. According to the Church, by 90 CE Paul's letters are sent, Mark's gospel is completed and Luke/John's are well under way, if not complete. Epictetus did not write any work himself, he was a philosopher and narrator of the Stoic style; his narrations were admired and recorded by Arrian, the Greek historian who gives us much of our knowledge of Alexander the Great. Epictetus is completely silent with regards to the New Testament; logically because as at 90 CE it is not yet widely known.

So we have looked at those who wrote polemics against literalist Christianity; what about the apologists? In literature, an apologist is not a person who is apologising for the existence of something, the meaning is quite different. An apology is the reverse of a polemic, they defend a concept. Therefore, we can also use the work of Christian apologists for a date stamp. The earliest known apologist work for literalist Christianity is Justin Martyr who wrote an apology of Christianity circa 155 CE. Justin Martyr was born around 100 CE and died circa 165 CE in Rome.

There are no pro 'literalist Christian' writings known (at the time of writing) which predate Justin Martyr. As stated in chapter one, the Church claim Clement of Rome, Mathetes, Polycarp, Barnabas and Papias to be early Church fathers writing between 90 and 150 CE, but none of their work contains any reference to the literal Jesus of Matthew, Mark, Luke, John and Acts. Ignatius aside, for the reasons given in chapter one, we do not find any specific New Testament gospel references until post-150 CE with Justin Martyr. The first obvious beacon for the origins of literalist Christianity is the fact that the earliest apologists all lived and died in Rome, as you would expect if this was the birth place of literalist Christianity. They did not live and die in the east; the realm of Gnostic Christianity.

Circa 180 CE we have a work from Irenaeus which is an attack on Christian Heresy; what we term today as Gnostic faiths. This comes five years after Celsus' attack on literalist Christianity. While this does not prove Gnostic faith predates literalist Christianity, or literalist Christianity predates Gnostic ideas, it does prove they both existed together and argued with each other circa 150 to 180 CE.

**Breaking the meme by thinking outside the box**

To give the material presented so far due consideration, a reader would need to be able to blank the position given to us by history, which has been heavily influenced by those most in a position to gain benefit from the promotion of such a position, i.e. organised religion, and think outside of the box. This is not something humans find easy to do once a meme is set in place. Let me put the inability some people have towards thinking outside the box in modern-day terms; I will use an example viewed from outside the box looking in. During 2006 a TV program set out to find new mediums in the UK; those people who have the supposed gift to communicate with the supernatural and the sub-conscious! They ran a TV audience participation game during the course of the show. At fifteen minute intervals, they displayed four symbols on the screen and asked the audience watching to pick one and write it down; they did this six times. At the end of the show, they revealed the six pre-selected symbols the show wanted the television audience to select; the show then invited those people who had just discovered they were psychic by selecting all six symbols correctly to contact them in order to join the next show. True to form, there were people that evening who had convinced themselves they had discovered they were psychic.

Now, think outside the box; let's say 1,000,000 viewers see four symbols and pick one, by the laws of average about 250,000 will get it right. Of that 250,000, 62,500 get the next one right and now have two correct predictions; and so on. The 62,500 becomes 15,625 for the third round, 3,906 for the fourth, 976 for the fifth and 244 for the sixth and final round. With 1,000,000 participants, statistically about 244 will get all six correct; but many of that would be 244 on the night completely convinced themselves that they had just discovered a psychic gift they did not know they had. 'Hook, line and sinker', as they say. In fact, only 4,100 need take part in order to stand a good chance of one positive outcome. My point here is: the New Testament is this exact same theory with a slight twist. There were loads of candidates Constantine could have picked for a new Christian religion with a messiah when he rose to omnipotent power, the literalist Jesus idea is no more than the one he decided to pick. If he had picked another, we might all be worshipping someone called Simon Magus or Seth or Manichee or some other quelled first century CE belief system equally unknown to us today. We would never have heard of, or understand the term 'Jesus'. People automatically assume, without looking outside the box, that because so much is made of religion and Christianity with churches, cathedrals and the New Testament, that it must be true. The view is formed that so many people, and so many artefacts, books and historic buildings cannot possibly represent a false idea. But it can and it does; the number of supporters of an idea can never be used as criteria by which to measure the validity of the idea itself. Those who hold that vast numbers of believers make a belief true by default, really do belong with the new converts to mystical power in the TV experiment above; those that were easily fooled into thinking they were psychic. We need to come to terms with the fact that millions of people of one accord does not automatically make the item they are in accord with correct, it can be wrong and has been proved to be wrong many times in the past; the concept of slavery being just such a belief system. It is easy to understand how many people can be in error, even although they are in accord, particularly when we use theology as an example itself; if the millions of Christians are right, then by default the millions of Muslims and the millions of Jews are all collectively wrong. The reason millions of people do believe in theology is because the meme (thought virus) has been successfully passed on to them, and the religious buildings from antiquity along with the state sanction of religion, help to reinforce and self perpetuate that meme within them. A very good example of the self perpetuation of a meme can be found in the responses to Orson Welles' radio presentation of H. G. Wells' 'War of the Worlds'. Listeners in 1938 began to believe they were listening to an actual news bulletin rather than a radio adaptation of a story. Some started to panic immediately and leave their homes in their cars while others listened on for more news; when the broadcast started to reveal the presence of black poisonous gas being emitted from the alien craft, and then cunningly cut broadcast to give the impression that the reporter had just died, more people panicked and the meme started growing in their mind. Turning to thoughts of evacuation they looked outside and saw masses of cars trying to leave the city, this reinforced the meme in their mind. But in actual fact it was being reinforced by people who had succumbed to the meme quicker than themselves, rather than the fact that it was true; so the meme became self perpetuating and the infected were reinforcing belief in the uncertain, who then became infected themselves and subsequently joined the infectors by adding to the numbers of the panic stricken. Religion does not involve the macabre circumstances of Orson Welles' broadcast or the speed of infection, but the self perpetuating spread of the meme is identical and has been achieved over a much greater time span.

Concerning Jesus, do we ever stop to think what the physical appearance of a Middle Eastern man might be in the first century CE; then wonder why every depiction of Jesus shows us a man who looks as though he comes from Western Europe? Should that not give us some clue as to who did actually commission the New Testament and when. As I have already alluded too, for me it was the Romans circa 70 to 150 CE who hijacked the ideas of Jewish converts to Gnosticism (probably in Rome as slaves); the ideas were then further refined by the French, English, Spanish etc in the Middle Ages. Why? Because to me Matthew; Mark; Luke and John are Western European connotations of ancient Greek or Latin names not Semitic names, and religious art depicting Jesus comes from the continent circa Middle Ages and Renaissance. To add weight to the claim that the concept of a literal Christ being crucified on a cross is a late first to early fourth century Roman concept; I challenge the religious world to produce an artefact that depicts Jesus being crucified (2-D painting or a 3-D sculpture) that can be viably dated between 30 CE and 70 CE. If the Christian claims are true, there would be first century art depicting the scene, where is it? There is, of course, no end of artefacts post-300 CE!

On November 8th 2005 (www.christiantoday.com) 'Christian Today' released an article with absolute glee; it concerned an early Christian church found under an Israeli prison. It had a mosaic floor containing the words "the god Jesus Christ". They confirm it is the earliest Christian church ever found in the Holy Land. They also date it at mid third to early fourth century, 250 to 300 CE.

www.jesuswalk.com has an article on the earliest crucifix artefact. In their own article they admit that the earliest image of a crucifix on a sarcophagus dates to around 390 CE; it is in the tomb of Sextus Petronius Probus. They also state: the earliest 3-D crucifix artefact does not appear until the early fourth century. Man has been creating his inner most thoughts in art since the early Stone Age; but where is the art depicting the crucifixion and nativity scene which should date from between 30 CE and 70 CE?

# --Chapter 4: Rampant Plagiarism--

The Christian faithful often ask: where is the proof that Jesus is a regurgitation of previous mythical characters. Well the proof is literally written in stone. The I-kher-nefert stele, which is currently housed in a German museum, has chiselled into it, 'The Passion play of Osiris'. The passion play lasts for several days in which Osiris is laid to rest in his tomb, then he is mourned, and after three days he is resurrected as a God. The play was enacted to people each spring equinox, modern-day Easter. This stone stele comes from Egypt and its origin is around 1900 BCE. This story, and many others like it, caused concern to the early Church fathers of the second and third centuries CE. They were concerned with the antiquity of the Osiris stories, among others, and their similarity to the literalist version of the Jesus story. They postulated the view that: the devil went back in time and placed the stories there to try and discredit the existence of Jesus in the future (Justin Martyr c150 and Tertullian c200). These early Church responses have been given the collective name of *'diabolical mimicry'*. I do not know whether that term came from the polemicists or the apologists, or whether it is ancient or recent; however, regardless of the origin of the collective term itself, *'diabolical mimicry'* remains the only official Church response to this quandary to the present day. Christian web sites go to great lengths to discredit the obvious advantage the *'diabolical mimicry'* stance gives to the supporters of the mythical Jesus argument. The current offering being: Justin Martyr explains that the myths of Dionysus, Attis, Bacchus,

Mithra etc were all themselves copied from the prophecies of Daniel in the Old Testament. Of course this supposes that the 'would be' Greek and Roman plagiarists were all 'making it up' until the Jesus character actually arrived and fulfilled the very prophecy they were mimicking. The supporters of this view clearly overlook the fact that the early Church might have done the exact same thing; that is, 'making it up' from the book of Daniel. Later in this chapter we shall see that the fact that the second temple destruction occurred in what is now termed 70 CE, an astrological number, proves the early Church did indeed concoct the Jesus story from the Old Testament book of Daniel. But that aside, the above defence is completely negated by the fact that the Osiris version, which was chiselled in stone circa 1,900 BCE, predates the Old Testament book of Daniel by more than 1,000 years.

Osiris' son Horus also suffered a death and resurrection scene. Our fullest version of the Horus mythology can be found on another stone stele called the Metternich Stele. The Metternich Stele was discovered in 1828 and a large part of the text was first translated by Professor Golénischeff. A further translation, which is repeated below, was made by Wallis Budge. The stele tells the story of the death and resurrection of the saviour god child Horus, the divine son of Osiris and Isis.

Wallis Budge describes the imagery on the stele as follows: the main image on the stele is that of Harpokrates or Horus the child, standing on two crocodiles and holding images of serpents, scorpions, a lion, and a horned animal, each of which are symbols of the allies of Set, the evil god. Above the head of Horus are symbols of Ra, the King of the gods, or supreme God. The solar disk takes the main position on the rounded portion of the front and is positioned above a lake of celestial water; it is flanked with four of the spirits of the dawn, which are in turn flanked on the right by the symbol of the rising sun Nefer-Temu, and on the left by Thoth.

Many other examples of this stele exist and can be seen in European museums, they are known as 'Cippi of Horus'. This particular cippi, known as the Metternich Stele, is the largest cippi yet found and incorporates the name of the reigning King at the time of construction, being Nectanebus I. This dates the construction of the stele to between 378 and 360 BCE.

### Excerpt from the translation by Wallis Budge:

*"At this point on the stele the spells are interrupted by a long narrative put into the mouth of Isis, which supplies us with some account of the troubles that she suffered, and describes the death of Horus through the sting of a scorpion.*

*Isis, it seems, was shut up in some dwelling by Set after he murdered Osiris, probably with the intention of forcing her to marry him, and so assist him to legalise his seizure of the kingdom.*

*Isis, as we have already seen, had been made pregnant by her husband after his death, and Thoth now appeared to her, and advised her to hide herself with her unborn child, and to bring him forth in secret, and he promised her that her son should succeed in due course to his father's throne.*

*With the help of Thoth she escaped from her captivity, and went forth accompanied by the Seven Scorpion-goddesses, who brought her to the town of Per-Sui, on the edge of the Reed Swamps. She applied to a woman for a night's shelter, but the woman shut her door in her face. To punish her one of the Scorpion-goddesses forced her way into the woman's house, and stung her child to death. The grief of the woman was so bitter and sympathy-compelling that Isis laid her hands on the child, and, having uttered one of her most potent spells over him, the poison of the scorpion ran out of his body, and the child came to life again. The words of the spell are cut on the stele, and they were treasured by the Egyptians as an infallible remedy for scorpion stings. When the woman saw that her son had been brought back to life by Isis, she was filled with joy and gratitude, and, as a mark of her repentance, she brought large quantities of things from her house as gifts for Isis, and they were so many that they filled the house of the kind, but poor, woman who had given Isis shelter.*

*Now soon after Isis had restored to life the son of the woman who had shown churlishness to her, a terrible calamity fell upon her, for her beloved son Horus was stung by a scorpion and died. The news of this event was conveyed to her by the gods, who cried out to her to come to see her son Horus, whom the terrible scorpion Uhat had killed. Isis, stabbed with pain at the news, as if a knife had been driven into her body, ran out distraught with grief. It seems that she had gone to perform a religious ceremony in honour of Osiris in a temple near Hetep-hemt, leaving her child carefully concealed in Sekhet-An.*

*During her absence the scorpion Uhat, which had been sent by Set, forced its way into the hiding-place of Horus, and there stung him to death. When Isis came and found the dead body, she burst forth in lamentations, the sound of which brought all the people from the neighbouring districts to her side. As she related to them the history of her sufferings they endeavoured to console her, and when they found this to be impossible they lifted up their voices and wept with her.*

*Then Isis placed her nose in the mouth of Horus so that she might discover if he still breathed, but there was no breath in his throat; and when she examined the wound in his body made by the fiend Aun-Ab she saw in it traces of poison. No doubt about his death then remained in her mind, and clasping him in her arms she lifted him up, and in her transports of grief leaped about like fish when they are laid on red-hot coals.*

*Then she uttered a series of heartbreaking laments, each of which begins with the words "Horus is bitten." The heir of heaven, the son of Un-Nefer, the child of the gods, he who was wholly fair, is bitten! He for whose*

98

*wants I provided, he who was to avenge his father, is bitten! He for whom I cared and suffered when he was being fashioned in my womb, is bitten! He whom I tended so that I might gaze upon him, is bitten! He whose life I prayed for is bitten! Calamity hath overtaken the child, and he hath perished.*

*Whilst Isis was saying these and many similar words, her sister Nephthys, who had been weeping bitterly for her nephew Horus as she wandered about among the swamps, came, in company with the Scorpion goddess Serqet, and advised Isis to pray to heaven for help. Pray that the sailors in the Boat of Ra may cease from rowing, for the boat cannot travel onwards whilst Horus lies dead.*

*Then Isis cried out to heaven, and her voice reached the Boat of Millions of Years, and the Disk ceased to move onward, and came to a standstill. From the boat Thoth descended, being equipped with words of power and spells of all kinds, and bearing with him the "great command of maa-kheru," i.e., the word, whose commands were performed, instantly and completely, by every god, spirit, fiend, human being and by every thing, animate and inanimate, in heaven, earth, and the other world. Then he came to Isis and told her that no harm could possibly have happened to Horus, for he was under the protection of the Boat of Ra; but his words failed to comfort Isis, and though she acknowledged the greatness of his designs, she complained that they savoured of delay "What is the good," she asks, "of all thy spells, and incantations, and magical formulae, and the great command of maa-kheru, if Horus is to perish by the poison of a scorpion, and to lie here in the arms of death? Evil, evil is his destiny, for it hath entailed the deepest misery for him and death."*

*In answer to these words Thoth, turning to Isis and Nephthys, bade them to fear not, and to have no anxiety about Horus, "For," said he, "I have come from heaven to heal the child for his mother." He then pointed out that Horus was under protection as the Dweller in his Disk (Aten), the*

*Great Dwarf, the Mighty Ram, the Great Hawk, the Holy Beetle, the Hidden Body, the Divine Bennu, etc., and proceeded to utter the great spell which restored Horus to life.*

*By his words of power Thoth transferred the "fluid of life" of Ra, and as soon as this came upon the child's body the poison of the scorpion flowed out of him, and he once more breathed and lived. When this was done Thoth returned to the Boat of Ra, the gods who formed its crew resumed their rowing, and the Disk passed on its way to make its daily journey across the sky.*

*The gods in heaven, who were amazed and uttered cries of terror when they heard of the death of Horus, were made happy once more, and sang songs of joy over his recovery. The happiness of Isis in her child's restoration to life was very great, for she could again hope that he would avenge his father's murder, and occupy his throne. The final words of Thoth comforted her greatly, for he told her that he would take charge of the case of Horus in the Judgment Hall of Anu, wherein Osiris had been judged, and that as his advocate he would make any accusations which might be brought against Horus to recoil on him that brought them. Furthermore, he would give Horus power to repulse any attacks which might be made upon him by beings in the heights above, or fiends in the depths below, and would ensure his succession to the Throne of the Two Lands, i.e., Egypt.*

*Thoth also promised Isis that Ra himself should act as the advocate of Horus, even as he had done for his father Osiris. He was also careful to allude to the share which Isis had taken in the restoration of Horus to life, saying, "It is the words of power of his mother which have lifted up his face, and they shall enable him to journey wheresoever he pleaseth, and to put fear into the powers above. I myself hasten to obey them." Thus everything turned on the power of the spells of Isis, who made the Sun to stand still, and caused the dead to be raised.*

*Such are the contents of the texts on the famous Metternich Stele. There appears to be some confusion in their arrangement, and some of them clearly are misplaced, and, in places, the text is manifestly corrupt. It is impossible to explain several passages, for we do not understand all the details of the system of magic which they represent. Still, the general meaning of the texts on the stele is quite clear, and they record a legend of Isis and Horus which is not found so fully described on any other monument."*

To illuminate the parallels with this story and the story of the saviour god child Jesus, consider the following points: The mortal Isis is made pregnant without intercourse by the deceased Osiris who is now a god. The fruit of this divine conception is the saviour god child Horus who is going to avenge his father's death and redeem the world by growing into adulthood and slaying the evil Set. The Book of Revelation tells us that Jesus will return and save all souls by defeating Satan in a final battle at Megiddo. Set is looking for the infant Horus in order to slay him, so Isis must hide the infant from Set, just as Moses was hidden from Pharaoh and Jesus was hidden from Herod.

In Egyptian mythology, Osiris is the divine Pharaoh who rules the heavens while Horus is the divine Pharaoh who rules the earth. Therefore, all new Pharaohs became Horus on their coronation, and were said to reincarnate as Osiris upon their death. Osiris ruled in heaven by the side of the supreme god Ra; just as Jesus was destined to rule in heaven after his resurrection when he will *"sit at the right hand of God in the kingdom of heaven"*.

There is a very slight parallel between the dilemma of both Isis and Mary in their endeavours to find shelter just prior to giving birth. Isis has a door shut in her face but is later allowed to stay and give birth, while Mary is told there is no room at the inn, but is then allowed to shelter in the animal keep. Isis then receives gifts of thanks after giving birth to Horus just as Mary and Joseph receive gifts for Jesus. In the text on the stele Horus is identified by Isis as *"The heir of heaven, the son of Un-Nefer, the child of the gods"* which parallels Jesus as *"The son of man and the son of God who will rule in the kingdom of heaven"*.

The Boat of Ra is the boat which carries the solar disk on its journey each day from sunrise to sunset. The passage in the stele referring to the boat being unable to continue its journey therefore depicts the winter solstice when the Sun is said to stand still; the death of Horus is therefore related to a solar event. The birth of Jesus is also related to the solar event of the winter solstice. Moreover, the death and resurrection of Jesus is likewise related to a solar event, being the spring equinox.

The sunrise is static on the horizon in terms of where it rises and sets, and almost static in terms of how high it reaches at midday, for about three days during the winter solstice. Solstice literally means in Latin 'sun stand still': sol (sun) and sistere (to stand still); this means in visual terms that at the winter solstice, the trace of the arc of the Sun from sunrise, to its highest point at midday, through to sunset, appears identical to the eye for about three days. After this short three day static period, the Sun's arc across the sky gets wider and higher. The Boat of Ra would therefore be deemed to be on the move again after the solstice, but static during the solstice. Since the story portrays the boat as not being able to continue its journey while Horus lays dead, and able to continue its journey after Thoth, acting on behalf of the supreme deity Ra, has brought Horus back to life, Horus would have undergone a three day death and resurrection. A gap of some degree can also be derived from the comment of Isis when she scolds Thoth for his procrastination in attending to the dead Horus.

In bringing Horus back to life, Thoth is acting for the supreme deity Ra, and uses the *"fluid of life of Ra"* to affect the resurrection. The saviour god child Horus can therefore be said to have been brought back to life by God himself.

As with many myths, this may be just one of many different accepted versions of the Horus myth from antiquity. From this story comes artefacts which depict Osiris, the divine father, standing with Isis, the virgin mother, who is holding Horus, the saviour god child; also from archaeology we have artefacts depicting as a pair, Isis the virgin mother holding Horus the saviour god child. Eusebius, the early fourth century architect of the New Testament content, would have been aware of the Osiris, Isis and Horus story because he quotes from the Egyptian scribe Manetho in his own works. Critics might well say that the parallels above have been hard searched for and could be coincidental. They might further claim that the two stories are actually very different; but consider the two plots of Arthur Laurents' 'West Side Story' and William Shakespeare's 'Romeo and Juliet'. There is a gap of 350 years between these two stories, and the stories may appear to be very different, but 'West Side Story' is a rewrite of 'Romeo and Juliet': and so it goes with the stories of Horus and Jesus above.

The concepts of astro-maths, and the idea of a god child have also been applied to emperors. Below is the account of the reign of Augustus by Suetonius. In Augustus chapter 5 we have an account of his birth date:

*5: Augustus was born just before sunrise on the ninth day before the Kalends of October:*

This equates to the 21$^{st}$ September, which is in turn the autumn equinox, a solar event. Also notice, the birth is reported to be at sunrise on the autumn equinox, the very moment of the solar event. In Augustus chapter 94 we find an account of his divine conception.

*94: I have read the following story in the books of Asclepias of Mendes entitled Theologumena. When Atia had come in the middle of the night to the solemn service of Apollo, she had her litter set down in the temple and fell asleep, while the rest of the matrons also slept. On a sudden a serpent glided up to her and shortly went away. When she awoke, she purified herself, as if after the embraces of her husband, and at once there*

103

*appeared on her body a mark in colours like a serpent, and she could never get rid of it; so that presently she ceased ever to go to the public baths. In the tenth month after that Augustus was born and was therefore regarded as the son of Apollo. Atia too, before she gave him birth, dreamed that her vitals were borne up to the stars and spread over the whole extent of land and sea, while Octavius dreamed that the Sun rose from Atia's womb.*

This passage does not suggest that Atia was a virgin, but is does imply that Augustus was conceived without sexual intercourse and by the seed of a main Roman deity, Apollo; also *"Theologumena"* means "to speak of God". Therefore, the passage depicts a divine conception and a resulting son of God. Augustus chapter 100 gives us his funeral scene:

*100: But though a limit was set to the honours paid him, his eulogy was twice delivered: before the temple of the Deified Julius by Tiberius, and from the old rostra by Drusus, son of Tiberius; and he was carried on the shoulders of senators to the Campus Martius and there cremated. There was even an ex-praetor who took oath that he had seen the form of the Emperor, after he had been reduced to ashes, on its way to heaven.*

The ex-praetor therefore witnessed a spiritual resurrection of Augustus, a reappearance of Augustus after his death and the ascent of Augustus to heaven. Of course, this is all poetic nonsense, but the point is, it is very popular poetic nonsense for its time. We have to ask the question, why would the theological world dismiss the above story of divine Augustus as fiction in an instant, but at the same time insist the exact same base line story applied to the Jesus character, from the same time frame in history. actually has substance? With regard to the book of 'Asclepias of Mendes' entitled 'Theologumena' which Suetonius cites as his reference; history knows nothing of this author, or when he lived. Our only knowledge of Asclepias comes from this reference to him by Suetonius. It could therefore be argued that the author Asclepias simply copied elements of the Jesus story when writing about Augustus. But, it is equally possible that Asclepias wrote first, and most probable that both Asclepias and the authors of Matthew, Mark, Luke, John and Acts are simply all copying the same base line god child stories from antiquity. We can give a date range to the work of Asclepias with the following data: Augustus became Emperor in 31 BCE and Suetonius wrote in 120 CE. Therefore, Asclepias wrote between 31 BCE and 120 CE. We already know that Matthew, Mark, Luke, John and Acts did not appear until after 70 CE.

We will now consider the main elements of the Matthew, Mark, Luke, John and Acts version of the literal Christ figure story, as adopted by Constantine on the advice of his religious sages Lactantius and Eusebius, and ultimately codified into the New Testament after the council of Nicaea in 325 CE. Given the opening of this book, where we considered the gap of 70 years: from within the Jewish faith for the time between the first temple destruction and second temple completion, from the Christian faith of the time from the birth of Jesus to the second temple destruction, and from the Muslim faith of the time between Muhammad's Hijra and the completion of the Dome of the Rock, we can now call into question the validity of the claimed biographical content of the Matthew, Mark, Luke and John stories. Particularly when we consider that, at the time in history when the second Jewish temple was destroyed, the date would have been collectively referred to as 'the second year of the reign of Vespasian'. The inclusion of Pontius Pilate and Caiaphas in the Matthew, Mark, Luke, John and Acts stories, and the date of 70 CE allocated to the temple destruction by Titus are very closely linked; this link also turns out to be deeply rooted in the concepts of astro-maths from chapter two. The existence of this glaringly obvious link is also the main evidence with which the Matthew, Mark, Luke, John and Acts stories are betrayed as manufactured rather than biographical; recall the analogy of the sword and the barbed wire in chapter one.

Consider how popular the number seventy is in religious thought. It is a common multiple of the most venerated number seven and does also have its own corresponding cosmic representation, along with the number seventy-two. Recall the experiment of tracking the movement of the sunrise in chapter two, we highlighted the fact that the constellations appear to move on the horizon at the rate of one degree every 71.6 years. This movement was used by the earliest astrologers to create the idea of epochs which lasted for 2150 years each. They allocated each epoch to star constellation which occupied the position of the sunrise on the spring equinox for the duration of the epoch; hence, the age (or epoch) of Pisces. Like seven and twelve, 71.6 also became a venerated astrological number; but not in its form as a fraction. It was rounded up to the nearest whole number to give seventy-two, an acceptable number for veneration since it is divisible by the venerated number twelve. It was also rounded down to the nearest multiple of ten to give seventy, also acceptable since seventy is divisible by the most venerated number, seven. And so, seventy-two and seventy became two highly venerated numbers representing the same cosmic event: the time in years for the stars to complete a one degree shift on the horizon.

The oldest known copies of the 'Old Testament' are from a work called *'The Septuagint'*, *or* simply *'LXX'*, literally *'The Seventy'* and it dates from the first half of the third century BCE; according to text within the Jewish Talmud: *"King Ptolemy once gathered seventy-two elders. He placed them in seventy-two chambers, each of them in a separate one, without revealing to them why they were summoned. He entered each one's room and said:* 'Write for me the Torah of Moses, your teacher.' *God put it in the heart of each one to translate identically as all the others did"* So, the book called 'The Seventy' was written by seventy-two scribes. The Islamic hadith 2687 states : *"The smallest reward for the people of heaven is an abode where there are eighty thousand servants and seventy-two houri,"*

Houri is taken to mean virgin, which is disputable, but it definitely refers to extremely voluptuous maidens. We also find discrepancies with these two numbers between the Greek and Latin bibles, with seventy and seventy-two both being used for the number of Noah's descendants and the number of apostles appointed by Jesus. In ancient Egypt, the heliacal rising of Sirius was celebrated by the Egyptians after a seventy day absence from the night sky; A Pharaoh's mummification ritual had to take exactly seventy days. As we morph away from mythology, and into the realm of theology, from the Old Testament we find the following captions involving the number seventy:

*Gen 4:24 If Cain shall be avenged sevenfold, truly Lamech seventy and sevenfold.*

*Ex 1:5 And all the souls that came out of the loins of Jacob were seventy souls: for Joseph was in Egypt already.*

*Ex 24:1 And he said unto Moses, Come up unto the Lord, thou, and Aaron, Nadab, and Abihu, and seventy of the elders of Israel;*

*Num 7:13 And his offering was one silver charger, the weight thereof was an hundred and thirty shekels, one silver bowl of seventy shekels*

*Num 11:16 And the Lord said unto Moses, Gather unto me seventy men of the elders of Israel*

*Judg 9:56 Thus God rendered the wickedness of Abimelech, which he did unto his father, in slaying his seventy brethren:*

*2 Sam 24:14 and there died of the people from Dan even to Beer-Sheba seventy thousand men.*

*2 Kgs 10:1 And Ahab had seventy sons in Samaria.*

*1 Chr 21:14 So the Lord sent pestilence upon Israel: and there fell of Israel seventy thousand men.*

*2 Chr 36:21 The land will lie desolate for seventy years, to make up for the Sabbath rest that has not been observed.*

*Is 23:15 And it shall come to pass in that day, that Tyre shall be forgotten seventy years, according to the days of one king: after the end of seventy years shall Tyre sing as an harlot.*

*Jer 25:11 And this whole land shall be a desolation, and an astonishment; and these nations shall serve the King of Babylon seventy years.*

*Ezek 8:11 And there stood before them seventy men of the ancients of the house of Israel,*

*Dan 9:2 In the first year of his reign I Daniel understood by books the number of the years, whereof the word of the Lord came to Jeremiah the prophet, that he would accomplish seventy years in the desolations of Jerusalem.*

*Dan 9:24 Seventy weeks are determined upon thy people and upon thy holy city, to finish the transgression.*

*Zech 7:5 When ye fasted and mourned in the fifth and seventh month, even those seventy years, did ye at all fast unto me.*

The number seventy also appears in the New Testament:

*Mat 18:22 "Jesus saith unto him, I say not unto thee, Until seven times: but, Until seventy times seven".*

*Luk 10:1 After these things the Lord appointed another seventy also, and sent them two and two before his face into every city and place, whither he himself would come.*

*Luk 10:17 And the seventy returned again with joy, saying, Lord, even the devils are subject unto us through thy name.*

If, given knowledge of the above, we conclude that the time gap of seventy years between the second temple destruction and the birth of Christ is suspiciously coincidental, and consequently not factual, one or both events are then considered to be fabricated. But we must remember that, the second temple destruction date cannot be moved in history, it did happen, and it did happen in the second year of the reign of Vespasian. Hence, the fabricated event would have to be the start event, the supposed birth of Christ.

Now consider the Old Testament prophesy from the book of Daniel: *In the first year of his reign I Daniel understood by books the number of the years, whereof the word of the Lord came to Jeremiah the prophet, that he would accomplish **seventy years in the desolations of Jerusalem**.* This passage claims that Jerusalem will lay in ruins for seventy years; but, taken in context along with the remainder of the chapter, and given different circumstances and a specific time in history, it can also be read as: if the people of Israel reject the messiah when he arrives, Jerusalem will be destroyed seventy years after his arrival. Given this passage, and the religious obsession with the number seventy revealed above, the date of 70 CE for the destruction of Jerusalem and the second temple is now either an amazing coincidence, or a self-fulfilling prophecy; a self-fulfilling prophecy derived from a story which was unknown until after the publication of Matthew, Mark, Luke and John, all believed to have been written some time after 70 CE, after the destruction of Jerusalem and its temple. It is clearly not an amazing coincidence, it is a self-fulfilling prophecy, and a reverse construction; and here is how it came about, and why it has to be the characters Pontius Pilate and Caiphas who are used to give the Matthew, Mark, Luke and John Jesus story its historical credentials.

Not until 523 CE, after a monk named Dionysius Exiguus created the dating system which recorded the number of years since the 'birth of Christ', did the second year of the reign of Vespasian (the year Jerusalem and its temple were destroyed) become referred to as 70 Anno Domini (70 CE); or in essence seventy years after the birth of Christ. Up until what is now termed 532 AD, or CE, dates were still stated with reference to the current ruling monarch. For example: the fifteenth year of Augustus, or the fourth year of Tiberius etc. This was workable, but very complicated; particularly when trying to work out the number of years between events.

To do this, one would have to know the year of the Emperor for the start event, the year of the Emperor for the end event, the length of rule for all the emperors in between, add up all the years, and adjust for any joint rulers or years with more than one ruler. To overcome this problem the monk named Dionysius Exiguus created the dating system of BC and AD, (Before Christ) and (Anno Domini, 'In the Year of our Lord'). Using the system which recorded the length of rule for emperors, Dionysius Exiguus calculated the year in which he carried out the exercise to be 532 years since the birth of Christ; he therefore set in place the current system of sequentially counting years from 532 AD onwards.

Using this system, the birth of Christ was considered to be year one and the destruction of Jerusalem, and the temple, by Titus in the second year of the reign of Vespasian now equates to 70 AD. Dionysius' concept of the birth of Christ being year one has since been thwarted by the fact that Herod the Great appears in the gospel of Matthew. Herod is stated to be upset about the birth of a prophesied messiah and therefore orders the death of all newborn males in Bethlehem (the slaughter of the innocents). Herod died in what would now be classed as 4 BC. Since Herod is alive when the Jesus child is said to be born, the child must have been born before year one. However, Herod only appears in Matthew; he does not appear in Mark, Luke or John. We know the slaughter of the innocents is a fictitious event since the Jewish scribe Josephus, who enumerates all of the tyrannies of 'Herod the Great' against his Jewish brethren, makes no mention of the alleged incident. This is considered suspicious since a more macabre assault on your brethren could not even be conceived of; if the slaughter of the innocents did happen, Josephus would have had plenty to say about it. I would maintain that: Dionysius saw the supposed episode as a conflict when trying to determine a year one and therefore simply ignored it; or, Dionysius miscalculated the death of Herod and did not even realise the conflict. It is also important to note that in this system there is no year zero between 1 BC and 1 AD.

With the background details of the BC/AD dating system explained, I will now progress the hypothesis for the course of events leading up to the inclusion of 'Pontius Pilate' and 'Caiaphas' in the stories of Matthew, Mark, Luke and John, and how the date for the second temple destruction came to be 70 AD under Dionysius' new system. The progression of this hypothesis also builds on the notion of the allegorical/literalist schism introduced in chapter two and enhanced in chapter three and proceeds as follows: at the end of the Age of Aries circa 100 BCE, and consequently the start of the Age of Pisces, a new religious movement occurs in the Levant to mark the dawning of the new astrological epoch. The movement creates an allegorical hybrid character known as Christ who is a cocktail mixture of the god child myths from the pagan mystery religions and the prophesied messiah from the Old Testament. The cult forms many different groups, all quite small in number, and each group worships the new allegorical Christ figure in their own way; they all create their own versions of the allegorical Christ figure and record these differing versions in written gospels. The groups are subsequently referred to as Gnostics, and their stories come to be known as the Gnostic gospels; only a few of these gospels have surfaced and with certainty many more versions have been lost forever, or, have survived and are waiting to be found.

The Gnostics preached about the secret hidden knowledge of heaven. When one obtained this secret knowledge, which was essentially to know oneself, the person became the allegorical Christ and could therefore rejoin God in heaven. I use the term rejoin because the Gnostic texts reveal that the Gnostic's believed their spirit came from God in the first instance, and their life journey is the quest for their spirit to be reunited with God. The Apostle Paul, preaching some eighty to thirty years before Titus destroyed Jerusalem, is in fact one such Gnostic preacher. We can make this assertion with confidence, since none of Paul's letters refer to a literal Christ; nor do they display any knowledge of the life of the literal Jesus character from the books of Matthew, Mark, Luke, John and Acts, which were all penned some time after Titus destroyed Jerusalem. There are many unique Gnostic passages within the fabric of Paul's letters, such as:

**Romans 16:25** *"Now to him that is of power to establish you according to my gospel, and the preaching of Jesus Christ, according to the revelation of the mystery, which was kept secret since the world began,"* A clear reference to the secret hidden knowledge.

**1Corithians 2:6** *"Howbeit we speak wisdom among them that are perfect: yet not the wisdom of this world, nor of the princes of this world, that come to nought: But we speak the wisdom of God in a mystery, even the hidden wisdom, which God ordained before the world unto our glory"* Another clear reference to secret hidden knowledge.

**1 Corinthians 3:1** *"And I, brethren, could not speak unto you as unto spiritual, but as unto carnal, even as unto babes in Christ. I have fed you with milk, and not with meat: for hitherto ye were not able to bear it, neither yet now are ye able."* This paragraph alludes to the concept of staged initiation; firstly to the allegorical outer mysteries with milk, and then progressing to the esoteric inner mysteries with meat. The pagan mystery religions such as Mithraism all employed the concept of staged initiation, and the pagan mystery religions do seem to have been influential in the formation of Gnostic beliefs.

**2 Corinthians 11:4** *"For if someone comes to you and preaches a Jesus other than the Jesus we preached, or if you receive a different spirit from the one you received, or a different gospel from the one you accepted, you put up with it easily enough. But I do not think I am in the least inferior to those "super-apostles." I may not be a trained speaker, but I do have knowledge. We have made this perfectly clear to you in every way."* This passage also refers to the Gnostic concept of secret knowledge.

**2 Corinthians 12:2** *"I knew a man in Christ above fourteen years ago, (whether in the body, I cannot tell; or whether out of the body, I cannot tell: God knoweth;) such an one caught up to the third heaven."* The reference to *'third heaven'* here is a specific reference to a particular Gnostic belief of ascending through eight heavens on the journey to God's realm. Recall from 'The Discourse on the Eighth and Ninth' in the last chapter: the seven heavens relate to the Sun, Moon and five wandering stars, the eighth to the realm of the fixed stars and the ninth to God's realm beyond the fixed stars.

We know Paul is only preaching one, of many versions of the Gnostic Jesus character prior to the sacking of Jerusalem, because Paul's letters were all written before the temple was destroyed in 70 CE and they make specific reference to, and complain about, the acceptance of other stories about other Jesus figures. Therefore we have literary evidence of the existence of multiple versions of an allegorical Jesus figure some thirty to eighty years before Jerusalem, and its Jewish temple to Yahweh, were destroyed:

**2 Corinthians 11:4** *"For if someone comes to you and preaches a Jesus other than the Jesus we preached, or if you receive a different spirit from the one you received, or a different gospel from the one you accepted, you put up with it easily enough. But I do not think I am in the least inferior to those "super-apostles." I may not be a trained speaker, but I do have knowledge. We have made this perfectly clear to you in every way."*

**Galatians 1:6** *"I am astonished that you are so quickly deserting the one who called you by the grace of Christ and are turning to a different gospel which is really no gospel at all. Evidently some people are throwing you into confusion and are trying to pervert the gospel of Christ. But even if we or an angel from heaven should preach a gospel other than the one we preached to you, let him be eternally condemned! As we have already said, so now I say again: If anybody is preaching to you a gospel other than what you accepted, let him be eternally condemned!"*

We need to be mindful that during this pre-70 CE Gnostic revolution the Jewish people, who shunned pagan and Gnostic worship, lived under a heavy yoke due to the Roman occupation of their land. Inevitably, the Jewish people invoked an uprising against Roman rule in the eleventh year of the reign of Nero. The resulting war between Rome and Judah lasted for four years and culminated in the destruction of Jerusalem, and its temple to Yahweh, by Titus in the second year of the reign of Vespasian. After the war, an unbearable retribution was extracted from the Jewish population by the Romans. Being Jewish carried a heavy taxation liability and Jews were freely abused physically at whim by the Gentiles and Roman citizens, without any recourse to legal protection. Being Jewish, just after the war's conclusion, becomes extremely difficult and perilous. Many Jewish people start to look for an alternative, and some start to join the existing Gnostic versions of the allegorical Christ cult.

Sixty-two years after the Romans quelled the Jewish revolt; a second Jewish uprising was invoked. This uprising was in response to the renaming of Jerusalem to 'Aelia Capitolina' and the building of a pagan temple to Jupiter on top of the second temple ruins. The revolt started in the fifteenth year of the reign of Hadrian. The resulting war between Rome and Judah lasted for three years and is therefore quelled by Hadrian in the eighteenth year of his reign. Hadrian's rebuke of the Jews after the war is far worse than that of Vespasian. Circumcision in the empire is forbidden and all Jews are ordered to leave the lands of Judah. Judah effectively ceases to exist, and all Jews find themselves without a homeland in a Roman Empire that extracts heavy taxes from them for being Jewish, and also allows and promotes the physical abuse of Jews. The majority of Jewish people now look for an alternative, and ever increasing numbers join the many Gnostic Christ movements.

After the defeat of the first Jewish uprising, at the start of the reign of Vespasian, and following a Jewish migration to Gnostic Christianity, a

114

new Judaic/Gnostic splinter group of the many Gnostic Christians starts to form from within the ranks of the Jewish converts; a group that are looking for, and require answers. They wish to know why they were so utterly abandoned by their God Yahweh. They construct their own answer: They start to claim that the Christ figure is not allegorical; they assert that the Christ figure is in fact the messiah prophesied in the Old Testament; they maintain that Christ is a very real character from history. The new splinter group claim that the Old Testament, in particular the book of Daniel, states that if the people of Israel reject the messiah when he arrives, Jerusalem will be destroyed exactly seventy years after his earthly visit: **Dan 9:2** *I Daniel understood by books the number of the years, whereof the word of the Lord came to Jeremiah the prophet, that he would accomplish seventy years in the desolations of Jerusalem.* They therefore conclude that since Jerusalem, and the temple, have now been destroyed, the messiah must have already come in the past, and was rejected. The rejection of the messiah would have been perceived as a fatal and terminal rejection, as in 'the putting to death' of the character, as opposed to mere social rejection. They calculate that seventy years prior to the destruction of Jerusalem in the second year of the reign of Vespasian would be the twenty-eighth year of the reign of Augustus; therefore the messiah's visit to earth, or his birth, would have taken place in this particular year. The basis of a new story is now born and starts to take form. The new splinter group are aware that the Gnostic groups they have joined collectively claim that Christ, as in the Gnostic allegorical Christ, was crucified and resurrected on the third day; this concept is adopted by the new Judaic/Gnostic splinter group as the basis for their perceived rejection of the messiah. Many previous pagan god childs resurrected at the vernal equinox, and so to follow this popular trend they surmise that any crucifixion would have taken place during a Passover festival. They further surmise (or just simply decide) that the messiah figure would have been about thirty years old at the time of crucifixion. Thirty is also a very common astrological figure, so to select this number follows the astro-maths trend.

The Old Testament book of Daniel states that it is Jerusalem that will suffer if the messiah is rejected by the Jews when he arrives; the splinter group therefore set the crucifixion scene in Jerusalem during Passover. It is worth pointing out at this juncture that no pre-70 CE text gives a location, or time frame for the crucifixion, so the splinter group are creating their own backdrop to an ancient mythical story. The stories created claim that only a Roman Prefect can pass the death penalty; whether or not this is true for the time is possible, but debatable; however, it does fit the purpose of the story being created. Since the Christ character is placed at the age of thirty at crucifixion; thirty years after the twenty-eighth year of Augustus would be the sixteenth year of Tiberius. The Proconsul of the province of Judah in the sixteenth year of the reign of Tiberius was one Pontius Pilate. It therefore follows that if the character is to be crucified in Jerusalem during the sixteenth year of the reign of Tiberius, the crucifixion would have been ordered by, or sanctioned by, Pontius Pilate; hence the inclusion of Pontius Pilate into the story. But the book of Daniel states that: Jerusalem suffers if the Jews reject the messiah, not the Romans. The new story therefore has to include the Jewish High Priest of Jerusalem during the sixteenth year of the reign of Tiberius, who is one Caiaphas. The story therefore evolves to: Pontius Pilate ordering the crucifixion of the Jesus character on the instigation of Caiaphas with the support of the Jewish populace. Hence Pontius Pilate and Caiaphas give the story its historic timeframe, location and rationale. Remember, the group forming this story are pointing out why God has rejected the Jews, and in doing so allowed the Romans to destroy their land and their temple. Their story therefore portrays the fulfilment of a prophesised retribution for the killing of the messiah. So the new Judaic/Gnostic group are both blaming the Jews, and distancing themselves from the Jews at the same time by creating this story and committing apostasy via a conversion to Gnostic Christianity.

The Old Testament also states that the saviour will come forth from Bethlehem. **Micah: 5.1** … *"But you, Bethlehem Ephrathah, though you are small among the clans of Judah, out of you will come for me one who will be ruler over Israel, whose origins are from of old, from ancient times."* We therefore now have a new group of ex-Jewish converts to Gnosticism, desperate to reject Judaism and not to be classed as Jews in order to evade crippling taxation and physical persecution, who have created a story about the birth of a literal, not allegorical, messiah in Bethlehem, during the twenty-eight year of Augustus. Their new god child is crucified and comes back to life during a Passover festival in Jerusalem in the sixteenth year of Tiberius on the orders of the Roman Proconsul Pontius Pilate, at the behest of the Jewish High Priest Caiaphas. This gives rise to the synoptic gospels of Matthew, Mark and Luke; followed closely by John and then Acts all post-70 CE; post second temple destruction.

The remainder of the story from birth to death, the fill-in, so to speak, can all be found within the pages of the Old Testament. Including such things as, they pierce my hands and feet, they cast lots for my vestments, 30 pieces of silver, etc:

**Malachi: 3.1** *"See, I will send my messenger, who will prepare the way before me. Then suddenly the Lord you are seeking will come to his temple; the messenger of the covenant, whom you desire, will come," says the Lord Almighty."*

**Isaiah: 7.14** *"Therefore the Lord himself will give you a sign: The virgin will be with child and will give birth to a son, and will call him Immanuel."*

**Hosea: 11.1** *"When Israel was a child, I loved him, and out of Egypt I called my son."*

**Isaiah: 9.1-2** *"Nevertheless, there will be no more gloom for those who were in distress. In the past he humbled the land of Zebulun and the land of*

*Naphtali, but in the future he will honour Galilee of the Gentiles, by the way of the sea, along the Jordan."*

**Isaiah: 35.5-6** *"Then will the eyes of the blind be opened and the ears of the deaf unstopped. Then will the lame leap like a deer, and the mute tongue shout for joy. Water will gush forth in the wilderness and streams in the desert."*

**Isaiah: 42.18** *"Hear, you deaf; look, you blind, and see!"*

**Psalms: 78.2** *"I will open my mouth in parables, I will utter hidden things, things from of old..."*

**Deuteronomy: 18.18** *"I will raise up for them a prophet like you from among their brothers; I will put my words in his mouth, and he will tell them everything I command him."*

**Zechariah: 9.9** *"rejoice greatly, O Daughter of Zion! Shout, Daughter of Jerusalem! See, your king comes to you, righteous and having salvation, gentle and riding on a donkey, on a colt, the foal of a donkey."*

**Psalms: 2.1-2** *"Why do the nations conspire and the peoples plot in vain? The kings of the earth take their stand and the rulers gather together against the Lord and against his Anointed One."*

**Psalms: 41.9** *Even my close friend, whom I trusted, he who shared my bread, has lifted up his heel against me.*

**Psalms: 55.12-14** *"If an enemy were insulting me, I could endure it; if a foe were raising himself against me, I could hide from him. But it is you, a man like myself, my companion, my close friend, with whom I once enjoyed sweet fellowship as we walked with the throng at the house of God."*

**Zechariah: 11.12-13** *"I told them, "If you think it best, give me my pay; but if not, keep it." So they paid me thirty pieces of silver. And the Lord said to me, "Throw it to the potter" the handsome price at which they priced me! So I took the thirty pieces of silver and threw them into the house of the Lord to the potter."*

**Psalm: 22.7-8** *"All who see me mock me; they hurl insults, shaking their heads: 'He trusts in the Lord; let the Lord rescue him. Let him deliver him, since he delights in him.'"*

**Zechariah: 12.10** *"And I will pour out on the house of David and the inhabitants of Jerusalem a spirit of grace and supplication. They will look on me, the one they have pierced, and they will mourn for him as one mourns for an only child, and grieve bitterly for him as one grieves for a firstborn son."*

**Psalms 22:16** *"Dogs have surrounded me; a band of evil men has encircled me, they have pierced my hands and my feet."*

**Psalms: 69.21** *"They put gall in my food and gave me vinegar for my thirst."*

**Psalms: 22.18** *"They divide my garments among them and cast lots for my clothes."*

**Psalms: 22.1** *"My God, my God, why have you forsaken me? Why are you so far from saving me, so far from the words of my groaning?"*

**Psalms: 31.5** *"Into your hands I commit my spirit; redeem me, o Lord, the God of truth."*

**Isaiah: 53.5-7** **"***But he was pierced for our transgressions, he was crushed for our iniquities; the punishment that brought us peace was upon him, and by his wounds we are healed. We all, like sheep, have gone astray, each of us has turned to his own way; and the Lord has laid on him the iniquity of us all. He was oppressed and afflicted, yet he did not open his mouth; he was led like a lamb to the slaughter, and as a sheep before her shearers is silent, so he did not open his mouth."*

**Isaiah: 53.12** *"Therefore I will give him a portion among the great, and he will divide the spoils with the strong, because he poured out his life unto death, and was numbered with the transgressors. For he bore the sin of many, and made intercession for the transgressors."*

**Hosea: 6.2** *"After two days he will revive us; on the third day he will restore us, that we may live in his presence."*

**Psalms: 110.1** *"The Lord says to my Lord: "Sit at my right hand until I make your enemies a footstool for your feet."*

**Zechariah: 6.13** *"It is he who will build the temple of the Lord, and he will be clothed with majesty and will sit and rule on his throne. And he will be a priest on his throne. And there will be harmony between the two."*

It can hardly be denied that all of the quotations from the Old Testament above, in the order they are displayed, plus many others that this work does not have the space to include, make up the major framework of the Matthew, Mark, Luke and John stories. The many sayings of Jesus in the Matthew, Mark, Luke and John stories can also be found in the works of Philo of Alexandria pre-50 CE, along with the works of the Greek philosophers' from circa 300 BCE; and for that matter, sayings which originate from the Far East, attributed to likes of Confucius.

The works of Matthew, Mark, Luke and John do not specifically allude to the actual day of crucifixion or birth; but subsequent Christian authors have selected the 25th December for the birth, which is - in effect - the winter solstice and the right hand stake in the experiment from chapter two; and the first Sunday, after the first full moon, after the vernal equinox for the crucifixion celebrations; which is - in effect - the spring equinox, the midpoint stake in the experiment. It should not escape our attention that many of the pagan god child myths from history, which predate the Jesus character, also include birth, death and resurrection scenes which are intrinsically linked to the main solar events.

Many of the miracles included in the Matthew, Mark, Luke and John stories are also to be found in ancient pagan myths, such as turning water into wine and bringing the dead back to life. Many of the pagan myths also include Eucharist rituals with symbolic food and drink. In short, none of the content of the Matthew, Mark, Luke and John stories was new at the time of writing; it can all be found in a host of ancient literature and verbal traditions which predate the Matthew, Mark, Luke and John stories themselves. As the title of this chapter suggests, the New Testament books of Matthew, Mark, Luke and John are indeed nothing more than rampant plagiarism.

The newly created 'literal Jesus' cult coexists alongside the Gnostic Jesus cults up until the conversion of Constantine circa 306 to 325 CE. After Constantine had decreed Christianity to be the state religion for the entire Roman Empire and set in motion the promotion of the new literal version, and the abolition of the original Gnostic allegorical versions, subsequent emperors enforced the new literal Jesus view and eradicated all Gnostic Jesus cults along with all pagan religions; this eradication was comprehensive in its conduct and achieved with the use of brutal force.

In 532 CE the monk named Dionysius Exiguus creates the new dating system and - counting forward from the twenty-eighth year of Augustus as year one for the birth of Christ - the temple destruction receives a date of 70 Anno Domini, or 70 CE. If the hypothesis above did in fact happen, no other date could have been allocated to the temple destruction, and remember it is a venerated astrological number. This is because Daniel 9:2 was used to create and date the story in the first instance and the reason why it has to be Pontius Pilate and Caiaphas who lead the persecution of the new literal version of the Jesus character in Jerusalem.

Daniel 9:2 can be, and clearly has been, viewed with two very different meanings, maybe more, but at least two. Which meaning is adopted is determined by who is reading it, for what purpose, and how the events of the time impact on the particular reader. Its intended interpretation was a reverse prophesy about the construction of the second temple, rather than a forward prophecy of its pending destruction. It predicts that, although Jerusalem has been destroyed by Nebuchadnezzar, the desolation will only last for seventy years, upon which time the city and temple will exist again. Hence the specific insistence in the Old Testament that the second temple was completed during the sixth year of King Darius, giving a modern dating system date range of 586 BCE to 516 BCE. The excerpt is written as a prophecy in order to suggest that the writing is taking place after the destruction, and before the seventy year period has expired. Clearly, it was actually written long after the second temple completion, and the second temple completion would have been sometime during the reign of Darius, not specifically in the sixth year of his reign. Our Judaic/Gnostic apostates from post-70 CE have applied a meaning to the work which suited their immediate circumstances and their desire to find acceptable answers; in this, they saw it as a prophesy concerning the recent second temple destruction (this mindset is confirmed by Tertullian 200 CE). Although Daniel 9:2 is seen by this group as a prophecy for the destruction of Jerusalem within the pages of the Old Testament, it is of course just coincidental that many hundreds of years after it was written Jerusalem was actually destroyed. In fact, it is not even a surprising coincidence, since major cities were being destroyed on a weekly basis in this time frame of our history. It was really only a matter of when, not if, Jerusalem would one-day be laid waste. However, once that day came, the text of Daniel 9:2 was used by terrified Jews:

- To explain the misfortune that had beset them,
- To create a story about a messiah that had already visited Earth in the past but was rejected,
- To date the story, and then to subsequently calculate who the main characters in that story ought to be, i.e. Caiaphas, Pontius Pilate, etc. given the dates calculated.

Vespasian's brutal edicts against the Jews in Jerusalem are given in 70 CE, followed a mere sixty-five years later by Hadrian's edicts against all Jews in the Roman Empire in 135 CE. It therefore adds weight to the main hypothesis of this work, that the Matthew, Mark, Luke and John stories are born out of desperation by breakaway Jews in an attempt to rid themselves of the persecution that being Jewish carries with it, sometime between 70 and 135 CE; particularly when we consider that none of the Christian writers pre-150 CE are aware of the existence of the Matthew, Mark, Luke and John stories; whereas, the Christian writers after 150 CE are. Tacitus, a Roman historian writing around 100 CE, does make mention of Christians worshipping a Christ figure. His commentary also contains the name of Pontius Pilate. We can therefore narrow down the time frame and conclude that the Matthew, Mark, Luke and John stories were conceived between 70 and 100 CE, and became more widely known and accepted by 150 CE.

Tertullian, a Christian apologist, gives us more evidence to support the version of the creation of a literal Jesus story given above. Tertullian lived from circa 160 to 220 CE. Around 200 CE he wrote a work called 'An Answer to the Jews'. In this work Tertullian indirectly confirms that the excerpt from the book of Daniel, viewed in a manner as to predict the destruction of Jerusalem and its second temple, was indeed used to create and date the Matthew, Mark, Luke and John stories: *"Accordingly the times must be inquired into of the predicted and future nativity of the Christ, and of His passion, and of the extermination of the city of Jerusalem, that is, its devastation. For Daniel says, that "both the holy city and the holy place are exterminated together with the coming leader, ... Vespasian, in the first year of his empire, subdues the Jews in war; and there are made lii (seventy) years, vi (6) months. For he reigned xi (11) years. And thus, in the day of their storming, the Jews fulfilled the lxx (seventy) hebdomads predicted in Daniel"*. That Tertullian uses this argument to support the validity of the Matthew, Mark, Luke and John stories circa 200 CE, betrays the fact that it was this precise text that was used to create and date the stories in the first instance. In reality, Tertullian is taking the text that begot the idea for the story, and putting it forward as evidence for the validity of the story itself. Tertullian also confirms the time of year for the crucifixion scene as the

123

vernal equinox. *"They exterminated my hands and feet." And the suffering of this "extermination" was perfected within the times of the lxx (seventy) hebdomads, under Tiberius Caesar, in the consulate of Rubellius Geminus and Fufius Geminus, in the month of March, at the times of the Passover,* **on the eighth day before the calends of April,** *on the first day of unleavened bread, on which they slew the lamb at even, just as had been enjoined by Moses."* The eighth day before the calends of April is March 25, the vernal equinox by the Julian calendar. Tertullian then further confirms the use of the Old Testament to create the Matthew, Mark, Luke and John stories by matching it with Hadrian's expulsion of the Jews from Judah, which would of course include Bethlehem. He argues that since the 'Book of Micah' states that the messiah will be a Jew that comes forth from Bethlehem, (**Micah: 5.1** ... *"But you, Bethlehem Ephrathah, though you are small among the clans of Judah, out of you will come for me one who will be ruler over Israel, whose origins are from of old, from ancient times."*), and there are no longer any Jews in Bethlehem, the messiah can no longer come forth from Bethlehem and must therefore have already come forth in the distant past.

It follows logic that: if we had to wait for Jerusalem and its temple to be destroyed before the stories in Matthew, Mark, Luke and John could be conceived and date stamped, the character Jesus cannot possibly be a character from history. It is prudent to remind the reader at this point that no literature prior to 70 CE, which includes all of the letters of Paul in the New Testament, confirm belief in a physical Jesus; they only confirm the existence of Christians (Allegorical/Gnostic Christians) and a belief in an allegorical/gnostic Jesus. Acts, which is written after Matthew, Mark, Luke and John, is the story of Paul's activities. It is, in fact, fraudulent and pure fiction. Acts was created by reading the Gnostic letters of Paul, mixing them with the literalist versions of the Jesus character in Matthew, Mark, Luke and John and from them all, making up a fictitious biography telling a story about Paul's missionary journeys; hence the dating conflict with the 'First Epistle of Clement' and the existence of an "*Ancient Corinthian Church*" witnessed in chapter one.

After Constantine had confessed belief in the literalist Matthew, Mark, Luke and John versions of the Jesus story, and his successors had forced acceptance of this belief onto the population upon pain of death and torture, and brutally oppressed all alternate Gnostic Christian views, along with pagan and astrological beliefs, the literalist Christian movement spread over the entire Roman Empire. It is often remarked by Christian apologists today that the Matthew, Mark, Luke and John stories must have a kernel of truth to them due to the speed of acceptance of the Christian message across the Roman Empire in the closing stages of the first century CE. However, this rebuff presupposes that no form of Christology existed before 30 CE. The views presented above reveal the existence of multiple Christologies which had been in existence for an unknown time frame, possibly centuries rather than decades, all over the civilised Mediterranean area, prior to 30 CE. Therefore, there was no rapid spread of Christianity post-30 CE, only a gradual morph from an allegorical to a literal interpretation over a 300 year period from 70 to 325 CE.

The New Testament had a specific architect; his name was Eusebius. Under the wing of the Emperor Constantine around 325 CE, Eusebius basically makes up the New Testament to his own liking. In doing so he rewrites history with fantastic lies. Eusebius completely changes the concept of Christianity from that of a mystery Gnostic faith with people looking to find the Christ in themselves, to one of a group of people following a character named Christ. He does this by rejecting all allegorical Christ literature and promoting the favoured literal Christ literature. In this act, Eusebius officially converts Jesus Christ from a fictional to a literal character and with the help of a quick succession of ruthless despotic rulers, people were compelled to accept the doctrine or suffer the consequences.

We know this process today as the Nicene Creed of 325 CE. Below is a translation of Eusebius's work.

*The Divine Scriptures that are Accepted and Those That are Not (from Ecclesiastical History 3.25.1-7)*

*[recognised]*

*At this point it seems appropriate to summarise the writings of the New Testament which have already been mentioned. In the first place must be put the holy quaternion of the gospels, which are followed by the book of the Acts of the Apostles.*

*After this must be reckoned the Epistles of Paul; next in order the extant former Epistle of John, and likewise the Epistle of Peter must be recognised. After these must be put, if it really seems right, the Apocalypse of John, concerning which we shall give the different opinions at the proper time. These, then, [are to be placed] among the recognised books.*

*[disputed]*

*Of the disputed books, which are nevertheless familiar to the majority, there are extant the Epistle of James, as it is called; and that of Jude; and the second Epistle of Peter; and those that are called the Second and Third of John, whether they belong to the evangelist or to another of the same name.*

*[spurious]*

*Among the spurious books must be reckoned also the Acts of Paul, and the Shepherd, as it is called, and the Apocalypse of Peter; and, in addition to these, the extant Epistle of Barnabas, and the Teaching of the Apostles [Didache] , as it is called. And, in addition, as I said, the Apocalypse of John, if it seems right. (This last as I said, is rejected by some, but others count it among the recognised books.) And among these some have counted also the gospel of the Hebrews, with which those of the Hebrews who have accepted Christ take a special pleasure.*

*[heretical]*

*Now all these would be among the disputed books; but nevertheless we have felt compelled to make this catalogue of them, distinguishing between those writings which, according to the tradition of the Church, are true and genuine and recognised, from the others which differ from them in that they are not canonical, but disputed, yet nevertheless are known to most churchmen. [And this we have done] in order that we might be able to know both these same writings and also those which the heretics put forward under the name of the apostles; including, for instance, such books as the gospels of Peter, of Thomas, of Matthias, or even of some others besides these, and the Acts of Andrew and John and the other apostles. To none of these has any who belonged to the succession of ecclesiastical writers ever thought it right to refer in his writings.*

*Moreover, the character of the style also is far removed from apostolic usage, and the thought and purport of their contents are completely out of harmony with true orthodoxy and clearly show themselves that they are the forgeries of heretics. For this reason they ought not to be reckoned among the spurious books, but are to be cast aside as altogether absurd and impious.*

*The Epistles of the Apostles (from Ecclesiastical History 3.3.5-7)*

*... Paul's fourteen epistles are well known and undisputed. It is not indeed right to overlook the fact that some have rejected the Epistle to the Hebrews, saying that it is disputed by the Church of Rome, on the ground that it was not written by Paul. But what has been said concerning this epistle by those who lived before our time I shall quote in the proper place. In regard to the so-called Acts of Paul, I have not found them among the undisputed writings.*

*But as the same apostle, in the salutations at the end of the Epistle to the Romans, has made mention among others of Hermas, to whom the book called 'The Shepherd' is ascribed, it should be observed that this too has been disputed by some, and on their account cannot be placed among the acknowledged books; while by others it is considered quite indispensable, especially to those who need instruction in the elements of the faith. Hence, as we know, it has been publicly read in churches, and I have found that some of the most ancient writers used it. This will serve to show the divine writings that are undisputed as well as those that are not universally acknowledged.*

So, as can be seen above, the world authorities of 325 CE decided what was, and was not, acceptable doctrine; and how that doctrine was to be interpreted. We also have to bear in mind here the amazing parallels between the New Testament story and the Egyptian story of Osiris, Isis and the god child Horus. As demonstrated earlier in this chapter, the Osiris story is ancient beyond imagination and involves a death and resurrection scene and a divine conception of the god child Horus. The birth takes place on the winter solstice (25th December at that time, by their calendar) and Horus, the god child of Isis, was Osiris reincarnated. Parallel this with the holy trinity concept: Jesus is not just the son of God, he is God, and so it is with Horus and Osiris. The reader will recall from the second chapter the commentary on the alignment of the three stars of Orion's Belt and the star Sirius which all point to the sunrise location at the winter solstice. To the Egyptians, the constellation Orion was Osiris (the father), Sirius was Isis (the mother) and Horus was the Sun being born on the winter solstice. Did Eusebius, the architect of the Nicene Creed and the New Testament content, know this story? Yes he did, he tells us himself in his own words that he is familiar with the work of the Egyptian scribe Manetho. So we have good cause to wonder just where the idea of Joseph, Mary and Jesus actually came from. Recall from chapter one, 'Clement and Barnabas', that it did not come from any of the pre-70 CE epistles included in the New Testament, because they make no mention of Joseph or Mary.

In conclusion to this section: the only similarity between Christianity pre-70CE, and that which is promoted by the Church today is the name. The content of the theology was completely changed to suit the political aims and despotic rule of the Roman Empire post-325 CE.

## Gilgamesh and Akhetaten rediscovered:

Just as the New Testament plagiarises from prior myths, so too does the Old Testament. In 1844 an English man named Austen Henry Layard began excavations on some mounds in what we know today as Mosul in Iraq. He began the work following rumours of there being antiquities buried inside the mounds. The mounds were identified as the ruins of palaces at ancient Nineveh; the finds were magnificent. Amongst the finds were thousands of clay tablets; over 25,000 according to Stephen Mitchell in the introduction to his book 'Gilgamesh'. The clay tablets contained the markings of an un-deciphered text. Some ten or more years later a story was discovered etched in gigantic proportions into a cliff face in Behistun, north-west Persia, which transpired to be an inscription left by the Persian King Darius circa 500 BCE. It was discovered by an English Army Officer named Henry Rawlinson. The etchings depicted a story in three different alphabets of which one was known and two were unknown dialects. Rawlinson scaled the cliff face and recorded the passages in all three dialects in order to take them in to a more comfortable environment for analysis. As all three writings told the same story, the known text, Old Persian, was the key to deciphering the lexicon to the two unknown ancient dialects. They were deciphered and identified as Elamite and Akkadian. Further work on the Akkadian text revealed that it had an origin in an earlier form, this form was recreated and identified as Sumerian. The tablets found at the ruins of Mosul could now also be identified as Semitic in origin and of the Akkadian language. Other tablets, now being found all over the region, contained the Sumerian text. Many of these tablets found their way to the British museum and in 1872 a British museum curator found and translated a tablet which contained an epic story with a very familiar chapter.

It was the story of King Gilgamesh; a poem as beautiful and thought provoking as the Iliad. It was also controversial because it told the self same story of the flood we know from the Old Testament. This was initially seen as proof that the Bible is in fact a historical document; this was of course just wishful thinking, a case of trying to make the facts and the evidence fit the scenario. The Gilgamesh story involved many gods, a different name for Noah and a different scenario leading up to the building of the boat; but the boat is built for the same reason. The story has a Goddess called Mami who made humans from clay on the seventh day of each month and it makes constant use of the number seven with regard to the time lapses between certain events in the story. The rest of the flood myth part of the story is identical to the Noah flood myth story with regard to: killing all life, releasing doves and ravens, two of each animal etc. So, the reality is actually quite the reverse. The clay tablets are hard factual evidence that the Bible, or the story of Noah and the flood at the very least, is complete plagiarism of stories from other lands. These stories originate from a time much further back in antiquity than the creation of the Torah or the forming of the Israelite Kingdoms.

The Clay tablets from Nineveh verifiably date to a civilisation in existence before the Egyptians; a civilisation which resided in Mesopotamia, the fertile land between the Tigris and the Euphrates rivers known today as Iraq. Given their content about a King Gilgamesh who is believed to have reigned circa 2700 BCE, they have been dated to about 2100 BCE and belong to a people with a history which goes back to 3500 BCE. This then, is currently the oldest known occurrence of a civilisation we have. So if the stories of the Flood in the Epic of Gilgamesh and the story of Noah's flood are similar, the Gilgamesh version predates Noah.

Given evidence skilfully presented by Israel Finkelstein and Neil Asher Silberman, which demonstrates that the Old Testament was probably penned between 1025 and 600 BCE, the Gilgamesh Epic predates the Bible by some 1,075 to 1,500 years. One other fact is certain, although the characters, places and number of gods in the two versions are different; the general underlying stories are identical. This means without doubt, who ever created the story of Noah, plagiarised and adapted the Epic of Gilgamesh or a later variation of the same story. In reality, the flood story exists in folklore in many variations, in many areas, from many time frames; indeed, even Greek mythology contains such a myth attributed to the displeasure of Zeus: Apollodorus' Library of Greek Mythology, Book II, The Deucalionids. Translated by Robin Hard: *"When Zeus wanted to eliminate the race of bronze, Deucalion, on the advice of Prometheus, built a chest, and after storing it with provisions, climbed into it with Pyrrha. Zeus poured an abundance of rain from heaven to flood the greater part of Greece, causing all human beings to be destroyed, apart from those who took refuge on the lofty mountains nearby."* The flood myth probably originally formed as an explanation for a disaster that no one understood, such as a tsunami. Events throughout history have given us the Noah version on a world-wide scale; this is mere chance and cannot possibly be used to assert any truth in the story. Had events in history taken any other turns, we might be more familiar now with some other, long since forgotten and not yet rediscovered, version of the story. It is entirely conceivable that we could have found ourselves teaching our children the Gilgamesh version and not even know of the Noah version.

One more interesting twist on the flood epic can be found in the research of Graham Hancock 'Fingerprint of the Gods'. He has visited and studied the ancient tribes of Peru and Bolivia, along with the writings made about these people by the Spanish just after the Conquistador invasion. These writings reveal a common character from folklore from all over the

Americas given the general name, among others, of Viracocha. Viracocha seems to have been the entity credited with the creation of all life. Interestingly he is credited with creating all current life, after the floods sent by him to destroy the humans (with which he was unhappy) had receded. More interestingly, these prior humans that displeased him so much were, according to the stories, giants. It is worth pointing out at this stage that had the people of Central America set sail and conquered Europe, we would all know Viracocha personally. We would know him because we would have spiritual organisations insisting that we teach our children all about Viracocha. This chapter would then be about the discovery of an ancient Middle Eastern cult that used to worship a god called Yahweh. But, the Spanish conquered the Americas so we preach to our children about a god called Yahweh, and this chapter introduces an ancient Central American deity called Viracocha!

The flood story of Viracocha is far too close to the Old Testament version to be a coincidence and probably gives some clue as to the place and time of origin for the story. However, many scenarios are possible. It is possible, although it flies in the face of modern orthodox history, that this story has travelled the globe in a westerly direction. That is, it started in South and Central America, travelled along the west coast of North America, over the Bering Strait between America and Russia and into Asia. From there the story could have travelled to the Persian Gulf and then on to the east Mediterranean coast. Modern teaching tells us that humans populated the Americas last; well, modern teaching could be just plain wrong, and a good read of Graham Hancock's work might even convince you of that, I can highly recommend it. A second scenario could be that the Persian Gulf was the start point for the origin of the Flood story. It would then have travelled left to the Mediterranean and Europe while travelling right to Asia, the Bering Strait and the Americas at the same time; with the story being evolved and amended a little bit by each new civilisation/generation who accepted the story. One-day, around 1532 CE, when the Spanish invaded the Incas of Peru, the story met itself again after its journey around the globe in different directions. The two meeting versions were still basically the same, but with many local twists added. I think the truth will lie somewhere between these two hypotheses. What we do know for certain is that: the story we adopt in Europe, the version from Mesopotamia and the version from South America, all have a common origin from somewhere in time and at some specific location on the planet. In fact Graham Hancock's book reveals the work of Dr Richard Andree in which he studied more than 500 different flood myths from around the globe.

I think Graham Hancock's hypothesis of a civilisation yet to be uncovered and confirmed by archaeology holds a great deal of water, pardon the pun; if found, it will completely upturn our accepted view of history and the rise of civilisations. Applying research into the origin of common base stories such as the flood myth might hold the key to the location in which to search, in order to find the very first civilisation.

What of the Old Testament concept of monotheism; was this unique or plagiarised? In 1885, while digging for mud blocks to use as fertiliser in the outskirts of El Amarna (ancient Akhetaten) in Egypt, a woman unearthed some clay tablets. They proved to be correspondence between the Pharaoh Akhenaten and his ruling body at the outposts of his empire. The tablets gave an insight into the radical thinking of this heretic Pharaoh and his, then unique, idea of monotheism. Akhenaten came to power in 1353 BCE. Contemporary archaeology demonstrates the earliest Israelite settlements did not appear in the Levant until circa 1200 BCE, over one hundred years after the rule of Akhenaten began. The unpopularity of Akhenaten's monotheistic concept became clear following his death; this is evident from his omission from, and removal from, many king lists found in Egypt today. But one more clue to the radical thoughts of this Pharaoh also came to light in the tomb of Akhenaten's chief minister and later Pharaoh Ay. It is the hymn to the Aten. So similar in content and concept is the hymn to psalm 104 in the Old Testament that the writing of one has to be influenced by knowledge of the other. Once again the facts are quite conclusive; the hymn to the Aten predates psalm 104 by some 300 years at least. The logic behind this figure is: Ay died 1321 BCE and the hymn to the Aten was etched in stone in the walls of his tomb. Therefore the hymn to the Aten must have been penned before this date. While the earliest settlements in the Levant appear in 1200 BCE, the Israelite Kingdom did not form until the start of the Iron Age around 1025 BCE and psalm 104 would have been written after this date. Hence 1321 BCE minus 1025 BCE equals a minimum of 296 years between the origins of the two texts. Even if psalm 104 originated with the early settlers in the Levant and before the formation of Kingships, the hymn to the Aten still predates psalm 104 by a minimum of 120 years.

The hymn and the psalm both relate how Aten 'the solar disk' and God respectively are responsible for creating everything on earth. They both reveal in their message what happens when the light fails and night arrives. They also describe what happens after the light returns. They tell the idea in different words but the theme and chronology is the same. In the hymn to the Aten, Akhenaten chooses to use a lion emerging from his den to illustrate what happens when the Sun sets:

*When thou sets in the western horizon the land is in darkness, in the manner of death.*

*They sleep in a room, with heads wrapped up nor sees one eye the other.*

*All their goods which are under their heads might be stolen but they would not perceive it.*

*Every lion is come forth from his den; all creeping things, they sting.*

*Darkness is a shroud, and the earth is in stillness, For he who made them rests in his horizon.*

Curiously, so does psalm 104:

*The Sun knows when to go down. You created night.*

*When it is dark, all the wild animals come out of their dens.*

*The young lions roar while they hunt.*

*They look for the food that God gives to them.*

*When the Sun shines again, they go back to their dens.*

*There they lie down.*

Once again, we have to accept that the Aten hymn predates the psalm and the psalm can only have been written with detailed knowledge of the content of the Aten hymn. This identifies clear plagiarism.

A History Channel documentary researching the date of the Dead Sea Scrolls revealed some quirks with the copper scroll. This scroll differed from the rest in that all the others were papyrus or parchment. The copper scroll was written in Hebrew with some Greek letters inter-dispersed into the text. The reason for this is bizarre and unclear. According to the TV exposé, the first Greek letters from the text, in the order in which they appear spell in Greek, 'Akhenaten'. We also know that following the campaigns of Alexander the Great, the written language of Egypt became Greek. So, if the claim stated by the programme is true and the scroll does contain the Greek spelling of Akhenaten, there is at least some direct link between Jewish monotheism and ancient Egypt's monotheistic King Akhenaten.

With regard to 'Abrahamic Scriptures' we have to accept that: the Epic of King Gilgamesh is a work of fiction from circa 2100 BCE Iraq, the concept of monotheism did exist in Egypt in 1350 BCE, the Torah did not begin its formation until circa 1025 to 600 BCE. Therefore, due to the obvious plagiarism in the Torah and the chronology of the Old and New

Testaments, the two books are, without question, works of fiction. That is: 'Man created God'.

When looking for the origin date of the Torah (Old Testament), just as we found for the New Testament, there are many clues from the manner in which it is written which can be used to arrive at a good date stamp. We must accept that today we are reading a copy of a copy of a copy etc. Until the discovery of the Dead Sea Scrolls in the 1940's, the oldest known full texts of the Old Testament were Greek copies of the Septuagint from about 300 to 500 CE. It is these copies that our modern King James version is derived from. All we can really ascertain from this is: not that the stories have any truth, but that this is what the people who wrote the copies believed, in that time period and that place. Following the translation and dating of the Dead Sea Scrolls, we can push that concept much further back in time.

The scrolls themselves are quite long when unrolled and were found in large clay pots in the caves on the north-west bank of the Dead Sea. Not far from the caves are the ruins of a settlement called Qumran. Archaeologists have found in the settlement, long thin earth tables, the same length as the scrolls unrolled, along with ink pots which contain ink of the same basic chemical structure as the ink on the scrolls. They also found pottery shards which match the pottery the scrolls were hidden in. This leads to the belief that the inhabitants of the settlement hid the scrolls in the caves. The settlement existed primarily as a place where ancient scripture was copied for circulation and the renewing of old worn out copies to avoid the knowledge of scripture being lost.

Archaeology also reveals that the site began life around the first half of the first century BCE. We know from history that it was destroyed by the Romans during the Jewish Roman war of 66-70 CE. It seems logical to assume that the inhabitants of Qumran knew the Romans were on route and placed the precious scriptures in the pots, and hid the pots in the caves, to save them from destruction, but did not survive the invasion themselves. The scriptures lay hidden in the caves until their discovery in the 1940's and have now been translated and published. Many of the manuscripts mimic Genesis and Exodus. This again only proves the mindset of these people at this point in history in this particular place, not any truth in what it was they believed. But the reading does give some interesting dilemmas for the Bible and its role as a historic document. We can guess at the time the ideas were conceived from some of the entries. For example the text uses the term Pharaoh as opposed to King for the leader of Egypt, a term that did not exist until the start of the New Kingdom circa 1570 BCE. The scripts also use the word iron as in 'iron tools' and therefore must have been conceived after the advent of the Iron Age in the Middle East circa 1025 BCE. The biggest clue is the inclusion of events unfolding around a camel caravan transporting goods. As Israel Finkelstein and Neil Asher Silberman point out, camels were not used as beasts of burden in the Middle East until after 1000 BCE. The trade in 'gum, balm and myrrh' did not exist in the Middle East until about 700 BCE. They further point out that excavations at Tell Jemmeh reveal a marked increase in the amount of camel bones occurring in the seventh century. These telling signs reveal that the Bible stories written in the Dead Sea Scrolls around 100 BCE to 70 CE originated from stories conceived circa 1025 to 600BCE.

I will elaborate on the issues concerning the validity of the Old Testament as a historical document in the next chapter, but for now I will prise out one interesting issue concerning the New Testament. The settlement of Qumran is only fourteen miles exactly due east of Jerusalem, and the site was inhabited between 100 BCE to 70 CE by people whose main task in life was writing scripture about God. The Church have always defended the argument *'there is no writing in existence today about Jesus which dates from the time of Jesus'*; with *'you cannot use an argument from silence'*. That is to say, just because there is no written documentation, this does not prove he did not exist. Well, this can now be positively countered because the inhabitants of Qumran have left us writings that are from the exact time frame concerned: being before, during and for forty years after all the events surrounding the character of Jesus. They also originate from the very place these events are supposed to have happened. These people were in the business of writing scripture and had a full forty years to write about Jesus, but they wrote nothing. I know that that is still an argument from silence but, Dead Sea Scroll 4Q521 fragment 2 and fragment 3 changes this situation emphatically.

*The heavens and earth will listen to his Messiah ...*

*Over the poor His spirit will hover and will renew the faithful with his power...*

*And he will glorify the pious on the throne of the eternal Kingdom..*

*He who liberates the captives, restores sight to the blind, straightens the bent...*

*For he will heal the wounded, and revive the dead and bring good news to the poor...*

*He will lead the uprooted and make the hungry rich...*

*...like those who curse and are destined for death when the life giver will raise the dead of his people...*

And Dead Sea Scroll (Gen, xlix 10)

*...until the Messiah of Righteousness comes,...*

This is undeniably a description of the Jesus Character in the New Testament. So, as late as 70 CE and just fourteen miles from Jerusalem, a group of Jewish priests known as the Essene are still waiting for the Christ figure to arrive. They have no idea he has already been and departed some forty years since. They do not seem to be acquainted with the man who preached to five thousand people and fed them all with just five loaves and two fishes, who healed the sick and brought the dead back to life. They seem to know nothing about the crucifixion just fourteen miles down the road which turned the sky black over the whole country for three hours. An event so pivotal, that it provoked violent thunder storms and earthquakes, and saw graves cracking open and their dead occupants coming back to life. As late as 70 CE, they are still waiting for him to arrive? This is no longer an argument from silence, the only logical explanation is: the Essene are still waiting in 70 CE because they are waiting for a created character, and a created character can never actually arrive. This also sits well with the concept postulated earlier in this chapter, that the destruction of Jerusalem in 70 CE was the event which prompted a migration from Judaism to Gnostic Christianity, and led to the Matthew, Mark, Luke and John versions of a literal Christ figure post-70 CE. The Essene sect from Qumran was destroyed just prior to 70 CE, and therefore before the creation of the literal Jesus character, and hence why, up to and including 70 CE, they are still waiting for him to arrive.

Do not forget, we in 2011 have the Dead Sea Scrolls; the Roman/Jewish literalist Christians of 70 to 300 CE - who placed the Jesus story in the time span of the twenty-eighth year of Augustus in Bethlehem to the sixteenth year of Tiberius in Jerusalem - did not. They could not have known that their dating of these events could ever be successfully challenged. The irony is: the Dead Sea Scrolls reveal an ideal that lived on as a meme for some 230 years and was then turned into an actual event and date stamped. This time and date stamping process has now helped to disprove the concept itself, and it has been disproved by the very thought process from which it originally evolved.

Given the above, how then, does a plagiarised fictitious theology become so widely accepted? Any movement, particularly a theological movement, needs a champion to be in power before it can really taste success. With the driving force of political power an ideology can have the accounts of its origins written about and forced on to the population. For Christianity, their moment came when Constantine adopted their ethos.

139

Without doubt, if Constantine had not been successful in his campaign to be the sole Emperor, we would not know the name Jesus today and there would be no Christian faith. It is as hard and cold as that; if there is no ruthless champion, there can be no unanimous, or even majority success. The most logical conclusion we can arrive at is that the literalist stories in the New Testament were created by ex Jewish converts to Gnostic Christianity between 70 and 100 CE. They were then introduced to the public at large after the forced conversion to literalist Christianity post-325 CE as the state religion, courtesy of Constantine I, closely followed by Theodosius II.

Plagiarism also runs rife in Constantine's memoirs and reported conversion to Christianity. The historic accounts of the 'Battle of Milvian Bridge' suggests that Constantine saw a mighty cross in the sky and believed this to be an omen and a call to become Christian, and that he heard the words "with this sign conquer". In reality, he was probably just courting the now massive Gnostic Christian movement in the eastern empire to secure their help in his battle aim of becoming the sole Emperor of Rome and Byzantium. However, a few years prior to the 'Battle of Milvian Bridge' in 310 CE Constantine is said to have seen a vision of the god Apollo in the sky holding an emblem which contained the figure thirty; Constantine is said to have interpreted this as a sign of his divine right to rule following the quelling of the northern Barbarians beyond the Rhine at Cologne, and the defeat of Maximian. He believed the figure thirty indicated that he will continue to conquer and rule for thirty years. If we consider what the figure thirty would have looked like to Constantine we have to accept that he would be claiming to have seen 'XXX' in the sky. It appears then that crosses in the sky seem to have been a popular vision for Constantine, as was having divine apparitions prior to and after battles. It is of course entirely possible, and highly likely, that the first account of a vision from Apollo was used by Lactantius, the Christian scribe, to create the version of the story of a vision of a cross in the sky at Milvian Bridge.

# --Chapter 5: Absurdity of Scripture--

It is almost pointless trying to disprove the existence of the Abrahamic God to most of its supporters, because the founders and supporters of such a being have created the concept of faith; blind faith. They also state that God is an entity that cannot be disproved. Well, creating an entity which is neither provable nor disprovable is something which is very easy to do; given five minutes of thinking time, a person could quickly create hundreds of different such entities. Indeed hundreds were created in the Iron Age. But when following the wrong entity resulted in being stoned to death or burnt at the stake, people generally gravitated towards the one their overlords demanded they follow and they abandoned all other dangerous theological entities. Despite this plainly obvious evolution of ridiculous ideas, any attempt in debate to persuade the followers of the three Abrahamic faiths about the absurd and physically irrational content inherent in their scriptures simply results in the use of the faith card. Apparently, religious belief requires no proof at all to be valid, it just requires faith. With a heart full of faith you can justifiably ignore all the overwhelming scientific and archaeological proof that makes the validity of these three theologies impossible. As the scriptures themselves claim, *"with faith you can move a mountain"* Matthew: 17.20. The same stance is used when confronted with the physical objects that have been found and carbon dated to be in excess of 6,000 years old; some of them circa 360 million years old. The irony is: not only can the faith issue be used to thwart the arguments against

143

theology, it is a necessary and integral part of the concept. Without the faith card, the core concepts behind the theologies cannot survive the overwhelming evidence which proves, without doubt, they are pure fantasy fiction. However, faith card aside, I will now put over logical arguments that completely disprove claims that the three books of the faiths (Old Testament, New Testament and the Koran) are the word of a god given to prophets.

Ignoring the seven days of creation, in order to overcome retorts from the faithful which claim a 'God Day' to be equal to 1,000 man years, the Old Testament gives us an unambiguous time span from the eighth day all the way up to the sacking of Jerusalem by King Nebuchadnezzar in 586 BCE, a historically verifiable event. That time span is only 3,571 years which, when added to the King Nebuchadnezzar sacking of Jerusalem date of 586 BCE, gives a date for the eighth day as 4157 BCE; 6,167 years before the present date (BP). So the Old Testament clearly states that the world began in earnest for man just 6,167 years ago, apparently on a Sunday! The time frame of 3,571 years between the eighth day and the sacking of Jerusalem by King Nebuchadnezzar can be calculated from the narratives within the chronology of the Old Testament, as demonstrated below:

- *When Adam was 130 he had a son called Seth*
- *When Seth was 105 he had a son Enosh*
- *When Enosh was 90 he had a son Kenan*
- *When Kenan was 70 he had a son Mahalalel*
- *When Mahalalel was 65 he had a son Jarad*
- *When Jared was 162 he had a son Enoch*
- *When Enoch was 65 he had a son Methuselah*
- *When Methuselah was 187 he had a son Lamech*
- *When Lamech was 182 he had a son Noah*
- *After Noah was 500 he had three sons Seth, Ham and Japheth*

- *Noah was 600 years old when the flood came*
- *Two years after the flood when Shem was 100 years old he had a son Arapchshad*
- *When Arapchshad was 35 he had a son Shelah*
- *When Shelah was 30 he had a son Eber*
- *When Eber was 34 he had a son Peleg*
- *When Peleg was 30 he had a son Reu*
- *When Reu was 32 he had a son Serug*
- *When Serug was 30 he had a son Nahor*
- *When Nahor was 29 he had a son Terah*
- *After Terah was 70 he had a son Abram*
- *Terah died there at the age of 205*
- *When Abram was 75 he set out from Haran*
- *Abraham was 100 years old when Isaac was born*
- *Isaac was 60 years old when they [Jacob and Esau] were born*
- *At the time when they spoke to the King Moses was 80 years old*
- *I [Moses] am 120 years old and no longer able to be your leader*
- *Jacob Lived in Egypt for 17 years until he was 147 years old*
- *The Israelites had lived in Egypt for 430 years*
- *On the day the 430 years ended, all the tribes of the Lord left Egypt*
- *480 years after the people of Israel left Egypt, during the 4th year of Solomon's Reign... worked started on the temple*
- *It had taken Solomon 7 years to build it [the temple]*
- *He [Solomon] was King for 40 years ... and his son Rehoboam succeeded him*
- *Rehoboam reigned for 17 years and his son Abijah succeeded him*

And so on...up to:

- *King Nebuchadnezzar of Babylon attacked Jerusalem in the eight year of his reign.*

Now, if the faithful insist the concepts of Judaism, Christianity and Islam hold water, they have to accept that Adam is the first human. We know as a proven fact that the Kebaran and Natufian societies lived in the area of Palestine circa 20,000 years Before Present (BP). This is some 14,000 years before the creation of the first human by God? Even blind faith cannot fail to see the dilemma here! This challenge to biblical authenticity is now commonly countered with, 'the time frames in the Bible are only symbolic'. Well, to start with they are not meant to be symbolic; they are clearly intended to be specific from the manner in which they are written, as can be seen in the Old Testament narratives included above. Further, to dismiss them as symbolic is to start to reject the tenets of the Bible. However, here is the nail in the coffin once the symbolic time frame stance has been offered. For the symbolic time frame argument to work the faithful are clearly stating that Adam was created by God long before the Kebarans and Natufians existed in the area of Palestine; because the Kebarans and Natufians were human and Adam was the first human. Adam therefore clearly has to predate the Kebarans and Natufians. There is however a colossal flaw with this argument. Cain and Able, the immediate offspring of Adam and Eve, (the first four humans alive) were, at some unspecified timeframe before the Kebaran and Natufian societies existed: farming land, farming animals, living in constructed houses and using tools of Bronze and Iron. We are also told that Cain built a city. Why then, were the Kebarans and - later - Natufians hunter-gatherers, living in rudimentary shelters and creating weapons and tools out of bone and flint? This would require mankind to take a monumental step backwards with regards to technological knowledge; yet we know from the archaeological record, and from our own experiences, that technological knowledge is exponentially progressive. So we can see that, human existence being just 6,165 years old cannot be correct because of the existence of the Kebarans and Natufians; nor can Adam and Eve existing before the Kebarans and Natufians be correct because Adam and Eve are using technology that did not exist for some 18,000 years after the Kebarans and Natufians. The rational thinker will have already spotted the flaw, and the flaw is this: the Old Testament is a fictitious story, a creation myth, a myth that was written in stages. A myth that was written long after the advent of farming, animal husbandry and the discovery of iron took place in the Levant; this would be circa post-1025 BCE.

I will now confront the claim: God informs us that he created the universe, everything in it and that his knowledge is boundless, which of course it would be if such an entity had existed and did create everything. This is a solid claim made in all three books of the Abrahamic faiths. I will prove beyond reason that the books were written by mere men, obviously, and that man created God; not God created man. Thereby stating with proof that God, as in Yahweh, God and Allah is a fictitious character or entity in three ancient novels with no more bases in reality than Cyclops or King Kong.

Since God is reputed to have created the universe, we can make the assumption that if this were a true statement God would then know a little bit about the universe. When God instructs man, being Abraham, Moses, Peter and Paul, and Muhammad about his creation, in order that man could log it down in scripture, we can expect that the record would be, by default, accurate. Why then, is God's view of the universe so small and microscopic when the universe is so vast, and why did God get planetary motion so completely wrong? How, according to the Bible does the universe come to be only 6,165 years old? Why does the word of God see the universe as a static finished product?

The total land mass mentioned in the Old Testament is no larger than the Levant, the east Mediterranean, the Nile Delta, Egypt and Persia. The only bodies in this universe are that land mass, which is presumed flat, the Moon, the Sun and the visible stars; God does not even realise that the five wandering stars are actually planets themselves, planets he is presumed to have created. What of: Australasia, Europe, America, the rest of Asia and the rest of Africa? If God created these landmasses, he must know of their existence. There were plenty of people living in those landmasses in the late Bronze Age and early Iron Age periods. But God makes no mention of them; it is as though they did not exist, or he knew nothing of them.

Why does the book of God age the universe, let alone the Earth, at 6,165 years old when it is clearly billions of years old? If God created the universe; he must know this is incorrect. God tells his prophets that the Sun was created after the Earth, Three days after actually. But we know the planets formed around the Sun, i.e. after the Sun. God must know this, he created them. Human life on earth can be proved to have started in east Africa around 130,000 years ago. But according to the word of God it started in Iraq about 6,165 years ago. This is a huge discrepancy. But God could not have made a mistake here; he created man. Perhaps the scribe wrote it down wrong and God neglected to edit the script before committing to print? Why does God not make his people aware of: the other planets in the solar system, the galaxy we inhabit, the other planets around other stars in our galaxy and the multitude of galaxies in the universe he created? It is as though he did not know they existed. But that cannot be true, he created them. How can it be that we have light separating day from night three days before the Sun, Moon and stars are created. Surely with no Sun, there can be no light? Why are we told by God that his work on the creation is finished and "*immovable*" when the universe presents itself as very much a work in progress; we are now well aware that the universe is expanding, and at an accelerating rate. We can also observe new stars being born, and we know that this can lead to the formation of new planets in a new solar system around these fledgling stars. But, here is the big one: the book of the word of God tells us that the Sun travels across the sky? But the Earth spins, and orbits the Sun does it not? The Sun does not orbit the Earth. This is a big problem; either God did not know this, or he has told his prophets a complete lie. But God must have known; he created the universe.

There is only one possible conclusion we can arrive at to explain the irregularities listed above. The scriptures were written by men - as if it really needs to be stated - who made up the concept of God. They purport to be writing what their made-up creation, God, is telling them to write. They make the mistake of writing about the creation of the universe, something they clearly knew nothing about. No one did in the Iron Age. Only astonishing credulity of the highest order can lead to the conclusion that a creating God narrated these books to men.

Here in the 21st century, we know quite a bit about the size of the universe and the mathematical and physical laws governing the universe in which we live. Between 1025 and 600 BCE (there is strong archaeological evidence to suggest that this is when the Old Testament scriptures were first written) man only knew what he could see from his physical surroundings. He only knew of the local area, of people from surrounding areas, and what he could see when he looked upwards during the day and the night. This is why the narration on the creation of the universe is so completely limited in scope and utterly wrong. The undeniable point is: if the Abrahamic version of a God did exist, and he had created the universe, passed this knowledge on to the prophets and instructed them to write it down, the narration on the creation of the universe would be absolutely correct in every detail. However, it is not. It is completely wrong in every detail. Fantastically wrong, and yet we teach this story to our children as a stated fact!

Having consigned the Creation and Adam to the realm of myth, what about Noah? Let's now look critically at his escapades. While secular people see the Noah story for what it is - 'a story' - and, indeed, many religious people view it as only symbolic, there are still many people from the Jewish, Christian and Islamic faiths who view it as factually based. There are even people alive today actually trying to locate the remains of the boat. This section is designed to help the credulous of this world separate fantasy-fiction from fact. In this section I will point out some chronological problems which make the events historically impossible, never mind physically impossible.

As we have already seen, the Bible itself gives a quite definitive time-line which can be linked and used to arrive at major biblical event dates. These dates can then be used to cross-reference the dates of biblical events with archaeological dates for other non-biblical events. We do have one problem though. The event dates given by the biblical text differ from the date of the Jewish calendar by 396 years. That is, according to the Jewish calendar the year for 2010 CE is 5771. So, 5,771 years since creation less 2,010 years since the start of the Common Era equals a date of 3761 BCE for the creation. However, the chronology in the Bible text gives a date for the creation of 4157 BCE; but no matter, since both of these dates prove problematic for the flood story. Despite the 396 year discrepancy, they both prove the story impossible when set against non-biblical archaeology.

From the biblical narratives we find that the flood took place at creation plus 1,656 years, giving the flood date of 4,157 less 1,656 equals 2501 BCE. This will be known as the 'Bible chronology flood date'. If we use the Jewish calendar which states the creation was 3761 BCE we get 3,761 less 1,656 equals 2105 BCE as the date for the flood. We will call this the 'Jewish calendar flood date'.

Now that we have an earliest and latest date of 2501 BCE and 2105 BCE respectively for Noah's flood, provided courtesy of biblical text and the Jewish calendar, here is where the problems start. The chronology of the fourth and fifth dynasty of the Egyptian Pharaohs, and the chronology of the eleventh dynasty, is where the clashes lie. There is unbroken rule from the start of the fourth dynasty in 2613 BCE to the end of the fifth dynasty in 2345 BCE. The passage from the fourth to the fifth dynasties is smooth with Userkaf, the son of Shepeskaf's half sister starting the new dynasty. The eleventh dynasty also runs unbroken from 2134 BCE to 1991 BCE. Listed below is the chronology of the fourth and fifth dynasties and the eleventh dynasty with the two possible flood dates interlaced:

**Fourth & fifth dynasty:**

| | |
|---|---|
| Snefru | 2613 – 2589 |
| Khufu | 2589 – 2566 |
| Djedefre | 2566 – 2558 |
| Khafre | 2558 – 2532 |
| Menkaure | 2532 – 2504 |
| Shepseskaf | 2504 – 2500 {Biblical flood 2501} Bible chronology flood date |
| Userkaf | 2498 – 2491 |
| Sahure | 2491 – 2477 |
| Neferikare | 2477 – 2467 |
| Shepseskare | 2467 – 2460 |
| Neferefre | 2460 – 2453 |
| Niuserre | 2453 – 2422 |
| Menkauhor | 2422 – 2414 |
| Djedkare | 2414 – 2375 |
| Unas | 2375 – 2345 |

**Eleventh dynasty:**

| | |
|---|---|
| Intef I | 2134 – 2117 |
| Intef II | 2117 – 2069 {Biblical flood 2105} Jewish calendar flood date |
| Intef III | 2069 – 2060 |

For the 2501 BCE date, why does the flood not break the Pharaoh's dynastic line, given that the flood killed all life on earth? We simply cannot have a fourth and fifth dynasty continuation and a flood event killing all

151

life, it is impossible. Either one happened or the other and the fourth and fifth dynasty continuation did happen. As for the 2105 BCE date we see exactly the same problem with the eleventh dynasty continuation.

It is actually ridiculous in the extreme that such an exercise should need conducting to prove to fully mature adults that such a blatant fantasy story is 'a story'. But, it seems we do need to. The above proves that even in the airy fairy world of theology, where it seems all manner of ridiculous things are possible, the Noah flood story is still not credible. We also need to question the validity of the story against the mammal life present on the planet today. The boat is reported to have landed in the Ararat mountain range, taken to be somewhere in the Middle East. All the animals and Noah's family alight here. So how did the marsupials get from the Ararat mountain range to Australasia? All of the marsupials mind, not just some of them.

One would hope that the Prime Minister and the Education Minister of our country are rationally minded people and not deluded, given the posts that they hold. So why does the government persist in teaching these fairy tales to our children at school, as though they are factually based? Or, more poignantly, if it offers nothing of any tangible benefit to a child, why even teach it at all?

These arguments do not attempt to disprove the existence/non-existence of a creative force for the universe, be it self-aware or totally inanimate; I am not venturing anywhere near that argument. They attempt to show, and succeed in showing, that the Old Testament is a work of fiction. That is undeniable just from reading its very first page. Not only is it a complete work of fiction, it is also full of plagiarisms of earlier myths and ideas. As already demonstrated, the story of Noah and the flood is a regurgitation of the Epic of Gilgamesh. Gilgamesh is a Mesopotamian story dating from some 1,000 years before the Old Testament; as is the story of creating man from clay. Likewise, psalm 104 is no more than a completely reworked copy of Akenhaten's ode to the Aten poem. Akenhaten was the originator of a monotheistic faith which worshipped the solar disc some 500 to 1,000 years before the supposed exodus of the Hebrews. So if the Hebrews plagiarised Akenhaten's poem, they were probably influenced by his monotheistic idea in the first instance.

Since the Koran high-jacks most of the Old Testament and is also purported to be the word of the very same God given to Muhammad, the Koran is also, by default, proved to be a complete work of fiction. If the personal Abrahamic God is proved never to have existed, he could not possibly have spoken to anyone; including Muhammad (It is probably a good time to bring to the reader's attention at this juncture that we are still plagued by the problem of world leaders, who talk to, and hear back from, this non-existent god: Bush and Blair). Moreover, Islam is as guilty of plagiarism for its faith as Judah. The oldest known religions, hypocritically called myths by the modern-day faiths, from the heart of Arabia and Mesopotamia Circa 2600 to 2440 BCE worshipped many gods, with the moon god being one of the chief deities. The symbol for the moon god was the new moon beginning to wax, the crescent. The calendars of these fledging religions were lunar not solar calendars; the followers of these lunar faiths were completely obsessed with predicting when, and where, the new crescent would first reappear early evening in the west each month, after having disappeared early morning in the east. The calendar and the crescent at the very least have been lifted from the pagan religions of ancient Persia and grafted into Islam. The name Allah is also under some debate at present and it has been suggested that it was in use in some areas of Asia as the name of the pagan moon god.

When analysing the Islamic faith and the figure head Muhammad we have to take account of the following issues. Jews had populated the Arabian Peninsula since the first temple destruction in 586 BCE. The invasion caused many Jews to migrate south to escape the onslaught of

King Nebuchadnezzar. They were fleeing Judah to avoid enforced deportation to Babylonia. A second wave of Jews migrated deep into the Arabian Peninsula populating Medina, Mecca and as far south as the Yemen after the failure of the Jewish uprising against Rome in 70 CE. The Roman persecution of Judaism was ruthless after the war and the only bolt hole available to the Jews was south to Arabia. This was due to the extent of the Roman Empire to the north and the strength of the Persian Empire to the east. A final immigration into the peninsular would have occurred by the Gnostic Christians around 379 CE to escape the persecutions of the Roman Emperor Theodosius II; a persecution aimed at eradicating all Gnostic thought and literature. These Jews and Gnostics would have lived and worked side by side with the Arabian farmers and Bedouin nomads. This cohabitation existed from 586 BCE right up to the purported birth of Muhammad in 570 CE, some 1,156 years. To suggest that Islam was a new revelation given to the Arabs by Muhammad around 610 CE quite frankly does not hold any water. The immigrations listed above would have made the Arabian Peninsula a live cocktail of Jewish, Gnostic Christian, and ancient Persian religious theology. Through time, all immigrants would have become aboriginal Arabs with monotheistic beliefs heavily influenced by Jewish, Gnostic Christian and Ancient Persian ideas; a fact which is plainly evident from the text of the Koran itself. This process culminated centuries before the Muslim invasions into Byzantine and Roman Catholic territory in 634 CE.

There is strong evidence of an Abrahamic based monotheism being present in the Arabian Peninsula pre-610 CE; the alleged date of a man called Muhammad receiving a divine recital. The Christian scribe Eusebius, who died around 339 CE, writes in his book 'The History of the Church' about the works of an earlier Christian scribe by the name of Origen who died circa 254 CE. In that book he quotes Origen's work as follows:

Chapter 6 Serverus to Decius, 37 'Unorthodox Beliefs in Arabia': *"While he was thus engaged, a new group appeared on the Arabian scene, originators of a doctrine far removed from the truth, namely, that at the end of our life here the human soul dies for a time along with our bodies and perishes with them: later, when one-day the resurrection comes, it will return with them to life."*

Compare this with chapter 56 in the Koran, 'That which is coming': *"When that which is coming comes...such are those that shall be brought near to their Lord in the gardens of delight: a whole multitude from the men of old, but only a few from the latter generations."*

Both concepts are the same and from the same area. The concepts are: you do not go to heaven when you die; rather, everyone goes to heaven on the same day, a day allotted by God, which is the day when God will destroy the Earth. On that day, those already dead and those alive who are about to die will all ascend together. Origen clearly wrote his comments before he died circa 254 CE; some 316 years before an Arabian prophet named Muhammad is said to have been born. Also, elements of the old Arab and Persian polytheistic ideas are present within the new evolving monotheistic base. Allah was also a god of the Polytheist pantheon, all be it the high god. But in the Persian 'God who rules all the gods' version, Allah had three daughters. In the rise of the new Islamic idea Allah had shed his human form, lost his daughters and became the only God. This grafted him neatly over the top of the Jewish version of Yahweh, with the three daughters being a casualty of the morphing idea. The new movement claimed Jesus, a venerated prophet, could not be the son of God since God has no form and therefore could not beget a son. Obviously, to promote this idea and place Allah into the seat of Yahweh and God, the old pagan daughters had to go.

The above scenario created two versions of Judaism, in much the same way as we saw the development of two versions of Christianity being Roman Catholic and Byzantine Orthodox. When, inevitably, a schism like this forms, the two sides splinter completely down tribal and cultural lines. Thus the Arabian born adopters of Abrahamic monotheism looked for a new name to distinguish themselves, and the two halves completely drifted apart with separate theological identities. However, the stories of a 'missionary of conversion' by Muhammad, and the uniting of the whole Arab peninsular under the banner of Allah and Islam, are not credible. Muhammad is reported to have died in 632 CE. Prior to 632 CE, the population of the Arabian Peninsula was still ruled by their Persian masters in the East and paid heavy taxes to them. The first Islamic battles and victories, which were against the Persians not the Byzantines, did not take place until 634 CE. Before this period, when Muhammad is alleged to be uniting the Arabs of Arabia, the Byzantine and Persian armies were at war with each other and raging havoc all over the region.

The Persians, not the Muslims, sacked Jerusalem in 614 CE and took it from the Byzantine Christians. However, the Byzantine forces won the war by eventually defeating and seriously weakening the Persian military capability. The Arabic monotheists (Muslims) took full advantage of this situation. It was their turn to strike out and claim an empire. The two mighty forces of the world, the Byzantines to their north-west and the Persians to their north-east had just finished depleting each others' military capability and the time was right for the Muslims to be the new masters. All this happened after the dates given for Muhammad, and there are no written records of Muhammad during his stated life time or rule.

The earliest writings we have are a commentary from a period dating more than 200 years after the reported activities of Muhammad. This is a copy of a copy in itself, with the original - which is no longer in existence - being written by Ibn Ishaq, who died circa 767 CE. He therefore wrote some 145 years after the supposed events. There is therefore no text, Arabic or non-Arabic, to corroborate the Muhammad story. It is entirely possible, although unlike the Jesus character not provable, that Muhammad is just another mythical hero figure created after a people became the dominant force in an area. He certainly scores high on the hero factor scale and he is the archetypal 'Chosen one'.

We can also imagine the human instinct to replicate popular ideas and contemplate the following concept simmering in the minds of the monotheistic Arabs post invasion success circa 750 CE. The Jews have one god called Yahweh, a main prophet called Abraham, and a book of scripture. The Christians have one god called God, a main prophet called Jesus and a book of scripture. We have one god called Allah and should therefore also have our own main prophet and our own book of scripture. Hence, to fulfil the fashion demand, we see the creation of Muhammad and the Koran. The Muslims then have one god called Allah, a main prophet called Muhammad and a book of scripture. It is also worth noting that within the story of Muhammad, we see copious use of the numbers seven and twelve.

The claimed story of Muhammad is as follows: Muhammad starts his mission by selecting twelve representatives from the tribes. He receives a first recital from Allah in 610 CE. After trying to convince the people of his home, Mecca, of the message from Allah he has to leave Mecca to escape persecution. This is called the Hijra and took place in 622 CE, twelve years after the first recital. Muhammad then takes residence in Medina and conducts three main battles against the Jewish tribes of Northern Arabia. He grows strong and returns to subjugate Mecca, and this process takes seven years.

The only thing which is certain from history is that out of the mêlée between Byzantium and Persia circa 614 CE, there grew a united Arab nation under an Abrahamic faith called Islam. Islam then proceeded to conquer the Middle East, Asia Minor, Persia, North Africa and Northern Spain. Their attempted advance into Europe through Southern France around 777 CE was halted. The Muslims clashed with the advance in all directions in Europe of the Christian Forces of Charlemagne led by Charles the Hammer. With regards to the birth of Islam: A new theology of the merciful omnipotent God it may have been, but - predictably - all it actually stood for was wholesale slaughter and bloody massacre in the name of Allah.

The New Testament demonstrates just as many impossible statements as the Old Testament and the Koran, but let us start with the main - obviously impossible - statement: 'Jesus is the son of God, born to a virgin'. Firstly, we are again in serious plagiarism territory here, but this time it is perennial habitual plagiarism. The Jesus myth really is a case of 'let's wheel the god child story out again'. The concept of a god child born of a god and a mortal virgin is very old-hat by the start of the Common Era and has been literally done to death over the preceding 200 years. It has created many god child mystery religions from all over the Mediterranean and the Middle East. Second, the concept is impossible, and not just because it is obviously physically impossible; the idea that a woman became pregnant without having had intercourse with her 'husband to be' in 1 BCE in Judah means she would not have survived the nine months to child birth. She would clearly have had sex with someone in order to be pregnant. If it was not her 'husband to be' she would have been stoned to death for having had sex out of wedlock, and with someone other than her betrothed. The result would be that the child was never born. I can imagine this argument being countered with the claim that, all was explained to both Mary and Joseph by the visitation of an angel. This would demonstrate just how weak and thin the Christian argument is. To further expose this weakness, consider the favoured romantic version of the nativity from Matthew; that of the three magi and the star of the east. As adults, should we not question why it is that the star led the magi to Herod first in Jerusalem, and then to Bethlehem. Had the star gone directly to Bethlehem, all the male children under the age of two would have been spared their gruesome fate. Should we not then blame God for their murder? Also, why does Herod need to slaughter all of the children under two years of age to ensure he achieves the murder of Jesus; why does he not just simply follow the same star the magi are following? The New Testament then, is also a complete work of fiction. It seems absurd that this even needs pointing out, but clearly there are millions of people in the world today who believe it is based on complete fact. It is frightening that there are members of the House of Commons and the House of Lords who adhere to this literal view of theology. One would hope that our MPs and Peers were able to apply good sound judgment in all issues, given their role of leading the country, and making our laws.

If we look for non religious literary evidence for the concept of God and his divine son Jesus Christ in publications other than the Bible in order to confirm the phenomenon, we find there is none; despite the claims of the theological world to the contrary, all of which are extremely weak and totally flawed, as will be revealed in the next chapter. However, we can draw the conclusion that there is strong evidence to suggest that twentieth century style Christianity - existing in 30 CE Judah - is a fabricated concept; particularly when we consider the work of three prominent historians, Philo of Alexandrea, Publius Cornelius Tacitus and Josephus Ben Matthias, all of whom lived in the Mediterranean area in the first century CE, and compare what they have written with the claims in the New Testament.

I will take one specific claim from the New Testament that, if factual, these three historians would have been completely aware of, due to when and where they lived. This claim is something so earth-shattering that they must have written about it. In fact, even if it were only fiction - but popular fiction created and spread by word of mouth at the time - they would have known about it. However, if it was fiction that was created and spread by word of mouth after their time, they would, of course, know nothing of it, and would not have been able to comment on it; which they

159

consequently did not. The example I will use comes from Matthew, Mark and Luke who all write about the moment of Jesus' death. According to the scripture, at noon on the day of the crucifixion the sky in the entire country turns black for three hours. Matthew goes even further, adding violent ground shaking and graves cracking open with the dead vacating their graves and walking the earth again. The entire country they say? That is a major event, attributed to God being angry over the death of his son. This would have been readily believed by his followers; it would certainly have convinced the sceptic Jewish that Jesus actually was the son of God, and immediately converted the extremely superstitious Romans; they would have believed that they had indeed killed a God. From this pivotal moment in history the Christian movement would have experienced an immediate phenomenal growth in popularity; just as we are led to believe it did by the leaders of today's Church.

The news of this event would have spread like wildfire to satisfy people's concerns over why the sky turned black for three hours during the day. This all happened when writing was already a well established and a widely practiced art form, method of recording events, form of communication and a means of correspondence. Such a major event would have given rise to countless eyewitness manuscripts at the time it occurred; just like the eruption of Vesuvius in 79 CE only 49 years later. Vesuvius motivated many written accounts. But for the God-induced events after the crucifixion there are none - not one! We do have a battery of Latin and Greek works that have survived from this time. But imagine the odds, not one of the crucifixion accounts exists in the works that have survived. As stated earlier, not even the Essene from Qumran wrote about the phenomenon; a group whose very purpose was to write scripture and were only fourteen miles from the supposed event; and we have in our possession some 9,000 of their documents.

As mentioned earlier, we do have writings from the three very prolific historians, Philo of Alexandrea, Publius Cornelius Tacitus and Josephus Ben Matthias. None of them mention the day the sky turned black for three hours during the day, or any other crucifixion event. Why? Because they did not know about them. They did not know about them because they did not happen. It did not happen because it was fabricated.

The Historian most likely to have written about the crucifixion is Philo; he is a Jew who lived in the area of Alexandria, and was about 49 at the time the sky over the entire country of Judah turned black. An event that was associated with an act of God showing his displeasure at the Romans and Jews killing his divine son. This news would have reverberated all over the Mediterranean and Philo would have received the news. In fact, not only does Philo not mention the event, he does not make any mention of the name Jesus, or Christ or make any reference to a movement of people called Christians. This is obviously because, at that particular time in history (circa 30 – 50 CE), the literal concept of Jesus did not yet exist. There was no massive following of people called Christians celebrating a resurrection; if there were, Philo would have been able to write about them and probably would have passed comment either adverse or favourable. We can assume Philo would have written about this event because he gave himself every opportunity to do so and demonstrates that he was well aware of the existence and exploits of Pilate. He records the events surrounding a delegation he led to Caligula 'Gaius Caesar' to request the removal of an effigy of Caligula that had been placed in the temple at Jerusalem. A request made on the grounds that it was insensitive and unacceptable to the Jewish people. In his commentary of his conversation with Caligula he makes reference to a similar issue under the rule of Tiberius' Lieutenant Pilate. Pilate placed shields in Herod's palace that bore Pilate's name and were inscribed to the honour of Tiberius. During this discourse he mentions Pilate's ruthless persecution of the Jews. Philo makes no mention of his reported actions against a man claiming to be the son of God. If Philo is so eminent a person as to have led a delegation to the Emperor, there is no conceivable way that he would not have known of, been involved in, or have commented on the execution by Pilate of a Jew claiming to be the son of God. Unless, of course it did not happen; in which case, he definitely would not have known about it. Early Christian writers often cite Philo and comment on how his work is influenced by Christianity. The reality is quite the reverse. The evidence suggests that it was the Christians of the late second century CE who were influenced by the writings of Philo, rather than Philo by the acts of a character called Jesus, or a movement called Christians. Although the works of Publius Cornelius Tacitus and Josephus Ben Matthias are silent on the events surrounding the crucifixion scene, small excerpts of their work are used by the Church as proof for a historical Jesus, along with other excerpts from later writers. It is this postulated Church proof that I turn to in the next chapter.

The absurdity of viewing the New Testament as a biography is further illustrated when we compare certain scenes in the New Testament against the difference between a biography and the plot of a fictitious story. In a biography, the writer cannot create multiple concurrent scenes since the object of the biography can only occupy one scene at a time; for example: including scenes that do not feature the main character, at a time when the main character is clearly embroiled in a plot in a parallel scene at the same time, but in another location, is not credible. It is not credible because no one, which includes the author, and least of all the main subject, could possibly know what was happening or being said in a parallel scene. With a biography, only one thread can be successfully reported at a time, and any narrative must come from the person supplying the data. Moreover, this person must have been in contact with the subject of the scene in its historic setting in order to supply reliable and truthful dialect within the biography. No such restrictions apply when creating the yarn of a story. In a story there can be multiple concurrent scenes, and the narrative of all the characters is supplied directly from the writer's imagination.

Now consider the scene of Judas meeting with Caiaphas and his priests, in the temple, after the arrest of Jesus. Judas throws the thirty pieces of silver across the temple floor in disgust with himself and explains that his guilt forces him to return the money. Caiaphas explains to the priests that they cannot accept the money back, as it is now blood money. The priesthood decide to donate the money in order to purchase the field of potters. Judas then leaves the temple and commits suicide. Any rational view of this text must lead a person to ask: how does the writer know this? The only people present are Caiaphas and his priests, who clearly did not supply any detailed information to the author, and Judas, who apparently hangs himself immediately after the scene. The writer cannot possibly know that any such events ever took place, they have to be fabricated. But the author then states that the purchase of the field of potters, for the thirty pieces of silver paid for the messiah, was prophesied by Jeremiah; and so it becomes evident that this scene has been created to effect the reverse construction of a self fulfilling prophecy tale. This is the clear signature of storytelling, not a historic account of events. To a biographer, this scene cannot exist, but to a story writer, it presents no problems.

Consider also the scene with Jesus and Pilate inside Pilate's palace, and the dialogue interchange here; Jesus is led away to execution after this scene, so who supplied the dialogue to the writer; even more so, Pilate's wife's conversations with Pilate in private, and in all confidence? The manner in which these scenes are constructed, and all other like them, are a clear indication that we are dealing with a story, not a biography.

Many of the scenes themselves also give good cause to question. Jesus appears before the Jewish priests late in the evening. So keen are the priests to see Jesus dealt with, that they rouse Pilate from his palace before sun-up the next morning and say to Pilate, *"we require quick judgment on this man"*, to which Pilate duly obliges. Now let us take this concept and criticise it. Pilate is the Roman Prefect of Judah; he does not dance to the tune of the Jewish priesthood, the priesthood dance to his tune. Any villain required to appear before a Roman governor in order to be tried was simply placed in prison, and stayed there until the next judicial session was conducted by the governor, in that area. This could, in some cases, be upwards of a year. This alone makes the passion narrative completely implausible.

Now to the crime and the sentence: Jesus is a Jewish citizen, not Roman, who is said to have created a disturbance in the Jewish temple and made claim to be the son of the Jewish god. While these actions would indeed be incendiary and offensive to high ranking Jewish priests, they are hardly going to bother, or offend a Roman noble. These are not items that would have qualified Jesus for a hearing in front of Pilate at all, let alone first thing the following morning, before sun-up. Such a matter would have been dealt with entirely by the Jewish authorities. The significance of this is: if the crime, in the eyes of the Jews, warranted the death penalty, it would have received the standard Jewish punishment of the time for capital crimes, namely death by stoning, not crucifixion. But, the prophesies in the Old Testament make such claims as, *"they pierce my hands and feet"*, *"they offered him up to die"*, *"The messiah will die on the tree"* etc. Hence we see that we have a story designed as a reverse construction to fulfil ancient prophecy, not a historic narrative of actual events.

The prophecies in the Old Testament foretell an execution by crucifixion because these particular sections of the Old Testament were penned during and after the 586 BCE exile in Babylon. They plagiarise Babylonian and Greek myths of god child passion stories, and a common form of execution in Persia and Hellenistic Greece during this period of history was crucifixion. The first five books of the Old Testament, the Pentateuch, were all written prior to the Babylonian exile; consequently they contain no such talk of a messiah to be crucified in the future. So handing Jesus to Pilate in the story, is a construct used to fulfil the post-586 BCE prophecies of an execution by crucifixion. As pointed out by G. A. Wells in his book 'Who Was Jesus?' a stoning is more of a 'knocking down', than the 'offering up' of a crucifixion.

# --Chapter 6: Weak Evidence--

Publius Cornelius Tacitus, was a Roman historian who lived from 55 to 120 CE. He was therefore born just twenty-six years after the supposed event of the crucifixion and wrote extensively about the time and the area concerned. Tacitus also gives a good account of Titus' sacking of Jerusalem in 70 CE, an event which took place during his lifetime. Josephus Ben Matthias (37 – 100 CE), was born in Jerusalem and died in Rome. Josephus wrote extensively for the Romans and covered the Jewish wars of 66 – 70 CE, particularly the destruction of Jerusalem. He is excellent testimony to the Roman Jewish war because he was actually involved in the entire war and the specific siege of Jerusalem for both sides, the Jews and the Romans.

Tacitus' work is extremely thought provoking with regards to the history of the Jewish people, and the early Christian movement. Being born just twenty-six years after the supposed earth shattering events of the crucifixion he would have had access to the writings of the time. He would have been able to talk to people who lived during this reported major event and had witnessed it. Tacitus would have written about the crucifixion. However, the fact is, that in his complete extensive works, most of which are still available to us today, the Christians get just one tiny mention when he covers the great fire of Rome in his Annals of 62 to 65 CE. In this work he states that Nero is reported to have blamed the burning of Rome on a group called Christians. For his account of Tiberius (book four: 23 to 28 CE and book five: 29 to 31 CE), when the crucifixion is supposed to have happened and the Christian movement is supposed to have got under way, he makes no mention of the event, or Jesus or the Christians.

So what did Tacitus write in the Annals of 62 to 65 CE with reference to the burning of Rome?

*[15.44] But all human efforts, all the lavish gifts of the Emperor, and the propitiations of the gods, did not banish the sinister belief that the conflagration was the result of an order.* **Consequently, to get rid of the report, Nero fastened the guilt and inflicted the most exquisite tortures on a class hated for their abominations, called Christians by the populace. Christus, from whom the name had its origin, suffered the extreme penalty during the reign of Tiberius at the hands of one of our procurators, Pontius Pilatus, and a most mischievous superstition, thus checked for the moment, again broke out not only in Judah, the first source of the evil, but even in Rome,** *where all things hideous and shameful from every part of the world find their centre and become popular.* We need to consider exactly what has been written here, and when it was written. We have to split this passage into two sections:

*"Consequently, to get rid of the report, Nero fastened the guilt and inflicted the most exquisite tortures on a class hated for their abominations, called Christians by the populace."*

This part relates what happened in 64 CE and only claims that in 64 CE a group of people called Christians existed; this does not confirm that what they believed was factual, nor does it confirm whether the group concerned considered their faith to be allegorical or literal.

*"Christus, from whom the name had its origin, suffered the extreme penalty during the reign of Tiberius at the hands of one of our procurators, Pontius Pilatus, and a most mischievous superstition, thus checked for the moment, again broke out not only in Judah, the first source of the evil, but even in Rome, where all things hideous and shameful from every part of the world find their centre and become popular."*

This section is purely Tacitus' take on who the Christians were. But Tacitus writes this work circa 100 CE which is some thirty-six years later, and during the period of the Matthew, Mark, Luke, John and Acts stories. So Tacitus' take on who the Christians were, is possibly tainted with the resulting evolution of Christianity from an allegorical concept to a literal concept by Rome-based Jewish converts to Christianity. A process that neither Nero, nor the group called Christians in 64 CE, have yet been exposed to. Furthermore, Tacitus may have been acquainted with the literal version of the belief and completely unaware that an allegorical version had ever existed. In short, this passage does not confirm Nero's Christians believed in a physical Jesus, it only confirms that Tacitus, writing circa 100 CE, believes they did.

Tacitus' knowledge of the Jesus story from Matthew, Mark, Luke, John and Acts is however only partial and very incomplete. It is probably merely hearsay knowledge since he only uses the term "Christus", which simply refers to the character prophesied from the Old Testament, 'the messiah' or 'chosen one' or 'anointed one' and not the actual name of the chosen one as per Matthew, Mark, Luke, John and Acts. Further, when Tacitus tackles the history of the Jews by era in his work "The Histories", for Judah during the reign of Tiberius he writes:

" *At Herod's death, without waiting for the imperial decision, a certain Simon usurped the title of King. He was dealt with by the governor of Syria, Quintilius Varus, while the Jews were disciplined and divided up into three kingdoms ruled by Herod's sons.* **In Tiberius' reign all was quiet.** *Then, rather than put up a statue of Gaius Caesar in the temple as they had been ordered, the Jews flew to arms, though the rebellion came to nothing owing to the assassination of the Emperor.* "

So all quiet in Judah in the reign of Tiberius then, no earth shattering event worth any mention occurred! This displays no knowledge of the account of the sky turning black for three hours over the entire country, accompanied by violent storms and earthquakes; events attributed to the belief of divine retribution by a God, following the execution of his son by Pontius Pilate. So in conclusion, the first entry by Tacitus referencing Nero only confirms the existence of a group called Christians in Rome circa 64 CE, not the existence of a person called Jesus of Nazareth.

Josephus Ben Matthias was born in 37 CE; he played quite a prominent role in Judah and had contact with the Roman high court. He is reported to have had personal interaction with Nero and Titus. He is recorded as having petitioned Nero for the release of Jewish hostages, which may or may not be true; but Josephus did have contact with Titus during his conquest of Jerusalem in 70 CE and Josephus wrote about many events of the era, writings which are dated to have been penned in 90 CE. Josephus lived in Judah and was born shortly after (less than one lifetime) the supposed crucifixion. His passions were to research and record history and current events. This man would definitely have something to say about the sky turning black for three hours following the crucifixion of a man who was claimed to be the son of God by a group called Christians. Regarding the name Jesus, there are three very small pieces in his entire extant works. They come from his Jewish Antiquities, and are repeated below. The first is from a writing the Church calls 'Testimonium Flavianum'. The Flavian dynasty of Roman emperors is as follows: Vespasian 69–79, Titus 79–81 and Domitian 81–96. The Church allocates this title to the writing because they view it as conclusive evidence for the existence of Jesus Christ. The translation below is by William Whitson.

Jewish Antiquities 18.3.3: *"Now there was about this time Jesus, a wise man, if it be lawful to call him a man, for he was a doer of wonderful works, a teacher of such men as receive the truth with pleasure. He drew over to him both many of the Jews, and many of the Gentiles. He was the Christ, and when Pilate, at the suggestion of the principal men among us, had condemned him to the cross, those that loved him at the first did not forsake him; for he appeared to them alive again the third day; as the divine prophets had foretold these and ten thousand other wonderful things concerning him. And the tribe of Christians so named from him are not extinct at this day".*

Although the hard and fast theological supporters of a historic Jesus are aware that there is ample evidence to suggest that this passage is a fake and a later interpolation, they are deaf to the evidence and continue to cite this passage as irrefutable evidence for the existence of a historic figure. However, the evidence that this passage is a fake is extremely compelling and convincing. The passage concerned is 18.3.3 and it clearly interrupts the flow from 18.3.2 to 18.3.4, so much so, that it screams insertion to the reader; it really is a square peg and a round hole. The passage itself was unknown until it was brought to the attention of the theological world by Eusebius of Caesarea circa 326 CE.

In just 126 words the passage covers the birth, life, teachings, miracles, betrayal, execution and resurrection. That is the entire story and it is extremely unlikely that the author would have condensed such a large story to such a small footnote in his works; particularly given the normal style of writing adopted by Josephus. But evidence for forgery aside, if we accept the idea that it is not a forgery, and was indeed written by Josephus, we then have to consider what has been written and when it was written. The author does not confirm the existence of a character called Jesus; he confirms the existence of, and knowledge of, the story in Matthew, Mark, Luke, John and Acts. The author writes this work circa 93 to 94 CE, and we already know that Matthew, Mark, Luke, John and Acts were written post-70 CE. The author also alludes to the existence of a group called Christians pre-authorship and present day (93 to 94 CE). Once again, this only confirms the existence of a group of people following a belief, not the physical existence of the person they believe in. The next two references to the name Jesus come in chapter twenty, paragraph nine:

*"Festus was now dead, and Albinus was but upon the road; so he assembled the Sanhedrim of judges, and brought before them the brother of Jesus, {who was called Christ}, whose name was James, and some others, [or, some of his companions]; and when he had formed an accusation against them as breakers of the law, he delivered them to be stoned: but as for those who seemed the most equitable of the citizens, and such as were the most uneasy at the breach of the laws, they disliked what was done."*

This passage is also used by the theological world as evidence for the existence of a historical Jesus. However, when doing so they always conveniently neglect to include the rest of the passage which goes on to identify this Jesus as 'Jesus the son of Damneus'. Critics might argue that Jesus is a common name and that the author is speaking of two different Jesus characters, being 'Jesus of Nazareth' and 'Jesus Ben Damneus'. But, the second mention of Jesus (the son of Damneus) in the same paragraph is made because he is promoted to the position of high priest in favour of the deposed high priest Ananus.

If we consider the first mention of Jesus, he is introduced during the explanation of a person called James being tried in court. He is mentioned because he is the brother of the accused, and he is introduced first, before the accused. If these two Jesus characters were not the same character, there would be no need to introduce the main character of the paragraph, being the accused James, via his brother, a person who has nothing to do with the story. It would be most peculiar to do so. But if they are the same Jesus character, it makes perfect sense to introduce the accused James via his brother Jesus, because the accused has his conviction and sentence squashed and his brother Jesus is made high priest in place of his accuser. Given that this scenario would make perfect sense, the text *"who was called Christ"* is a clear interpolation. At some stage in history, a scribe has seen the relationship of James and Jesus, two very common names, and taken the opportunity to insert *"who was called Christ"*.

With Josephus, the controversy is the use of the term Christ in the text, and the reference to the resurrection. Josephus was a high ranking Jewish priest; he would not have made reference to a Christ figure or passed positive comment on a resurrection. These comments have almost certainly been added to Josephus' narratives after their compilation.

Another interesting fact about Josephus' Testimonium Flavianum has been highlighted by G. J. Goldberg, and concerns Luke 24:19 – 27

*"what things?" he asked. "The things that happened to Jesus of Nazareth," they answered. "This man was a prophet and was considered by God and by all the people to be powerful in everything he said and did. Our chief priests and rulers handed him over to be sentenced to death, and he was crucified. And we had hoped that he would be the one who was going to set Israel free! Besides all that this is now the third day since it happened. Some of the women of our group surprised us; they went at dawn to the tomb, but could not find his body. They came back saying they had seen a vision of angels who told them he is alive. Some of our group went to the tomb and found it exactly as the women had said, but they did not see him." Then Jesus said to them, "How foolish you are, how slow you are to believe everything the prophets said! Was it not necessary for the messiah to suffer these things and then to enter his glory?" And Jesus explained to them what was said about himself in all the scriptures, beginning with the books of Moses and the writings of all the prophets.*

At school, do you recall being given the following task: *"For homework, copy out chapters* x *to* y *in your own words"*. This is probably what has occurred here. The 'Testimonium Flavianum' entry in Josephus and the entry in Luke are so alike in structure, content and chronology that one has most likely copied the other. The assertion being that, the Josephus entry is an interpolation which has been derived from the above entry in Luke.

One more interesting excerpt from Josephus is a comment about John the Baptist's execution by Herod Antipas. Curiously he does not mention that John the Baptist baptised the so-called Christ; but he does mention that James, brother of the so-called Christ, was being prosecuted? I would venture to guess that the scribes responsible for doctoring Josephus' work took the first opportunity, but missed this one?

The entry referencing Herod Antipas casts even more doubt on the authenticity of the Jesus passage. Josephus not only writes about Herod Antipas, he also writes about his Grandfather Herod the Great. In fact, he writes extensively about Herod the Great and in some detail about his grandson Herod Antipas. For Herod the Great, Josephus seems to revel in highlighting his more bloodthirsty deeds. This is probably due to the contempt Jews had for Herod the Great because Herod was not himself Jewish and was forced upon them by their Roman masters. But despite Josephus' pleasure in highlighting the bad nature of Herod the Great, he does not mention the slaughter of the innocents. You simply cannot get a more macabre incident or a bigger affront to your nation. Consider, a figure you hate and despise is responsible for slaughtering all Jewish boys in Bethlehem under the age of two, and when writing about his crimes against Judah you neglect to include this particular act. This is simply not credible. Unless of course; you knew nothing about the act, because it did not happen. Today, the slaughter of the innocents is probably the only act Herod the Great is renowned for; its omission from Josephus' work can only be due to its fictitious nature, and that it was a story fashioned after Josephus wrote his histories. The slaughter of the innocents is also, of course, complete replication of the Old Testament story of Pharaoh ordering the killing of all male Hebrew children in Egypt, and the events which saved Moses from this fate; it also replicates the story of Isis hiding the god child Horus from Set. As for Herod the Great, the same is true for his grandson Herod Antipas. Josephus seems to know nothing about Pilate sending Jesus

174

to Herod Antipas; nor anything about Herod mocking Jesus and sending him back to Pilate prior to execution. However, he does seem to know that Herod Antipas decapitated John the Baptist? Nor does he mention that Herod Antipas thought that Jesus was John the Baptist in another body.

To reiterate, if the events of Jesus' death recorded in the gospels of Matthew, Mark, Luke and John, had happened and a character called Jesus of Nazareth did have a massive following, just as the story of 'feeding the five thousand' and 'sermon on the mount' suggest, Josephus would definitely have written about Jesus in quite some detail; as would have Philo and Tacitus, but they did not. They did not because the dramatic version of an execution did not happen and there were no five thousand plus supporters of the new Logos (the Word). Not only did these events not happen, the myth of these events as being literal rather than allegorical had not yet been fully formed, fully recorded and fully circulated circa 90CE.

Philo, Tacitus and Josephus are the closest we can get to primary sources for the character of Jesus of Nazareth, but as demonstrated above, Philo is completely silent on the matter, Tacitus only confirms the existence of a group called Christians, and the text of Josephus has clearly been doctored. If we remove the interpolation from Josephus, he too is silent on the subject. The Church do cite other, later writers who do no more than mention Christians, and submit these works also as proof of the physical existence of Jesus; we will now consider each of these claims in turn.

One such work is 'Lives of the twelve Caesars', a history written by Suetonius circa 121 CE. In his chapter on Claudius, Suetonius makes the following entry:

*"...since the Jews were continually making disturbances at the instigation of Chrestus, he expelled them from Rome."*

Suetonius dates the chapters which contain this passage as 800 AUC, meaning 800 years since the formation of Rome in 753 BCE; this equals 47 CE. Suetonius therefore dates this passage to 47 CE or just after. It appears in a passage which covers decisions made by Claudius relating to several ethnic and religious groups including the Druids of Britain, the Gauls, the people from Ilium, German ambassadors and the Eleusiian mysteries of Attica. In the passage above, it is the Jews who are expelled from Rome because they strongly disagree with a notion being communicated that the Old Testament messiah has already visited the world. Once again, the name of the messiah is absent and the passage only confirms the existence of the believers, not the physical existence of the character they believe in. Nor does the passage confirm the view of the believers as to whether they consider the character allegorical or literal; the passage reveals nothing of the Jesus version from Matthew, Mark, Luke, John and Acts. When Suetonius covers the life of Nero he makes the following observation:

*"In his reign many abuses were severely punished and repressed, and as many new laws were instituted; a limit was set upon spending; public banquets were reduced; the sale of cooked food in taverns was forbidden, except for vegetables and greens, while formerly every kind of food was available; punishment was inflicted on the Christians, a set of men adhering to a novel and mischievous superstition; he put a stop to the wild activities of the charioteers, who for a long time had assumed the right of ranging at large and cheating and robbing for amusement; the actors and their companies were banished."*

While this passage can be seen as corroboration of the passage from Tacitus regarding Nero blaming the fire of Rome on a sect called Christians, we also have to consider the order of authorship. The events mentioned are set in 66 CE, Tacitus wrote circa 100 CE and Suetonius writes in 121 CE. Suetonius could be using Tacitus as his source material, or Tacitus and Suetonius could both be using the same earlier source material; in these instances, the Suetonius passage is not corroborative, but merely a restatement of the same assertion. Tacitus and Suetonius could be using different source material which would move the statements towards the corroborative realm. However, even if the Tacitus and Suetonius accounts are corroborative and the events of the persecution are factual, it still only confirms no more than the presence of a group called Christians in Rome circa 66 CE. Suetonius dates the Christian persecutions by Nero as 819 AUC, which is 66 CE or just after.

Pliny the Younger is also cited as proof of the existence of a physical Jesus. While governor of Bithynia (Northern Turkey) during the reign of Trajan, Pliny wrote letters to, and received letters back from, Trajan. One such correspondence mentions Christians in his province. The letter and the response are dated to 111 CE and are reproduced below.

*Pliny to Trajan: "It is a rule, Sir, which I inviolably observe, to refer myself to you in all my doubts; for who is more capable of guiding my uncertainty or informing my ignorance? Having never been present at any trials of the Christians, I am unacquainted with the method and limits to be observed either in examining or punishing them. Whether any difference is to be made on account of age, or no distinction allotted between the youngest and the adult; whether repentance admits to a pardon, or if a man has once been a Christian it avails him nothing to recant; whether the mere profession of Christianity, albeit without crimes, or only the crimes associated with it are punishable, in all these points I am in great doubt.*

*In the meantime, the method I have observed towards those who have been denounced to me as Christians is this: I interrogated them whether they were Christians; if they confessed it I repeated the question twice again, adding the threat of capital punishment; if they still persevered, I ordered them to be executed. For whatever the nature of their creed might be, I could at least feel no doubt that contumacy and inflexible obstinacy deserved punishment. There were others also, taken in by the same infatuation, but being citizens of Rome, I directed them to be taken away.*

*These accusations spread (as is usually the case) from the mere fact of the matter being investigated and several forms of the mischief came to light. A placard was put up without any signature, accusing a large number of persons by name. Those who denied they were, or had ever been Christians, who repeated after me an invocation to the gods, and offered adoration, with wine and frankincense, to your image, which I had ordered to be brought for that purpose, together with those of the gods, and who finally cursed Christ, none of which acts, it is said, those who are really Christians can be forced to do, these I thought it proper to discharge. Others who were named by that informer at first confessed themselves Christians and then denied it; true, they had been of that persuasion but they had quit it, some three years ago, others many years, and a few as much as twenty-five years ago. They all worshipped your statue and the images of the gods and cursed Christ.*

*They affirmed, however, the whole of their guilt; or their error, was, that they were in the habit of meeting on a certain fixed day before it was light, when they sang in alternate verses a hymn to Christ as to a God, and bound themselves by a solemn oath, not to do any wicked deeds, but never to commit any fraud, theft or adultery, never falsify their word, nor deny a trust when they should be called upon to deliver it up; after which it is their custom to separate, and then reassemble to partake of food, but food of an ordinary and innocent kind.*

*Even this practice, however, they had abandoned after the publication of my edict, by which, according to your orders, I had forbidden political associations. I judged it so much the more necessary to extract the real truth, with the assistance of torture, from two female slaves, who were styled deaconesses, but I could discover nothing more than depraved and excessive superstition. I therefore adjourned the proceedings, and sought immediately your counsel. For the matter seemed to me well worth referring to you especially considering the numbers endangered. Persons of all ranks and ages, of both sexes, are and will be involved in the prosecution. For this contagious superstition is not confined to the cities only, but has spread through the villages and rural districts; it seems possible, however, to check and cure it. It appears now that the temples, which had been almost deserted, will be frequented and the sacred festivals, after a long general demand for sacrificial animals, which for some time past have met with few purchasers. It is easy to imagine what multitudes may be reclaimed from this error, if a door be left open to repentance."*

**Trajan to Pliny:** *"The method you have pursued, my dear Pliny, in sifting the cases of those denounced to you as Christians is extremely proper. It is not possible to lay down any general rule which can be applied as the fixed standard in all cases of this nature. No search should be made for these people; when they are denounced and found guilty they must be punished; with the restriction, however, that when the party denies himself to be a Christian, and shall give proof that he is not by worshipping the gods he shall be pardoned on the grounds of repentance even though he may have formerly incurred suspicion. Information without the accuser's name inscribed must not be admitted in evidence against anyone, as it is introducing a very dangerous precedent, and by no means agreeable to the spirit of the age."*

Once again, as with all previous offerings; the content proves no more than the existence of a group called Christians in Northern Turkey circa 111 CE. That is all it proves! Also note, despite the confessed torture of two females from the group by Pliny, in order to establish the basis of their belief, Pliny is unable to present to Trajan the name Jesus; nor is he able to say that the Christians believe Jesus was executed by a Roman governor of Judah called Pontius Pilate, and then resurrected from the tomb. One would have thought that this would be the bare minimum information that would result from the torture sessions, and that once Pliny was in possession of such knowledge, he would have communicated it to Trajan in his letter. We can only assume that the two unfortunate women being tortured did not know this version of the belief system themselves, since it would not have been secret or forbidden information, and to reveal it would have ended their torment. This leads to the realisation of different versions of the story, existing in different areas and in different time frames; this should not surprise us, as today we have many different versions of all the major faiths all over the globe. It is unreasonable to assume that there was ever a time in history when this discord did not exist. Indeed, it would fly in the face of all we know of human nature to assume that there was a time when all were of one accord about any faith system. Only ruthless despotic rule can create a reluctant unanimous adherence to a doctrine in any given area; Pliny's letter is written circa 111 CE, 214 years before that despotic enforcement arrived. As with Suetonius, None of Pliny's comments confirm the existence of a historical Jesus; moreover, it adds weight to the argument of an allegorical Jesus which was subsequently proclaimed literal by a splinter group (authors of Matthew, Mark, Luke, John and Acts), residing in a certain area, during a certain time period.

There exists a letter by one Mara Bar Serapion which has an unknown date of authorship. The supporters of a historical Jesus constantly claim this letter was written 'just after' 70 CE. However this cannot be deduced from the content of the letter, it is simply beneficial to the aims of the claim for a historic figure. The letter is reproduced below:

*"What advantage did the Athenians gain from putting Socrates to death? Famine and plague came upon them as a judgment for their crime. What advantage did the men of Samon gain from burning Pythagoras? In a moment their land was covered with sand. What advantage did the Jews gain from executing their wise King? It was just after this that their kingdom was abolished. God justly avenged these three wise men: the Athenians died of hunger; the Samians were overwhelmed by the sea; the Jews ruined and driven from their land, live in dispersion. But Socrates did*

*not die for good; he lived on in the teaching of Plato. Pythagoras did not die for good; he lived on in the statue of Hera. Nor did the wise King die for good; he lived on in the teaching which he had given. "*

First we need to be mindful of the possible date of this letter; the letter makes specific mention of the outcome of a Roman/Jewish war which followed a Jewish uprising from within Judah, against Roman rule in Judah. However, there were two suppressed uprisings in Judah; the first ending in 70 CE which was quelled by Vespasian and his son Titus, the second ending in 135 CE which was suppressed by Hadrian. If the letter is referring to the first uprising, all we can say is that the letter was written after 70 CE, but we cannot state how long after, and we certainly cannot state 'just after'. We know that the Matthew, Mark, Luke, John and Acts stories are also post-70 CE. Therefore, all this letter would demonstrate - if the *"wise King"* refers to the Jesus character - is knowledge of the story in Matthew, Mark, Luke, John and Acts, not the existence of a historical Jesus. However, Jerusalem and the temple were destroyed in the 66 to 70 CE uprising, but the Jews were not driven from the land. It was Hadrian in 130 CE who drove the Jews from the land around Jerusalem. Hadrian built a pagan temple to Jupiter on the site of the ruined second Jewish temple, renamed Jerusalem 'Aelia Capitolina', drove the Jews out and forbade the practice of circumcision within the Roman Empire. The letter is therefore more likely to be making reference to the events post-130 CE, and would consequently have been written after 130 CE. But this does not change the conclusion arrived at as for the post-70 CE interpretation; moreover, it makes the conclusion stronger because of the greater time lapse.

We must also bear in mind that the leader of the 132 to135 CE Jewish revolt was Simon Bar Kosiba. This man claimed to be the prophesied Jewish messiah, and this accolade was also bestowed upon him by the Jewish High Priest Rabbi Aqiba. He renamed himself Simon Bar Kochba which meant 'Sun of Star'. During the revolt, coins were minted by the rebels with the phrase 'SHIMON NASI YISRAEL' which translates to 'Simon Prince of Israel'. It is therefore equally possible that the *"wise King"* referred to in the letter by Mara Bar Serapion is making reference to Simon Bar Kochba rather than the Jesus character from the Matthew, Mark, Luke, John and Acts stories.

We now turn to Lucian of Somasata who wrote a satire called "The Passing of Perigrinus" Circa 165 to 180 CE.

*"The Christians, you know, worship a man to this day the distinguished personage who introduced their novel rites, and was crucified on that account. You see, these misguided creatures start with the general conviction that they are immortal for all time, which explains the contempt of death and voluntary self-devotion which are so common among them; and then it was impressed on them by their original lawgiver that they are all brothers, from the moment that they are converted, and deny the gods of Greece, and worship the crucified sage, and live after his laws. All this they take quite on faith, with the result that they despise all worldly goods alike, regarding them merely as common property."*

Peregrinus Proteus lived between 95 and 165 CE. The satire is basically making fun of the gullibility of the group called Christians and highlights how easy it is for those so motivated to take advantage of their good nature and gullibility, for personal gain. Again, the story only confirms the existence of groups of likeminded people who call themselves Christians, and what it is that they believe; it does not confirm the physical existence of the *"crucified sage"*, only the existence of a belief in such a character. As is common with such passages, the author fails to name the *"crucified sage"* as Jesus.

Around 177 CE Galen wrote a work called 'De pulsuum differentiis' roughly translated to 'on the knowledge of the pulse'.

*"One might more easily teach novelties to the followers of Moses and Christ than to the physicians and philosophers who cling fast to their schools.*

*. . . in order that one should not at the very beginning, as if one had come into the school of Moses and Christ, hear talk of undemonstrated laws, and that where it is least appropriate."*

Here Galen is promoting the idea of learning by experiment and observation; he is deriding the faith position of the *"followers of Moses and Christ"* for being too ready to accept, on faith only, that which is not demonstrable. Galen is also mocking the opposing dogmatic position of philosophers who will not adjust their position even after the observable results of experimentation cast doubts on their assertions. The very nature by which Galen refers to the faith position of the *followers of Moses and Christ,* which is clearly derogatory, should by itself exclude these entries from those being presented as proof for the existence of a historic Jesus by religious groups.

Two modern books cited by the religious world as 'scholarly books which prove the existence of a historical Jesus' are: Frank Morison's 'Who Moved the Stone' first published by Faber & Faber in 1930 and Roderic Dunkerley's 'Beyond the gospels' by Pelican published in 1957. Both of these books were written, and first published, before the publication of the content of the Nag Hammadi Gnostic gospels. An interesting fact is: Roderic Dunkerley makes positive reference to Gnostic beliefs. This proves that the modern-day theological alumni are as well acquainted with the concept of a spiritual, allegorical Gnostic version of Jesus as were the literalists of post-70 CE onwards. The modern theological world is well versed in the eradication of the Gnostic view of Christianity by the Catholic Church post-300 CE through to the 1600s. We therefore have to question why this historic religious material is not part of the modern-day school curriculum, while Catholic and Protestant Christian ideas are. Roderic

183

Drunkenly brings up the term Gnostic each time he wishes to dismiss a particular text as irrelevant and "*clearly fictitious*", as opposed to Matthew, Mark, Luke, John and Acts which he views as "*clearly factual*".

In 'Who Moved the Stone', Frank Morison puts forward the concept that the whole 'resurrection of Jesus story' has to be real because:

- The stone in front of the tomb had been moved.
- The three women that first went to the tomb on the Sunday morning could not possibly have moved it.
- The tomb was empty.
- The Jewish and Roman authorities would have nothing to gain by stealing the body.

Incredibly, this is relayed as irrefutable proof of the physical resurrection of Jesus, and the religious faithful quote Frank Morison's 'Who moved the stone' as a conclusive piece of scholarly work; a copy can sometimes be found in Church lending libraries. Frank Morison's investigative style is solely as follows: If 'A' happened then 'B' is the next logical occurrence. Since 'B' then happens in the story, 'B' must be correct. If 'B' is correct then 'C' is the next logical step and 'C' does seem to happen and therefore must be correct; and so on. The start point of 'A' is the fact that the stone was moved; all other events are deemed factual because they stem from this point. Frank Morison has begun his work with the assertion that there clearly was an execution and a burial in a tomb, without stating what evidence there is to lead him to this conclusion. He never once considers that the whole episode might be a mythical story. If we start from the view point that one of Matthew, Mark, Luke or John wrote a story around the allegorical version of a Christ figure and set the story in the past, and in the location of Jerusalem, by using Pontius Pilate as a main character; and that the other three authors copied and embellished the same story, Frank Morison's entire work is destroyed; yes, three women would not have been able to move the stone, but then there was no crucifixion, no burial, no women and no stone to move!

Roderic Dunkerely takes a different approach, he looks to find non-canonical writings about Jesus and put them forward as proof of his existence. He sees no problem with time frames, any work will do. He uses texts written in languages such as Greek and Latin that clearly date to the third, fourth and fifth centuries CE which mention Jesus. So long as these texts mention Jesus in the physical sense, they are put forward as proof of his existence. If they mention Jesus in the allegorical sense, or in the physical sense but in contradiction to the story of Matthew, Mark, Luke and John they are simply dismissed as *"obviously fake"*, without any explanation as to why they are *"obviously fake"*. However, it is plainly clear that they are considered *"obviously fake"* simply because they cannot be considered valid without also questioning the validity of the base canonical material. As For Frank Morison, Roderic Dunkerley does not even entertain the idea that the Matthew, Mark, Luke, John and Acts stories might themselves be fakes.

The above, along with Tacitus and Josephus, are currently all the evidence submitted by the theological alumni as proof for a historical Christ figure. However, from a courtroom perspective, the only thing proved by the literature put forward is the existence of a group of people who followed the idea of a character called Jesus. Every item put forward fails to provide any direct evidence for the historical existence of the character himself. As for the work produced by authors writing post-150 CE which make reference to the gospels of Matthew, Mark, Luke, John and Acts; these references only prove that the authors have read, and are regurgitating myth from, the three synoptic gospels and John and Acts. None of this work proves the physical existence of a character called Jesus Christ during the period 1 to 30 CE.

We know that the gospels called Matthew, Mark, Luke John and Acts exist; and that they were all composed post-70 CE. We also know that pre and post-70 CE, groups of people who worship the main character from the five works, in both allegorical and literal terms, existed; that is indisputable. The actual physical existence of the main character is not. Indeed, before and after the Jesus time frame, there is ancient literature referring to the god Mithra. There is also positive archaeological evidence of a massive following from Persia and the Roman Empire for the god Mithra. We know that, just like Christianity, Mithraism was very popular. But none of this Mithraic literature, or any of the Mithraic archaeology and artefacts, proves that Mithra actually existed. Perversely, the supporters for the existence of a physical Jesus would also agree that none of the evidence for the existence of Mithra proves Mithra existed. Paradoxically, they have to; if they did not, they would be admitting to the existence of two gods, and monotheism - the core of Christianity - becomes a duality or polytheism. So the Christian groups who claim that the literal evidence they supply for the existence of Jesus is valid, also claim by default that such evidence can only be considered valid for the existence of their deity; any identical literary evidence for the existence of other deities is not to be extended the same level of credence! This has to be the most precise elucidation for the word 'hypocrisy' one could possibly produce.

Allow me to furnish some modern-day analogies which expose the weakness in the evidence above: we also know of a massive group of people that can be termed a global group, and number in the millions, who call themselves 'Trekkies'; devoted fans of the Star Trek franchise of programs and films. Does the size of this following prove the physical existence of one 'Captain James T Kirk'; or is he still just a character from a story? Also, in the last UK census of 2001, over 390,000 people put 'Jedi Knight' as their religion; does this prove the existence of 'Luke Skywalker'?

We need to understand the main ingredients of a myth; these are generally numerous physically impossible events - conveniently termed *"miracles"* - which are performed by a God or gods. Myths also usually contain a pre-ordained *"chosen one"* as the main character of the story. The authors of Matthew, Mark, Luke, John and Acts have simply taken a contemporary 70 CE myth and portrayed it as factually based, setting the factual version some forty plus years into the past and in the area of Jerusalem by using Pontius Pilate as one of the main characters in their version of the myth. All else, from 300 CE to date, is simply a colossal misinterpretation of the events leading up to the writing of these five works. On a flippant note: if the Romans were aware that they had in their custody a man that could feed five thousand people with five loaves and two fishes. I think they might have put him in charge of the grain supply for the empire. rather than crucify him.

A common response from the Christian faithful with regards to the legitimacy of a Jesus character is the amount of writing about the character; but what the promoters of this defence of the Jesus character constantly refuse to accept is that none of this writing is either contemporary or corroborative. If the argument is based purely on the volume of writing about the character, then Robin Hood, King Arthur, Sinbad and Count Dracula would also exist in history. Ironically, it is the verbal introduction to the Jesus character as literal while children from authority figures such as teachers, priests and parents, while we are apt to accept, without question, what we are being told by our elders, which is later reinforced into the psyche of would-be Christians by this volume of written work on the character. This process successfully implants the religious meme into a person's mind. The meme is therefore self perpetuating because the teachers, priests and parents were themselves infected via the very same method; and so on back through the generations, all the way back to the writers of the books they refer to. The writers of the books are the product of the brutal regimes from our history which forced Christian acceptance on to the population upon pain of death and torture. It is to this brutal enforcement that we now turn our attention.

# --Chapter 7: Cruel Origins--

As identified in previous chapters, any movement, particularly theological movements, need a champion to be in power before they can really tastes success. With the driving force of political power and military might, an ideology can have the accounts of its origins, largely mythical, written about, codified and forced on to the population. For Christianity, their moment came when Constantine adopted their ethos. Without doubt, if Constantine had not been successful in his campaign to become the sole Emperor, we would not know the character Jesus today and there would be no Christian faith, it is as hard and cold as that; if there is no ruthless champion, there can be no unanimous, or even majority success. Had Maxentius, Maximinus Daia or Licinus emerged victorious and become the sole Emperor in the battles of 313 to 324 CE, we would be teaching our children about the sun god Mithras in religious education lessons today; we would be visiting iconic statues of Mithras slaying the bull, housed inside constructed underground rooms to imitate caves, in order to offer worship.

The brutal religious edicts of Constantine's successors, a small handful of which were presented in chapter two of this book, had a profound effect on the British Isles, because most of Britain was, at the time, part of the Roman Empire. In fact, Constantine resided in Britain when he was first proclaimed Emperor by his own troops. When the Romans abandoned Britain to its own devices circa 400 CE, Britain entered the so-called Dark Ages; Roman influence and Constantine's Christian beliefs had already had a long lasting impact all over Europe by this time, including Britain.

## Dark Ages Britain 400 to 800 CE

Official British Church history records the earliest Christian Saint and first Martyr in England as Saint Alban. However, there are no actual records of him other than an entry by Bede. Bede was a monk who lived in Britain between 673 and 735 CE. He completed many works on English ecclesiastical history and was referred to as the Venerable Bede and the father of English history. Through comments in the entry made by Bede about the persecution of Christians in Britain by the Roman Empire pre-Constantine, historians tend to place Alban as being executed in 304 CE. The persecutions are linked to the Emperor Diocletian who was renowned for his ruthless edict against Christian worship. Other historians link the reference to earlier persecutions between 209 to 245 CE. We do however, have to ask some searching questions about the readiness of historians to use Bede's work in a historic context. Bede lived between 673 to 735 CE; so if this is the only account of St Alban, and Bede himself had no verbal or written testimony to go by, how can Bede's account be so descriptive? It includes an explanation of exactly what happened and where; complete with the exact dialogue that was used by all the characters concerned. It is a very detailed and romantic story with the usual concoction of fairy tale magic mixed in.

We are asked to accept that: at the very moment the executioner decapitated Alban, both of the executioners eyes popped out of their sockets and hit the floor at the same time as Albans head. Also thrown in are a couple of miracles on route to the execution spot. We have a mini version of Moses' parting of the waves on the river Ver and the creation of fountains of water from the ground at the execution site. Seriously! If Bede is writing such utter fantasy in the late fifth and early sixth centuries, why do historians give it any credence at all and try to analyse the text in an attempt to find out when Alban lived and when he was killed. Bede's work simply indicates that there are no limits to the lengths religion will go to in order to give each newly converted area its very own piece of religious fantasy. I have included below the events as laid out by Bede and translated by Rev. William Hurst, 1814. I have to take the Reverend's word for the accuracy of the translation as I could not possibly translate Bede's text myself; but from the writings in and around St Albans city, particularly in the museum, I feel that this is a pretty accurate translation.

### The Martyrdom of St. Alban and his Companions

*When the judge perceived that he was not to be overcome by tortures, or withdrawn from the profession of the Christian religion, he sentenced him to be beheaded. Being led to execution, he came to a river, which was divided at the place where he was to suffer with a wall and sand, and the stream was very rapid. Here he saw a multitude of persons of both sexes, and of all ages and ranks, who were doubtless assembled by a divine impulse, to attend the most blessed confessor and martyr; and had so occupied the bridge on the river, as to render it almost impossible for him and all of them to pass over it that evening. Almost everybody flocking out of the city to see the execution, the judge, who remained in it, was left without any attendance.*

***St. Alban therefore, whose mind was filled with an ardent desire to arrive quickly at his martyrdom, approached to the stream, and, lifting up his eyes to heaven, addressed his prayer to the Almighty; when, behold, he saw the water immediately recede, and leave the bed of the river dry, for them to pass over.*** *The executioner, who was to have beheaded him among the rest, observing this prodigy, hastened to meet him at the place of execution; and, being moved by divine inspiration, threw down the drawn sword which he carried, and prostrated himself at his feet, earnestly desiring that he might rather suffer death, with or for the martyr, than be* *constrained to take away the life of so holy a man. Whilst he of a persecutor became a companion in the true faith, and the rest of the executioners hesitated to take up the sword from the ground, the most venerable confessor of God ascended a hill with the throng.*

*This very pleasant place was about half a mile from the river, enamelled with a great variety of flowers, or rather quite covered with them; where there was no part very steep or craggy, but the whole of it was levelled by nature, like the sea when it is calm: which beautiful and agreeable appearance seemed to render it fit and worthy to be enriched and sanctified with the martyr's blood.* **When St Alban had reached the summit of this hill, he prayed to God to give him water; and immediately, an ever-flowing spring rose at his feet, the course being confined; so that everyone might perceive that the river had been before obedient to the martyr.** *For it could not be supposed that he would ask for water at the top of the hill, who had not left it in the river below, unless he had been convinced that it was expedient for the glory of God that he should do so. That river, nevertheless, having been made subservient to the martyr's devotion, and performed the office which he enjoined it, returned; and continued to flow in its natural course as before.*

*Here, therefore, this most valiant martyr, being beheaded, received the crown of life which God has promised to those who love him. But the executioner, who was so wicked as to imbrue his sacrilegious hands in the martyr's sacred blood, was not permitted to rejoice at his death;* **for his eyes dropped to the ground at the same moment as the blessed martyr's head.** *At the same time was also beheaded there, the soldier, who before, through a divine inspiration, had refused to execute the sentence on the martyr: concerning whom it is evident, that, though he was not baptised at the baptismal font, yet he was cleansed with the laver of his own blood, and made worthy to enter into the kingdom of heaven.*

*The judge then, astonished at the novelty of so many heavenly miracles, ordered that the persecution should cease immediately, beginning thus to honour the saints for their patience and constancy, in suffering that death by the terrors of which he had expected to have withdrawn them from their adherence to the Christian faith. St Alban suffered on the 20th of June, near the city of Verulam, now, from him, called St. Alban's; a church of most exquisite workmanship, and suitable to commemorate his martyrdom, having been afterwards erected there as soon as peace was restored to the Christian Church;* **in which place there cease not to this day the miraculous cures of many sick persons, and the frequent working of wonders.**

If there are any elements of the story that stand a chance of being true they are that: Diocletian did viciously persecute the Christians just prior to 300 CE, and a man named Alban may have been executed for being foolish enough to say he was a Christian in such a regime.

The irony of this legend is, the story tells us of brutal, vicious, persecution of the innocent Christians just before 300 CE in England; but how soon the persecuted became the persecutors, and how well they implemented their own persecutions. We need also to be mindful of the fact that, while the non Christian literature from history does comment on Christians being killed, mostly they allude to the death sentence being administered because the victim broke the law as opposed to specifically because they were Christian; for instance, refusing to offer public sacrifice to the gods in times of hardship such as a drought, or a plague, was considered a capital crime. Remarks from Pliny the Younger suggests that when Christians were faced with such a choice, most overlooked their Christian belief and carried out the required ceremony. This is a natural human instinct, and it makes perfect sense to do so; it was the diehard few who stood their ground and refused to sacrifice who fell foul of the persecutors. These individuals would have suffered the death penalty for breaking a capital law. The accounts of 'the land running red with the blood of Christian martyrs' prior to 300 CE are accounts given to us by the Christian Church leaders from 400 CE onwards, which is irony in the extreme since at this particular time in our history the land was indeed running red with blood, but the blood of those who denied the Christian faith. One feels that there may have been a case of portraying the atrocities the Christian Church were themselves conducting against non-Christians, as events that had happened to themselves in past times; this they did to shed the guilt of their own atrocities, or to somehow perversely justify their actions.

Christianity arrived in Britain around 325 CE after Constantine decreed it to be the official religion of the Roman Empire. The Romans had been ruling Britain since 44 CE so the forced introduction of the theology is quite rapid once the order is given. Events from then would have run something like the following. A few small Roman churches are built for Christian style worship but the theology is short lived. The Romans abandon Briton around 410 CE to return to - and protect Rome against - invasion from Germanic tribes. This left a power vacuum that the religiously unconvinced and still mainly pagan Celts could not fill; the Celts soon found themselves defending Britain against invasion from the Picts of the north. One of the Celtic leaders named Vortigern courts the Saxons to help defeat the Picts; Vortigern double crossed the Saxons in agreed payment terms for their help, an event which led to the pagan Angles, Saxons and Jutes invasion. These Dutch-Germanic invaders conquered the South East of Britain and the land they claimed became known as Angle Land (England); the Celts of what is now England migrated to occupy Cornwall and Wales.

With the first forced Christian period of Briton now extinct, the country moves into almost 200 years of Anglo-Saxon pagan rule. During this time the Roman Catholic Church in Europe evolves into an absolute super-power while England becomes divided into many small Saxon Chiefdoms; through battle and conquest these Chiefdoms morph into seven well defined Kingdoms: Kent; East Anglia; East Saxon (Essex); West Saxon (Wessex); South Saxon (Sussex); Northumberland and Mercia. These pagan lands are now virgin ground for religious conversion; with a new East/West divide growing between Europe and an emerging Middle Eastern religion called Islam, the race is on for the Pope to conquer and convert as much pagan land as possible.

In 597 CE Ethelbert the King of Kent, through his European wife Bertha, agreed to meet Augustine, sent from Rome by Pope Gregory I. This meeting concluded with Ethelbert being baptised and Augustine being allowed to bring his missionaries to Kent and set about converting the serfs to Christianity. It will be no coincidence that this meeting, and subsequent change of faith, help Ethelbert in his campaign against Ceawlin of Wessex. One can imagine an agreement to accept the authority of the Pope in religious matters and allow the subjects of Kent to be converted, in exchange for political or military help of some sort; maybe in arms, or man power, or money, or maybe even by protection from invasion itself. But one could bet, with no more the even money on offer, that the conversion of the people was not conducted as romantically as we are led to believe; this being an image of the serfs instantly accepting the words of wisdom which are being preached to them. The more likely scenario would be that: resisting the invitation to convert would have been brought to the attention of the King's officers, and that would have been the end of this life for the serf. As previously stated; if a theology is to achieve almost universal acceptance in a given area, in this case a kingdom, it has to be forced on to the people upon pain of death and torture. Inviting a people to convert would result in a mixed response, not unanimous acceptance. In addition to being forcefully converted, and in order to keep whatever agreement Ethelbert made with Pope Gregory I, the serfs would have been used as labour to start the construction of churches and cathedrals in England for the Pope.

For Augustine's part, the Pope rewarded him by creating the position of Arch Bishop of Canterbury and made Augustine the first man to hold this post. All that remains now is for the poor unfortunate serfs to build his cathedral and his quarters. Many of the people forced to build the Pope's cathedrals would have died doing so. They would have taken little comfort in being told they were toiling and dying in the name of the Lord. Two of the more torturous tasks in building God's cathedrals were lime burning and operating the cranes on the high scaffold. Lime burning involved burning chalk until it became what is known as quick lime, a very dangerous caustic material that emitted toxic fumes. The furnaces used for this process were huge and had to be operated constantly. Lime burners did not live long lives, if they did not succumb to the toxic fumes, or fall foul of the huge furnaces, they suffered painful disfigurement from spitting quick lime when they immersed the compound in water. The power supply of the crane used to transport stone and mortar up the construction levels was a large hamster's wheel, large enough to house two humans; they were very unstable, prone to falling apart and were operated from enormous heights, supported on very dodgy scaffolding. Many young men would have lost their lives operating these death traps. As for Ethelbert, he goes down in British history as being the first Christian King of Kent.

Following hot on the trail of Ethelbert comes Offa, King of Mercia, 757 to 796 CE. He was a psychopathic killer who became King of all Mercia by brutally removing any opposition. To further his ambitions, he too looked to the power of Rome and made an alliance with the Roman Catholic Church. He allowed the Pope to send missionaries to conduct forced conversion on to his people; we can say forced with some confidence since this is the same timeframe allocated to Charlemagne's brutal conquest of mainland Europe. Charlemagne's forty-six year conquest saw a reported

4,500 people beheaded with an axe for following pagan rituals rather than converting fully to Christianity. Given Offa's personality, to say he was converted to Christianity is rather hard to contemplate; he did not convert, he made a deal to further his own ambitions. It was Offa's subjects who had to convert as a part of that deal. Once again, resistance from the serfs toward the missionaries would have been met with merciless treatment from the ranks of King Offa. In 793 CE King Offa commissioned the building of St Albans Cathedral, a first phase in the construction of the Cathedral which stands there today.

By King Offa's time the Islamic world had been born and through its own bloody conquest had spread to Europe. Islam enjoyed successful campaigns over, and forced conversions to Islam upon, the population of Northern Spain circa 710 CE. There exists a clue which might suggest Offa played Islam off against Christendom in order to see which allegiance would give him the better deal. There are some gold coins in existence that have Offa's name on the front and Islamic inscriptions referring to Allah on the back. Assuming the coins are genuine, and since there are no examples of Islamic construction or art in the area of Mercia from the Dark to Middle Ages, we might assume these are a diplomatic gift rather than an artefact from a spell of Islamic belief in Britain. After his death, Offa's son received England's first Christian coronation.

Soon after this event, all Kings of England were paying homage to Egbert, King of Wessex 802 to 839 CE, who became accepted as the first outright King of all England. The trend of converting the serfs to Christianity continues up to this time and the Christian Church slowly creeps back in, all over England, some 200 to 400 years after the Romans abandoned the country. Later kings, by varying methods, affect the Union of England and Wales (1536), Scotland (1707) and Ireland (1800); the resulting United Kingdom of Great Britain becomes completely infected, by way of force, with the Christian strain of the religious thought virus. And so, for the three Abrahamic faiths alone we now have a historic legacy of some 2,600 years of blood-stained religious enforcement and sectarianism. From this blood soaked history of Abrahamic religion, if humans have learnt nothing else, they should have learnt by now that opposing religious beliefs cause conflicts on all scales; conflicts ranging from playground bullying, through racism and terrorism and on to full blown military campaigns.

In order to challenge the blind faith so many people have in religious superstition today, we will now consider how religion has really conducted itself; Christianity certainly has been remarketed and repackaged along the way. This repackaging is something I fear people do realise but choose to conveniently ignore, in much the same way that the faithful collectively conveniently ignore the fact that: religious theologies are demonstrably incorrect in all their base statements and claims. We must not forget that all three 'faiths of a so-called loving God' were – and still are being - spread by the sword. This is easy to forget because this blood thirsty episode of our past has left the most fantastic architectural footprint all over Europe and Asia, buildings that are splendid in their size and beauty. We have to accept that these buildings are dramatic historic markers of our social evolution and that they are structures of stunning grandeur and breathtaking architecture: churches, cathedrals, synagogues, mosques and castles alike. One could be forgiven for coming to the conclusion, certainly in Britain with so many cathedrals and churches, that there must be something in this religious kick for so many labours of love to have existed in the name of the Lord. However, to arrive at this conclusion would be to completely misconstrue why, and how, these buildings were erected, and the toil of the poor unfortunate serfs who had to build them. They certainly were built for the Lord, but that would be the despotic land lord, not the biblical Lord.      A Cathedral is no less than a power statement from the Lord of the land, a consequence of Europe's medieval feudal system. It is a statement that says to the land lord's peers and adversaries 'I am better and more powerful than you, because I can build a bigger and better church to God', and in a true twelfth to thirteenth century 'keeping up with the Jones' attitude, up went church after church and cathedral after cathedral. To follow on from this, we must remember that in the 13th century, while these magnificent buildings were being erected, the British Isles was the wealthiest place in Europe with gold and silver trinkets a plenty. At the same time, ninety percent of the population were the poorest in Europe living in squalor with very little to eat and living a life of serfdom and servitude; but who to? Who were the ten percent with all the silver and gold trinkets, full bellies and luxurious lifestyles? It was the Church; the Church was even wealthier than the Monarchy. Not a very Christian attitude to the distribution of wealth! Still, they must have been, as they would have maintained, very pious, because they did give alms. So long as they tossed a penny in the direction of a poor starving beggar they could carry on their luxurious lifestyle with complete satisfaction in their Christian attitude toward unfortunate poverty; the poverty they themselves created and maintained in a cruel, vicious and uncompromising fashion. That is the true historical culture of the Christian religion within the British Isles, and for that matter, all over Europe.

Whether the Christian faithful like to hear it or not, the early Christian Church was founded on, and thrived on, brutal oppression and slavery in exactly the same manner as the Roman Empire, Hitler's Nazi regime and Stalin's Communist establishment; the Clergy and the Monarchy did very nicely thank you because of it, and without a prick of guilt. What is more concerning, and the religious leaders and hierarchy of this country would hate to admit to, is how recently that concept ended. The level of brutal oppression did diminish in stages over the centuries, but would it surprise you to know that if we look for a date to identify when the Church finally let go of brutal force as a tool to ensure adherence, we would be talking about no more than 175 years ago, that is only 3 lifetimes! However, although 1833 marks a major turning point in the remarketing of the Christian message with the emancipation of the slaves, it was only the beginning. A lot of vile evil practices were still perpetrated by the defenders of the faith long after that date.

Given that Abrahamic religion arrived in the British Isles around 325 CE when Constantine made it the official religion of the Roman Empire, in its 1,700 year British history it has very little to boast about in the way of kind compassionate deeds and much to be deeply ashamed of. Constantine himself used it as a tool to gain political and omnipotent power, and very soon after his openly confessed conversion to Christendom, he killed his son, his second wife and other family relatives and close friends in order to quell any fears of opposition; and Constantine is the foundation stone of the Christian religious presence in the world. From Constantine's religious edicts around 325 CE, things on the moral front went from bad to much worse for the next 1,508 years. We have witnessed people being burnt at the stake for heresy, something we call free speech these days, and women being tortured and then burnt at the stake by the Witch Hunter General for the heathen crime of being a thing called a witch; as to what a witch actually is in the real world I have no idea, but the Witch Hunter General appeared to be able to identify them. We have seen people being hung for stealing food because they were so poor and destitute they could not afford to buy food. We have seen small five and six year old children being forced to work dangerous jobs seven days a week in cotton mills and up the chimneys of industrial factories to help the land lords earn massive profits. We have seen young men being shot for refusing to fight, or losing their nerve in battle, or succumbing to shell shock. Most prominently, we have seen the very worst torture a regime can inflict on a people in the slave trade. All of these barbaric acts were carried out with the consent of, or blind eye of, our past Christian leaders; the defenders of the faith.

# Cruel Origins

Around 1350 John Wycliffe began a movement that was to pick up momentum over the following three centuries. Wycliffe read the Greek and Latin scriptures and came to the conclusion that the Pope and the Roman Catholic Church were not administering the word of God; rather, they were just using it to obtain wealth and power. He proclaimed that the wealth of the Church was illegally gained and should be handed to the Crown; He also called for the scriptures to be written in the vernacular so every person could read them and make of them what they will, rather than what the Church insisted. However, in the 1300's it was detrimental to one's health to have such thoughts, let alone voice them. Wycliffe did voice them and was charged and found guilty of heresy, as usual for the time. He did however escape execution and died a preacher in Lutterworth in 1384.

John Wycliffe sparked a desire for reformation, but his followers were not as fortunate as he, they experienced the most horrific form of discipline and punishment any despotic rule has ever devised, that of being burnt at the stake for dissent; dissent in our eyes, intolerable heresy in the view of the Church. In the 1500's, with all bibles still in Greek and Latin and the Pope pulling the strings all over Europe, and immensely wealthy because of it, the Church could tell the people whatever they cared to about the scriptures. Very few people from the 1500's could speak or read Greek or Latin; so the Church literally just made it up as they went along, to suit themselves of course, not the people. The eye-watering wealth of the Roman Catholic Church today is absolute testimony to this brutal period of its development. To increase their wealth, the Church comes up with a fantastic con trick; one that would be classed as a protection racket in today's terms. But interestingly, some people still actually believe in purgatory and the Church's ability to have a word in the right ear, pull a few strings, and reduce the time spent in purgatory by a sinner; this is said to ensure a soul's ascendance into heaven. Here is the scam: send a representative to an area, have him preach the word of the Lord and the horrors of hell that await all who have not lived their lives fully by the word of God. Have the local people completely convince themselves that they are doomed to hell because of things they have done in the past. This is achieved by including pretty much all things people might do in a lifetime and classing them as a sin; like masturbation for example. Once you have every one fully convinced they are going to hell, apply the sting. The Pope, by power invested in him from God can grant 'Indulgence'. This indulgence negated all sin and ensured a soul passage from purgatory to heaven no matter what sin had been committed. But how does a lowly sinner obtain indulgence? Well, indulgence came in the form of a written document signed by a representative of the Pope and sold by him to the public. Yes, you had to purchase indulgence from the Church. The advertising slogan is cited as being *"As soon as the coin in the coffer rings, the soul into heaven from purgatory springs'"*. People fell for it hook, line and sinker, and the Church becomes even richer. This same concept can be found in ancient Egypt. At one time, only the Pharaohs were considered capable of surpassing death with a soul, and they used the 'Book of the Dead' to help them navigate safely from this world to the next after death. As time went on, the idea that all people could ascend to heaven after death, or descend to hell if they did not possess their own 'Book of the Dead', emerged. Needless to say, having your own personal 'book of the dead' drawn up was extremely expensive and could only be purchased from the priests of Amun. With regard to the Catholic Church's version of this religious scam, an example of an indulgence certificate from 1521 is reproduced below.

*Ego, frater Jeronimus Munghofer ordinis Sancti Benedicti, Confessor et poenitentiarius Monasterii et Capelli Sancte Marie Virginis divinis consecrate loci eremitarii Constantie dyocesis, putatus penibus regnosco discretos honestos fratres Johannes & Oswaldus Burgi dictum locum et capellam visitasse missique sua petam in forma ecclesie confessis et auctoritate sede apostolica mihi in hac parte concessa iniuncta penitentia salutari absoluti in quorum fide penitentes litteras tradidi sigilloque in huiusmodi litteris consueto signavi.*

*Anno M.ccccc.xxi Datum nonadecima die decembris*

Rough English translation:

*I, brother Jeronimus Munghofer of the Order of St Benedict, confessor and penitencer of the monastery and chapel of St Mary the Virgin consecrated in the diocese of Constance, recognise the penitences made by Brothers Johann and Oswald Burgi and that they have visited the said place and chapel, and submitted their petition according to the form of the Church, and I, by the authority granted to me by the Holy See, absolve them of their penance, and in witness thereof I have granted them these letters and sealed them according to custom.*

*In the year 1521, on the nineteenth day of December.*

Things are going well on the protection scam front devised by the Pope for the Church coffers until someone upsets the apple cart. Martin Luther also calls for reformation and for the scriptures to be made available in the vernacular in order that it can be accessible to all. He too wanted to stop the Church 'making it up' as they go along. In 1526 William Tyndale assisted this reformation; he had his translation of the New Testament in to English printed to make scripture available to all in England. In order to maintain supremacy in religious matters, the head of the Church opposed the idea of printing and distributing this book; they try to have the translation made illegal and Tyndale arrested as a heretic. Things were not good for Tyndale, then he makes a fatal error, in one of his works he criticised Henry VIII's divorce. Henry petitioned the Pope to have Tyndale arrested and returned to England for trial. In 1536, a spy betrayed Tyndale's whereabouts to the authorities and he is captured, tried for heresy and burnt at the stake; he was throttled with rope while tied to the stake prior to the fires being set. Tyndale suffered this horrific death because his actions, that of translating the Bible into the vernacular, were considered a threat to the

Church's position of supreme dictatorial power in religious matters. What happened to all those copies of the Tyndale Bible? We do not know, probably burnt, but we do know what happened to everyone in England found in possession of one of Tyndale's bibles after it was banned; they suffered the usual sixteenth century Christian response to naughty people that did not do what the Church had instructed them to do, they too were burnt at the stake for heresy.

From here on, the Reformation starts to take hold and translating the Bible becomes a free for all with many different versions in circulation. This causes great concern and culminates with King James I insisting on one version, his version, being the only 'authorised version' in Britain. His version is collated by employing theologians of his choice to work on his translation, under a set of 'rules for translation'. Why did they need rules for translation, surely translation is translation? The answer is purely propaganda and censorship. The King James I version was not allowed to contain certain items which appear in the Greek and Latin versions. These were words and phrases that even remotely challenged the need for the Monarchy and its divine right to rule; this ensured the need for a Monarchy to be the head of the Church and to be God's voice on earth. This idea was indoctrinated into his son and successor Charles I. This view was, however, in complete contrast to the Puritan view point which claimed that access to God was free to every man, and required no divine representative on earth. The Puritans saw Charles I as a person creating his own mini-papacy out of the Church of England. We are all well aware of how many people had to die hideous painful deaths because of these two conflicting views on the issue of access to God. The King James I Bible was first printed in 1611; this all happened before the spread of the British Empire and as a result the King James Bible followed the British into their new worldly conquests.

**The Christian Inquisition:**

The above events are predated by the start of the first Catholic inquisition in Europe and the duration of all the Inquisitions subsequently run concurrently alongside all of the above. Pope Gregory IX established the first inquisition in 1231, its purpose was to eradicate all non Catholic beliefs in existence and leave only one version of Christianity being preached and practiced in Europe. By eradication, we mean eradication by brutal force and by any means necessary. The Inquisitions spanned continents and centuries, they lasted from 1231 to 1834, over 600 years. They were presided over by eighty-three Popes from Gregory IX to Gregory XVI. In 1245 Pope Innocent IV agreed to absolve Inquisitors and their agents of all acts of violence; he sanctioned the use of torture for as long as required to obtain confessions in cases of heresy, in other words, do not stop torturing until a confession is obtained. Pope Sixtus IV (1471-1484) appointed the most virulent Inquisitor in Spain, Thomas de Torquemada, he is credited with the burning of 2,200 people. Pope Paul III reassigned the medieval inquisition to Holy Office in 1542. Mass public burnings were common place and known as 'auto-da-fé'. It is shocking to consider that the literal translation of auto-da-fé is 'act of faith'. So these poor unfortunate victims of brutal Catholic edicts where being burned to death out of an act of benevolence by the Church, burnt, for their own good, as it were! Below are a few quotes from history; my main source here is 'The Dark Side of Christian History' by Helen Ellerbe.

Pope Innocent III 1198 – 1216: *"Anyone who attempts to construe a personal view of God which conflicts with Church dogma must be burned without pity".*

Barnard Gui, Bishop of Lodve, appointed Inquisitor of Toulouse 1307 – 1323 by Pope Clement V: *"The layman must not argue with the unbeliever, but thrust his sword into his belly as far as it will go".*

In 1521 Pope Leo X states: *"No questioning of, or appeal against, the sentence of the ecclesiastical judges"*

Francisco Pena; Inquisitor 1578. *"We must remember that the main purpose of the trial and execution is not to save the soul of the accused but to achieve the public good and put fear into others"*

**Malleus Maleficarum:**

The need to hunt, torture and execute witches was explained in a document called Malleus Maleficarum 'The Hammer of Witches' in 1486. Its construction was inspired and approved by Papal bull from Pope Innocent VIII in 1484. The 'Witch Hunts' had however already begun: the document was merely retrospective approval. The hunts lasted from 1401 to 1782: This represents 381 years of Christian Church sanctioned torture and execution of women, accused of the ridiculous notion of being a thing called a 'Witch'. Another fictitious creation by the Church used to install total fear into a community in order to obtain absolute obedience and power. There was also plenty of money to be made, since any property owned by the victim of this farce was confiscated by the inquisitor. The last medieval witch trial and execution in Europe was in 1782, that is only 229 years ago; the Church was also actively seeking and executing women for witchcraft in the Dark Ages under Charlemagne. The last burning for heresy in Europe was in 1834, that is only 177 years ago, less than three lifetimes. So the persona of love and forgiveness portrayed by the Church today is a very recent diametric re-branding of Christianity.

The general process for identifying and dealing with witches, carried out in most of Europe, is also a far cry from that fed to us by the Church of today. Being drowned in a ducking stool would seem a bad enough end, but compared to what actually happened, it could also be viewed as a quite pleasant option. The actual process carried out throughout most of Europe, with the blessing and encouragement of the Church, was as follows:

- Strip the accused naked in order to locate any of the tell tale signs of the devil: moles, warts, birthmarks etc. If necessary remove all hair from all parts of the body.
- Locate the devils spot, the area where the skin will not bleed. Do this by repeatedly cutting and stabbing the victim to see if any one area does not let blood.
- Administer torture to extract a confession. "*A Witch will only confess under extreme pain*".
- Sentence the convicted Witch to be burnt alive (if still alive) at the stake.

Britain's paranoia with witches began in earnest in 1401. In 1401 the Archbishop Thomas Arundel was instrumental in the construction and passing of the first Witchcraft Act. This act classed witchcraft and sorcery as an ecclesiastical offence and therefore carried the penalty of death by burning at the stake; burning because the Church does not like shedding blood, and fire cleanses the soul. Quite how one defines a witch, or locates one is beyond me, given that the concept of a witch is fabricated nonsense: however, the Church seemed to have no problem in doing so. Once again the meme is hard at work here infecting the minds of a population like a virus and making people think witches really do exist, and are a serious threat to society. The real reality is: it was a wonderful conceptual tool for a despotic organisation called the Church with which to keep the population in check, and ensure no one, but no one, ever dared question the instructions of the Clergy. The act was further refined in 1541 and again in 1563 by Queen Elizabeth. By this time the act of witchcraft was deemed so heinous that it was punishable by death without the benefit of clergy, that is: it now became a felony and was tried by the courts of common law rather than the ecclesiastical courts. This removed the penalty of death by burning, and any chance of leniency for first offences, and replaced it with death by hanging. It also brought with it the penalty of escheat: the forfeiture of all money and land to the Crown. This lit the blue touch paper and hunting witches became a popular and profitable pastime. It became popular because the Crown gave a kick back to the land lord and the land lord gave a kick back to the finder of the witch on his land. This gave rise to the new self-proclaimed, self-governed, occupation of Witch-finder General. The methods of proving a person to be a witch were mind-bogglingly barbaric. The most popular being: tying the left toe to the right thumb and the right toe to the left thumb and throwing the victim into a river. If they sink they are innocent, small comfort; if they float, they are being saved by the interference of Satan protecting his own, and therefore guilty. The only problem is, anyone fully clothed, in this crouched position, with a lung full of air, floats by design and so everyone was found guilty. However, although the victims floated, due to the manner in which they were trussed they floated faced down in the water and often drowned before being retrieved. If they miraculously survived and were still alive when they were retrieved from the water, their guilt was even more confirmed; then they had to face the horrors of being hanged.

Our most notorious self appointed Witch Hunter was Matthew Hopkins; he is credited with the execution of more than 300 witches alone, or should we say the murder of 300 innocent women? He became quite wealthy.

I will leave general examples of the cruel origins of Christianity now and look at a few specific examples of past high ranking religious officials. First under the spot light is Rev. John Newton 1725 to 1807; He wrote the most beautiful and famous hymn 'Amazing Grace'. If we consider the fantastic sentiment of the words with lines like "*who saved a wretch like me*" it can seem very moving. Well, the author certainly was a wretch, very wretched; he was the captain of a slave trader ship. He forcibly removed people from their home land, tortured them and chained them in squalid conditions below deck, which most did not survive, while he ate heartily in his spacious cabin. Then, once in England or Jamaica, these souls were sold in to life-long cruel slavery. They were haggled over and purchased by vicious, wealthy, supposedly religious people, who trained them to be utterly obedient with a whip. John Newton was paid handsomely for his work and his bosses made enormous profits from the sale of their human cargo. It is recorded that the slavers encouraged their sailors to rape the women slaves while they were chained to their wooden platforms which constituted their bed; to get them pregnant while still en route at sea was considered beneficial because mixed race children fetched an enormous price as house slaves, thus increasing the profit margin in the cargo.

John Newton is on record as having thumb screwed slaves as punishment for trying to escape by rebellion, and having buried slaves at sea due to not surviving the horrific journeys to their enslavement; John Newton is also on record as converting to religion in 1748, two years before the above events. If we need to comprehend how people in the eighteenth century could claim to be religious and square away in their consciences the promotion of slavery, we can look at the text of the Old Testament, New Testament and the Koran, which all permit, and to a certain extent positively promote the owning of slaves. John Newton then wrote the hymn Amazing Grace in 1772, but do not be fooled into thinking it reflects the Lord leading him away from the cruelty of the slave trade, not a bit of it. The hymn reflects his own selfish pig headedness and feelings of self importance in the fact that he managed to survive a violent storm at sea in 1748; he puts this good fortune down to God's personal love for him and God's intervention to personally deliver him from danger. Recently, a film has been made which recounts William Wilberforce's struggle to end the slave trade. The film does suggest that the Rev. John Newton did write this hymn to thank God for opening his eyes to the cruelty of the slave trade; not so, according to the Cowper and Newton Museum.

Our second character under the spot light is Henry Philpot, Bishop of Exeter 1830 to 1869. Despite being a Bishop, Henry owned a plantation and 665 slaves. It seems that inflicting such life-long misery on African people was quite acceptable by the Christian hierarchy as little as 178 years ago. The slave trade started in the fourteenth century; the Church provided the argument and justification for taking the African people and forcing them into slavery, destined for a life of servitude to the rich. That pitiful excuse was *"providing an opportunity for Africans to become Christians, accept Jesus and so allowing them to save their souls after death"*. In the Seventeenth Century the slave trade had become a lucrative trade passed off as a holy cause which was fully supported by the Christian Church. After all, all three of the Abrahamic faiths do quite freely justify slavery. Moreover, it was the African Muslim societies who were capturing and selling these poor souls to the Christian slavers. To both the Muslims and the Christians of the time, the African was seen as no more than a kafir or an infidel heathen and therefore fair game for enslavement.

The abolition of slavery arrived in 1833, after nearly fifty years of opposition to the parliamentary bill from the Lords of our country at the time. These very pious loving Lords (who of course had their own slaves and plantations) still required personal appeasement and inducement to agree to the concept of setting the slaves - including their slaves - free. Slave owners were to be compensated out of tax payer's money following the freeing of their slaves. Our man Henry Philpot (The Bishop of Exeter remember, a very pious man) received the tidy sum of £12,700 for his 665 slaves. That is a considerable sum of money in today's terms, it would have been a life changing sum of money in 1833, given to a man already filthy rich from the misery and toils caused by human trafficking and slavery. One feels the money should have been given to the slaves by way of some kind of apology, although no amount of money could have really compensated them for what they had been put through by the fine upstanding church-going, God-fearing Christians of this country. We can be sure that Mr Philpot was by no means unique and the clergy as a whole grew very rich off of the back of the slave trade. Other owners included 'The Society for the Propagation of the Gospel in Foreign Parts'. Their slaves were easy to identify; they had the word 'Society' branded into their backs with red-hot irons.

Moving back a little further in time, we are taught about one of our most romantic and brave kings, King Richard, and not just any old Richard but 'Richard the Lion Heart'. However, should that not be Richard the psychopath who, on the 20th August 1191, ordered the systematic beheading of 2,700 hostages, in the name of God; hostages he had already agreed to free for ransom. History tells us Richard carried out this act reluctantly, and had no choice. He could not logistically keep hold of the prisoners, and to set them free would mean they would rejoin the fight against him again. Had no choice? He could have chosen not to instigate a war to capture the 'Holy Land' for Christendom in 'the name of God' in the first instance. How hypocritical the teaching of our own history has been made in order to cover up the actual beginnings and uses of religion. Moving about in time the list can grow endless. Take Agincourt; sold today as a great English military victory against overwhelming French forces. But when reading this story of English gallantry, for the sake of the Church, we should ignore the part about Henry V sending his serfs to war and massacring French people and soldiers because he is being denied his 'God given right to be divine ruler of England and France'. We should ignore, for the sake of the Church, the fact that thousands succumbed to barbaric butchery and the most appalling bloody murder to appease one man's religious bigotry. What was Shakespeare's take on the men that were not at the battle, those at home in England instead of in France fighting the religious cause of God with their King? They should *"Hold their manhood's cheap"*!

We could go on indefinitely reciting from British, let alone world history, the times a despotic leader has forced men to fight for them, citing their 'divine right to rule' and that the war is 'in the name of God'. The 'Lord Protector' Cromwell carried out indescribably barbaric acts to appease his Puritan beliefs. This, then, is what God wanted us to do according to our past religious and spiritual leaders: spend our lifetimes butchering each other, in order that they could obtain even more land; wealth and power. So if you believe that the root of religion stood for loving thy neighbour, you need to understand that this is a very recent remarketing of the idea; but long enough to be more than two lifetimes, so no one alive today has actually experienced its origins or could speak to anyone who had. Our ancestors were religious through necessity and it was dangerous to their very existence to appear to be anti-religious; they had to walk the tightrope of which denomination, or section of a denomination, they openly confessed to worship in relation to the time period and area in which they lived, lest they get it wrong and ended up being another tortured and burnt offering to God. People who worship today have simply succumbed to the success of the religious meme and its ability to spread through distance and time; they have been, in general, indoctrinated into religious belief by religious parents and schoolteachers; they have been infected with a very efficient religious thought virus.

If the Christian manifesto had to be repositioned to rebrand the Christian message out of embarrassment, in order to hide the vile origins of the Church, why not turn our back on theology completely; why not come to the conclusion that a person does not need a religion to be a good compassionate person, they simply need the personal desire to be a good and compassionate person. Reflecting on my own schooling, in which I received what the state called religious education, but was really religious instruction (I was told in no uncertain terms that I was a Christian), I can see absolute cherry picking; cherry picking which completely dismissed nearly 1,700 years of absolute abominable behaviour on behalf of, and by, the Church. We were only taught the nice frilly pretty bits. Passages like: the nativity, the sermon on the mount, the good Samaritan, the resurrection and Noah with that lovely bouncy 'Two by Two' song that really catches the imagination of four year olds.

If the amount of love created by religion, and the amount of hate expunged by religion were the benchmarks in a project plan by which the introduction of religious beliefs were gauged for success, any organisation running such a project today would grade the project as a complete failure. This is a sad indictment for a system that proclaims it is based on love. If the core concepts of religion are based on fiction, the main concepts clearly do not work and the diametrically opposed beliefs cause hatred and have been used to justify murder and genocide (in the eyes of the perpetrators), then why on earth do we persist with such a ridiculous charade? We should have the courage to state that religion is simply superstitious, fictitious, baloney which causes harm and hatred. To use tradition and history to justify the continuation of religious belief is also a weak argument. The three monotheistic faiths are only long standing traditional belief systems when gauged against a human life span. When matched against the more realistic scale of human evolution and development (scaled down to a 24 hour period); Abrahamic religion is an idea that just got here two seconds ago and will disappear in about two seconds time and its duration will have been nothing but a small blip in our total history . Given these arguments, it really is time for religion to be consigned to the dustbin of extremely bad ideas.

# --Chapter 8: The Right to a Free Mind--

The teaching of religion in schools and the ability to preach religion to minors in places of worship should be withdrawn to protect a child's right to grow up with a free mind; just as minors are forbidden to smoke, drink alcohol and watch X-rated movies until their minds are judged to be old enough to comprehend what they are doing, watching or listening to. We deny these things to minors in law to protect them because we know that at a very young age they are inherently impressionable. It is therefore immoral that we should take advantage of that same impressionability to selfishly enforce personally held superstitious belief systems on to children. Some might argue there is no comparison here, because being religious does not necessarily point a person toward religious conflict. However, smoking does not condemn someone to die of lung cancer, but it might, so we protect minors from it. Drinking alcohol does not necessarily turn a person into an alcoholic and destroy their liver, but it might, so we protect minors from it. More poignantly, X-rated movies do not necessarily create psychopathic problems in people, but they might, so we protect minors from them. Why? Because we know that at a young age their minds are susceptible to believing what they are being told and what they see and hear, so to expose them to such material is deemed dangerous. We appreciate that minors would be more likely to nurture psychopathic problems after watching X-rated horror movies than adults. By the very same token, exposing young people to religious beliefs does not necessarily turn them into radicals; it will not aim to lead them in to a path of conflict against other beliefs or into religious martyrdom; but we know to our pain that it can and frequently does. So using the X-rated movie concept, religion should not be preached to minors.

An equally strong argument for removing the teaching of religion in schools would be that schools should concentrate on teaching children facts and developing hypotheses about the world and the Universe. Religion is a complete null hypothesis. It is - demonstrably - a completely incorrect concept. The world is provably older than 6,000 years, water cannot run uphill, humans cannot walk on water, women cannot give birth without having intercourse (IVF treatment aside) and when a person is brain dead, they do not come back to life; to name but a few of the ridiculous religious claims children are exposed to via Sunday school and the religious education classroom; and we start this thought indoctrination process of children when they are only four years old with the kindergarten nativity play.

The proof that preaching and/or teaching children religion at a young age denies them the right to a free mind comes from the fact that, on a percentage basis (there are always statistical outliers and exceptions) if you are a devout Jew, it is because your parents are devout Jews, likewise Christian and Muslim. Even down to Protestant and Catholic or Sunni and Shia. One wonders, if an Israeli child born in the Levant to devout Jewish parents is orphaned, and is by chance adopted and raised by devout Muslims, would that child turn out to be a Muslim or a Jew, and vice versa. Almost certainly, in either scenario, s/he would not be a Christian, pagan or atheist; the right to choose between the five options, or any other option, would be denied to the child before they were even old enough to realise they had such a right. Let us hypothesise further, Triplets are born in the Levant to a non religious couple and are orphaned at two months old. The triplets are each adopted, one by a Christian couple, one by a Muslim

216

couple and one by a Jewish couple. We can guess what the religious persuasion of the three children would be as they grow to adulthood. If, like me, you assume they would all follow the persuasion of their adoptive parents, you will have confirmed to yourself that they were religiously indoctrinated and had no conscious choice in the matter. One further wonders whether they might one-day fight each other because of their indoctrinated beliefs; or how different they would have turned out had they not been orphaned.

Any person should have, and does have, the right to hold religious beliefs, and has the right to discuss those beliefs openly with other people. But no one should have the right to force those beliefs on to other people. Whilst parent/child communication inside the family environment is a matter for the parents of a child, outside of the family environment, people should not possess to the right to indoctrinate a young mind, pre-thought development stage, with religious beliefs. To do so, is to force your beliefs onto another person and that is fundamentally wrong.

All children are born without any perception of race, skin colour or historic culture; they are born without the handicap of religious belief, and they have no conception of religious theology; it is us who provide them with these tools with which to hate each other and we have no right to.

It is our obligation to let children make of their future what they will and not to encumber them with the burden of religious belief that we find hard to shake. We have no right to fill their minds with the current and historic unsubstantiated conflicting views on creation, in order that they can continue our arguments into their future on our behalf. Religious indoctrination by a religiously biased school, Church sermons and the teaching of religion by seriously religious parents at a young age is intended to force religious beliefs, along with the cultures and historic traditions that religions cling to, on to children; this denies children the right to grow up with a free mind before they are even old enough to realise that they should have such a right. What is morally reprehensible is that we all know at a certain age children will readily accept, and for many children believe for the rest of their lives, what their authority figures, parents, teachers, etc. tell them; the religious alumni knowingly take full advantage of this human growing process, they use it to plant religious beliefs into the minds of children to ensure those religious beliefs live on into the future, through the children of the present.

Culture is just another term for history; cultures change, they have start points, they evolve, and they die out. We can therefore talk in terms of future culture. If we can accept that there will be future culture, we should accept that any future culture belongs to the children of today, not to us; we have no right to influence what that future culture might be. Our children are entitled to create that future culture for themselves, based on their life experiences, not ours. True, that future culture might turn out good or bad, but that will be their concern not ours. We cannot, by any stretch of the imagination, claim to be able to give expert advice in this area. A future culture will never exist, while we continue to rape the young forming minds of our children and fill them with the systems of hateful, conflicting theologies that have caused nothing but war on all levels for the last 2,600 years.

Statistical outliers' aside - because there are always some - in general, any religious person of any persuasion is basically religious because their parents, school teachers and ministers told them they were. The seed is set at a very young age and grows. Many religious inductees then move into a period of denial. Deep down, they know religion is a flawed concept, but they cannot bring themselves to admit they have followed a theology which is clearly nothing more than 'Iron Age ignorance'. The religious inductees then openly defend their inherited theology as factually based, in order to justify their acceptance of it. This category of religious devotee is then most apt to repeat the induction process with their own children. The indoctrination of religious theology and culture can also cause the inductee reconciliation problems later in life when they discover that there are groups in existence that are seriously diametrically opposed to their indoctrinated belief. This inevitably leads to conflict.

I find that I fully agree with Richard Dawkins and share his irritation at such terms as 'Catholic Child' or 'Muslim Child'. These labels are vindications of the argument against religious indoctrination in this book. There is no such thing as a 'Catholic Child' in the same way as there is no such thing as a 'Liberal Democrat Child'; there cannot be, when a child is born, it has no concept whatsoever about religious theologies. What is really meant when we hear the term 'Catholic Child' is: *"Here is the child of Catholic parents who are going to take advantage of the child's available developing thought process to convince the child that they too are Catholic, and that the parents will begin the religious indoctrination process immediately to ensure maximum effect and minimum chance of failure"*. The same is true of culture, when a child is born it has no culture, it is just another baby. Any notion of culture a parent tries to apportion to the child is the culture of their parents and grandparents. They are past cultures; the child will grow up in a future culture, one s/he and their peers will form.

For the sake of all the children in Britain from all backgrounds, we should accept that we now have mixed past cultures in Britain, and we need to stand back and let our children integrate free from those cultural constraints by forming their own, future culture. The available mind moulding period in a child's life should be used to teach them the things they need to know in order to be safe in life and live in harmony in society with their peers. For pre-school age this is: do not run across a road, learn to share etc. Schooling should concentrate only on facts, skills and science such as: maths; reading; writing; foreign languages; chemistry; biology;

physics; and physical education. Religion is not 'education', it is most resolutely 'miss-education', the intentional installing of false statements into the minds of young children. I remain convinced that if we do not foist religion and culture onto our children, they will naturally form friendships blind to race, creed, colour and our past bigotries. We just have to have the courage to stand back, let go, and give them the opportunity and the breathing space in which to try.

## Education reform act 1996

It is a legal requirement under the 1996 Education Act for all schools to conduct religious education and collective worship. So, it is not possible for any parents to send their children to a state school which does not conduct collective worship and religious education, regardless of the views of the parents towards the religious tenets. The curriculum for the religious lessons is left to the school authorities, under guidance from established religious groups. The guidance states that while other religions should be explored, the main content of religious education and collective worship has to be broadly Christian in nature; but it does not have to be biased to any particular Christian denomination in order to reflect the religious make up of the country. Circular number 1/94 from the Department for Education "Religious Education and Collective Worship" opens with *"All maintained schools must provide religious education and daily collective worship for all registered pupils and promote their spiritual, moral and cultural development"*.

With regard to promoting a pupil's spiritual development: this really has nothing to do with the school, the government or the Church. The idea of a spirit existing separate from the person is also a personal point of view and not a scientific or biological fact. With regard to moral development, are we sure we should use the tenets of the Bible to teach our children morals?

*Exodus 12:29* *"At midnight the Lord killed all the firstborn sons in Egypt"*
*Exodus21:3* *"If you buy a Hebrew slave, he shall serve you for 6 years and the seventh he is to be set free". "If a man sells his daughter as a slave, she is not to be set free as male slaves are".*
*Deuteronomy 22:20* *"but if the charge is true and there is no proof that the girl was a virgin... (referring to the wedding night) She will be taken to the entrance of her father's house where the men of her city are to stone her to death".*
*Exodus 31:14* *"You must keep the day of rest because it is sacred. Whoever does not keep it, but works on this day, is to be put to death"*
*Leviticus 26:14* *The Lord said, "If you will not obey my commands, you will be punished. If you refuse to obey my laws and commands and break the covenant I have made with you, I will punish you. I will bring disaster on you; incurable diseases and fevers that will make you blind and cause your life to waste away...."*
*Genesis 19:6* *Lot went outside and closed the door behind him. He said. "Friends I beg you, do not do such a wicked thing! Look I have two daughters, they are both virgins. Let me bring them out to you, and you can do whatever you want with them..."*

These are just six quick examples of why the Bible is not the place in which to look for moral values. But we should be in no doubt, we could carry on reciting examples of nauseatingly immoral passages from the Bible and double the word count of this book.

The content of RE lessons is left up to individual schools, but must be created to follow guidelines laid down by the government. The creation of these guidelines are then farmed out to groups set up to advise in these matters; these groups are called SACRE "Standing Advisory Council on Religious Education". The SACRE are themselves advised by a body set up to advise government on religious issues. They are "The National Society for Promoting Religious Education". The National Society and the Church of England's Board of Education (now Education Division) produced specific guidance about the place of Christianity in the agreed syllabus in 1994.

***Religious Education: The Church of England's Education Division's Policy on Religious Education and the Teaching of Christianity:***

*The Board of Education of the General Synod of the Church of England strongly urges the government to ensure that at least 5% of curriculum time in all schools is available for the teaching of religious education. This percentage would not include the time allocated to collective school worship.*

*The Board of Education is also of the view that two-thirds (66%) of the RE teaching programme in schools should be allocated to the teaching of Christianity. There are schools with a significant number of pupils from other faiths and the Board recognises that such schools, though few in number, have a particular concern. Even in these schools, however, the Board would expect at least 50% of the programme time available to RE to be spent on teaching about Christianity. Equally there may be some schools which for their own purposes may wish to teach up to 75% of the time on Christianity. This would be acceptable to the Board, but in general the Working Party believes a figure of 66% in most schools to be reasonable. The remaining time would be sufficient for one or two other religions at the appropriate Key Stage to be taught properly and at sufficient depth to be treated with the respect and intellectual integrity they require.*

*The Board's view is that within the given time limits available for RE it is unrealistic to expect pupils to give the same amount of attention to all the principal religions in Great Britain. It recommends that pupils should be expected to study no more than three religions (one of which would be Christianity) in depth at any Key Stage.*

*The Board is most concerned that the central beliefs and practices of Christianity should be taught to all pupils in all schools. This booklet includes a general and helpful guide to those central beliefs and practices.* Application of the above can be quite mild in state schools, but in faith schools it can be, and often is, quite fanatical. Below is the religious education curriculum (2007) for Loreto Roman Catholic School in St Albans.

### RELIGIOUS EDUCATION:

*The religious education Department puts into practise the lessons learnt in class through the life and liturgy of the school and out work in the wider community. We organise liturgies on Fridays, Holy Days and at the end of each term. We also encourage the whole school to raise money for their chosen charity. Each class or Year Group has a day retreat at All Saints Pastoral Centre and sometimes visit places of worship of other religions. Every summer holiday the Sixth Formers have the chance to go to Lourdes as Red Cap helpers. Sixth Formers can also take part in our Catechetic course where they learn to pass on their faith to younger children and experience teaching children at primary schools. We have links with 'Open Door' – helping the homeless in our local community and organise hampers for the less fortunate at Christmas time. We also sponsor a child in the Developing World.*

**Year 7:**

*The Way.*
*The Word of God.*
*God's Call.*
*The Sacraments.*
*Sacraments of Healing.*
*Leadership in the Church.*
*The Church's Mission.*

***Year 8:***

Creation.

Covenant.

The Mass.

The Easter Mystery.

The prophetic role of the Church.

The Church of Britain.

***Year 9:***

Being a Christian today – issues of racism, poverty, homelessness.

The Background to Mark's gospel. Pupils begin an introduction

course on St Mark's gospel that is carried over to their G.C.S.E. studies.

***Years 10 & 11:***

<u>This is compulsory for all at G.C.S.E. Level.</u> We will be studying the AQA Specification A. Option 1C The Christian Life and St Mark's gospel and Option 2A Effects of Christianity on Behaviour, Attitudes and Lifestyles. This will include two coursework assignments, one on each aspect of the course. It is worth 20%. The Scheme of assessment is not tiered.

***Year 10:***

Christian life and Marks gospel.

The topics covered:

The person of Jesus.

The Kingdom of God.

Faith and Prayer.

Discipleship.

Leadership.

Worship.

Baptism.

Suffering, death and resurrection.

***Year 11:***

Effects of Christianity on behaviour, attitudes and lifestyles.

*The topics covered:*
*Decisions on life and living.*
*Justice and reconciliation.*
*Christian responsibility.*

Note the use of the word compulsory in the passage *"compulsory for all at G.C.S.E. level"*! Attending religious education lessons at school is not compulsory and children can be withdrawn from all religious content within the school environment at the parents request; it is only compulsory for the school to provide religious education. Making the attendance of religious education lessons compulsory is in effect breaking the law, and moves most definitely away from the realm of education and toward the realm of forced indoctrination. As a pure coincidence, between the writing up of my research in 2007, and the completion of the write up in 2010, there appeared a news item which made reference to Loreto Roman Catholic School in St Albans:

**2 May 2010**

*A parliamentary candidate has been suspended from his position as a parent governor of a Catholic school because of his party's critical position on faith schools policy. A report in the Herts Advertiser newspaper says that Loreto College decided to suspend Jack Easton, Green parliamentary candidate for St Albans, because it believed that the Green Party policy criticising the idea of religious organisations running state schools could be incompatible with his role at the school.*

The most disturbing form of Christian indoctrination in the civilised west today comes from North Dakota where a woman called Becky Fischer runs a children's summer camp which she calls Jesus Camp. It can be viewed on the internet at http://topdocumentaryfilms.com/ 'Documentary list', 'Religion section', 'Jesus Camp'. It is extremely disturbing. This is not just hard core evangelical indoctrination of children;

it is positively militant and vile. The children are being indoctrinated as soldiers of Jesus ready to act positively on his behalf in the near future, as opposed to mere Christian followers of Christ. It has to be said that Becky Fischer is indeed totally insane; she holds the belief, like many American evangelicals that she can 'pray in tongues', and demonstrates this gift by babbling complete tripe while praying. The disturbing part of this issue is that she gets all the children in the hall, very young children, to join her. She not only attempts to demonstrate to the children that they can also pray in tongues, but pretty much convinces them that they can. Whilst mimicking the adult teacher Becky Fischer in her demented act of talking in tongues, they are also encouraged to fall about on the floor and writhe in imitated ecstasy; most of the children can be seen to be physically disturbed by this experience and positively beside themselves in floods of tears. This woman is not only completely mad, she is also extremely dangerous. In one scene she gives a piece to camera and states that we need to out-fanaticise Islam, and clearly admits that she views the way to do this is to brainwash our children with the same vigour as does Islam. Fischer feels this should take place while the children are young enough to be successfully indoctrinated to such a fanatical level. In a session with the children she rants "*Kids, This is a sick old world, so let's fix it. Kids you got to change things, Boys and girls can change the world. I need you to get serious serious with God, say God, I'm here to get trained, I'm here for an education, I'm willing God. I will do what you want me to do and say what you want me to say, in Jesus' name*" The children responded by repeating her rants with excitement, and then Fischer shouts "*Are you willing to die for Jesus*" and makes the children publicly promise to do so. This is followed with "*don't you be no promise breakers!*" Fischer then completes her piece to camera with the vile statement of "*I want to see our young children laying down their lives for the cause of Jesus because, excuse me, but we have the truth.*"

Most of these children are in fact home-schooled and are being taught the Bible as science and denied access to children from backgrounds outside of the evangelical circle. At the end of the documentary Ted Haggard, president of the National Association of Evangelicals, makes a contribution; he informs the young congregation not to take notice of the hype regarding climate change and the burning of fossil fuels. We can accept that the burning of fossil fuels as a dangerous accelerant to climate change, although very convincing, is still not totally proven. But this is not the basis of Haggard's statement to the congregation of minors. He goes on to explain: *"Use all the fossil fuels, burn them up, the world will end soon anyway"* referring to his personal belief in Armageddon and the rapture. Not the sort of utter tripe we should be allowing completely insane adults to preach to very young children.

OK, so this is America, but there is no reason why such fanaticism will not find its way to our shores, and there are organisations in the UK that would willingly run such camps. If we continue to ignore this disturbing phenomenon, we will look around one-day and find out that we have ignored it for far too long. In fact, the only thing Fischer is correct about is the fanaticism with which Muslim children are indoctrinated into the faith of Islam, and that concept does already happen in the UK today inside the madrasas.

**The dangers of indoctrinated belief:**

I often feel that the western faithful respond to the accusations of religion being divisive and bigoted as, 'maybe, but not our religion'. They seem eager to portray Christianity as the mild, loving, caring religion. How could something that stands for love and good be considered in any way harmful? I wonder? What if our political leaders are deeply Christian; could that faith spill over into their international policy making? Let's hop back in time just ninety-four years and test this theory. Our Prime Minister is David

Lloyd George, and we are at war with Germany and her ally Turkey. Turkey is holding on to the last remnants of the Ottoman Empire. The Arabs in Arabia have been under Turkish Ottoman rule for centuries and want to rule their own Muslim states. Britain seizes the opportunity and offers to help create this vision of a united Arab state ruled by the Arabs, if the Arabs help Britain in their military aim of defeating the Turkish Forces in the Middle East. The Arabs do help the British and together they succeed in defeating the Ottoman Turks. But the British did not, and had no intention of, creating a unified Arab Muslim state. Even before the promise was made, M. Georges Picot and Sir Mark Sykes had produced for their respective governments a plan to split the Arab territories between France and Britain as soon as the Turkish forces had been defeated. The Sykes-Picot agreement understandably caused serious damage to Arab/British relationships after the war, but not nearly as much as the declaration waiting to be unleashed in the background.

As part of the Sykes-Picot agreement, Britain found themselves the new rulers of Palestine. On 11th Dec 1917 General Edward Allenby marched into Jerusalem and the British started pondering on the fact that they had just achieved what Richard I failed to do; they had won the Holy Land back from the Muslims for Christendom. In November 1917, a month before Allenby took possession of Jerusalem, under the instruction of the Prime Minister Lloyd George; the Foreign Secretary Arthur Balfour wrote a letter to Lord Rothschild which came to be known as the Balfour Declaration. Under this declaration Britain supported and implemented a program which gave the Jews of Europe a homeland in Palestine. Thirty violent and bloody years later came the nail in the coffin of peace; in 1947 the United Nations approved the British Mandate for Palestine and, against Arab wishes, divided the land into two states, one Jewish and one Arab. The Jews got the contentious holy sites of Jerusalem. In 1948 The Jews declared independence and created the country of Israel. The most damning consequence of these events was that tens of thousands of Palestinians lost their homes in the thirty years from 1917 to 1947 to European Jews whose ancestry had nothing what-so-ever to do with first century CE Middle Eastern Judah or Israel. The only thing Jewish about these people was the fact that they had decided to follow a particular religion. They were, and still are, of European ancestry, not Arabic, as the original inhabitants of the Israelite Kingdoms would have been. The original Jews of Jerusalem and Judah were completely decimated and dispersed by Vespasian and his son Titus in 70CE, along with the destruction of the temple. Following the fall of the Roman Empire the land was re-inhabited by the indigenous Arabic people who, by 600 CE became Muslim; they had been Muslim from circa 600 CE until the unwanted and unwarranted interference of the British Government in 1917.

How do we know that the British reneged on their word to the Arabs, and that their plan to offer the Jews a homeland in Palestine to the detriment of the Palestinians was born out of Christian religious bigotry? Balfour wrote a memorandum in August 1919 in which he freely admits that the four great powers are committed to Zionism, *"be it right or wrong, good or bad"*. He further stated that this commitment to Zionism was *"rooted in ancient traditions, present needs and future hopes"*. In stating ancient traditions he is referring to the Old Testament, a story, and therefore a travesty that such bloodshed should be caused by bigoted belief in the text of a novel. In his comment on future hopes, he is referring to the prophecy of the second coming of the Lord, who will return and preside over Armageddon and then rapture all the faithful, alive and dead, to spend eternity with him in heaven.

1 Thessalonians 4:15-17 *"For this we say to you by the word of the Lord, that we who are alive and remain until the coming of the Lord will by no means precede those who are asleep. For the Lord himself will descend from heaven with a shout, with the voice of an archangel, and with the*

*trumpet of God. And the dead in Christ will rise first. Then we who are alive and remain shall be caught up together with them in the clouds to meet the Lord in the air. And thus we shall always be with the Lord."*

Passages like this in the New Testament have given rise to a belief in 'the rapture' following seven years of pestilence. Fanatical believers further suppose that Jesus will not return again to invoke Armageddon and the rapture until the Jews once more live in the land promised to them by God. The rationale behind Lloyd George and Arthur Balfour's declaration, two seriously religious men, now takes on an altogether frightening and more sinister manifestation. So, the answer is yes, religious indoctrination of the young is, and has proved to be, very dangerous. Could the above be repeated today? I feel I only have to supply two names: Bush and Blair!

That such bloodshed should have been caused by the passages in a story is so often excused by today's theologians and politicians as a consequence of peoples beliefs not being respected. It is this very stance which helps the concept of fighting for a belief in the tenets of a book to exist. It is most resolutely the 'ostrich burying his head in the sand'. We absolutely should not have to respect such ridiculous Iron Age ignorance as having any relevance to today's world. No more than we could excuse two groups forming today that believed the Arthurian chronicles to be absolute truth; with one group believing that Queen Guinevere was unfaithful to King Author with Sir Lancelot, and the other group believing that Queen Guinevere remained faithful and did not have relations with Sir Lancelot. If two such groups did form, and did both fervently believe their mutually exclusive stories to be the absolute truth, and took to killing each other over the issue of Sir Lancelot, would we say 'Oh well, it's all to do with peoples' beliefs? Of course we would not, we would not tolerate it and we would readily point out to both groups how ridiculous their claims were. So why do we not take the same stance with Catholic and Protestant tensions, Sunni and Shia, Christian and Muslim, Muslim and Jewish etc!

# --Chapter 9: Concluding Thoughts--

The Church maintain that religious education is neither indoctrination nor divisive and merely attempts to make young people aware of the existence of religion and different cultures. They do not accept that the whole exercise is designed to supply lambs for religious recruitment and insist that the faiths can exist without bigotry, hatred and religious racism.

On Friday 30th November 2007 a Radio Four news item relayed that the Pope had issued a statement which blamed the woes of the world today on the increase in Atheism. He called on world leaders to tackle the growing *'atheist problem'* and pay more attention to the religious and spiritual needs of the young. The very next item on the programme was the fact that Gillian Gibbons had just been found guilty in Sudan of insulting Islam by naming a toy teddy-bear Muhammad. She was sentenced to fifteen days in prison while the Sudanese public remonstrated and called for her to be executed. I think the Pope really does need to reconsider his views on where the problem in the world today is coming from.

As stated in the introduction: primitive man of the earliest civilisations did not understand the natural causes of anything. Out of this ignorance religion was born; then came theology, which is essentially the art of verbally expressing the ignorance of religion. This 'religious' concept has morphed into a gigantic feeding trough called 'The Church' from which a multitude of clergy feed, and live extremely comfortable lives. 'Feeding trough' might seem a stark term, but it is also an extremely accurate one.

We cannot ignore the obscene wealth of the Church, both Protestant and Catholic, nor the hypocrisy of the two churches in owning such wealth. This can be demonstrated with the following logic: if we conclude that the concepts are totally flawed and that neither the Abrahamic God nor Jesus actually existed, the wealth of these two organisations will most definitely have been obtained by the perpetration of a total lie. However, if we accept that the tenets of Christianity are completely true, and that the messiah Jesus did visit Earth to preach the word of God, do we think that the wealth of the two main organisations created in his name would be what he had in mind? Of course not; in which case, his message has been misused by greedy parasites in order to create immense wealth. In either scenario the wealth of both churches is utterly disgusting.

Consider, why is it that the job of 'Clergy' comes to be a full time post? Those who are fanatical about football and play in the lower non professional leagues are 'Part Time Footballers'. They work a paid job during the week, and play football, for free in many cases, on a Sunday, and attend training sessions on weekday evenings, after a full day's work. As with camera enthusiast, canoeing clubs, rugby clubs etc. We might also include the volunteer services of the Police, Fire Brigade and the Territorial Army. Ask yourself a serious question: what do the clergy do, which requires full time attendance? In Nov 2000, the BBC tackled this question. *"Being a vicar is more than just a Sunday job. Each day typically starts and finishes with personal prayers. Sundays are taken up with services at 8am. 10 or 11am, and 6.30pm - and some vicars tend to more than one parish. Between services, the vicar may visit housebound parishioners. As well as spreading the word of God and tending to parishioners' spiritual needs, vicars also carry out a number of secular tasks. They are expected to keep parish accounts, chair meetings and run fundraising campaigns. They may also sit on the Board of Governors of a church-run school, or head a community project for the homeless or the elderly. As the Church of*

*England is keen to turn around falling attendance figures, the vicar often leads a team of lay volunteers charged with taking the word to the streets - modern-day missionary work."* There is nothing above that cannot be conducted in the realm of part time evening and weekend work, paid or voluntary, after a normal full-time position in society. We certainly cannot class having to say prayers at the start of every day as particularly arduous. Many devout Muslims pray five times a day, while also conducting a full time post.

The BBC also listed the remuneration for the above tasks as at Nov 2000: Curates: £14,680-£15,820, Parish Clergy: £16,420, Cathedral-based Canons: £20,200, Junior Bishops: £24,790, Diocesan Bishops: £30,120, Archbishop of Canterbury: £55,660. It is highlighted that the average of these salaries is below the average wage, but also, more than double the average minimum wage; while at the same time in line with many key workers and serviceman salaries, people who do offer real tangible benefit to society and work a minimum, hard graft, 40 hour week. Also, we have to consider that many of the above salaries for the clergy come with the supply of generous accommodation for the duration of the post; negating the need for a mortgage or the paying of rent, thus allowing money to be saved over a working lifetime toward the purchase of a retirement home.

The longevity of the religious gravy-boat which the priesthood feed from is dependent on how well the partakers, 'the Priests', can convince the populace that society simply cannot do without the intangible services of their organised religion. In order to keep the gravy-boat flowing, and so sustain the livelihood of the clergy, a constant supply of future followers is vital, and hence the need for the indoctrination of children via a faith school system.

It is time for society to wake up, and see this 1700 year old confidence trick for what it really is: a 'thought virus', perpetrated solely for the benefit of the clergy, and by the clergy. If we take as a prime example

Rowan Williams, we see an extremely intelligent and articulate man. Does this man actually believe: the concept of a mortal virgin being impregnated by an invisible supreme supernatural being, or the concept of a boat large enough to contain a family, two of every animal on earth and all necessary supplies to sustain such a group for nearly a year, or a man living inside a whale for three days, or feeding five thousand people with five loaves and two fishes, or coming back to life three days after having been thoroughly and ruthlessly tortured and executed? Of course he does not; but he does have a well paid career, lives in Lambeth Palace and will receive a handsome pension without the need to do, what most of us would consider, real work and toil in exchange for such extravagant rewards. As stated, a 'very intelligent man'. Now compare Rowan Williams with the late L Ron Hubbard of the 'Church of Scientology' fame, who lived a luxurious life from the donations of his followers. Is there actually a vast difference between the two men, or is the difference merely the longstanding existence of Christianity over the short life to date of Scientology? In short, is not Scientology only doing what the Christian Church has been doing for centuries, i.e. selling, for hard cash, indulgences to guarantee absolution of sins? A form of religious protection racket perpetrated against parishioners in order to increase the wealth of the Church and so keep the feeding trough full!

The trough which is known as 'The Church' affords the higher echelon of ordained members of 'The Church' an alternative to facing up to the real rigours of life; while at the same time ensuring the necessities of life, being food, clothing and shelter, are amply supplied to them out of the profits of pedalling religion. Those profits being organised religion's obscene wealth in land, buildings and gold. Wealth which is extracted today from its followers via voluntary donations sustained by peer pressure and a promise of a better afterlife for their generosity in this life; but originally extracted in blood, and upon pain of death and torture, from our ancestors;

wealth which has not, to date, been returned. Supporters of the existence of the Church as a wealthy organisation would, and do, insist it is a force for good because of the charitable donations it attracts from its members for good causes. But this is hypocrisy in the extreme, such an argument presupposes that religious followers only give to charity because of the existence of the Church, and would not donate otherwise. It is poignant to consider that secular members of society need no such compulsion to donate to good causes. It is also noteworthy that 100% of secular donations go direct to their intended good causes, while donations made via church services are apportioned: part goes to the cost of the keeping the feeding trough full, and the remainder to good causes. Hence, secular donations are far more effective.

From the 2001 Census, 72% of England and Wales recorded 'Christian' to the question *"What is your religion"*; this was in stark contrast to the fact that, at the same time in our history, only 4.5% of the population actually attend regular church services. This question in the 2001 census was clearly answered from a historic cultural view point, and not from a standpoint of a personal conviction in religious belief. The Church have used this 2001 72% response figure as a whip against the government to aid it in forwarding the Christian agenda for the last ten years. As a result, today, faith schools are in the ascendancy and set to grow in number exponentially. Many of these faith schools are extremely virulent in the manner in which they proselytise their personal religious beliefs to young developing minds. This, in turn helps to ensure the trough will remain full for generations to come.

At the time of writing we are approaching the 2011 census, and a fear that this too will be answered by many from a historic cultural, rather than personal perspective. From the perspective of 'being a Christian', one cannot be 'Somewhat Christian'. Either a person believes in the miracle virgin birth of the son of God, the death and miracle resurrection of the son of God, the ascension into heaven of the son of God to sit at the right hand of God, and the pending rapture of all the Christian faithful to heaven (with the expulsion of all non-believers to an eternity in hell) when the son of God returns to preside over the final conflict with Satan at Megiddo (Armageddon), and is therefore a Christian; or a person does not concur with these ideas and is therefore not a Christian. There is no salad bar concept on offer; selecting the parts one likes and rejecting the parts one finds hard to accept, such as: "*and Noah was 600 years old when the flood of waters was upon the earth*", "*Thou shall not suffer a witch to live*", "*Slaves, obey your earthly masters*", "*If a man also lie with mankind, as he lieth with a woman, both of them have committed an abomination, they shall surely be put to death*". It is hypocrisy to say, we reject the fantastical miracles, ridiculous statements and vile phobias as purely symbolic and just concentrate on the message of love. The desire for love and peace is a secular human condition, not the self appointed bastion of organised religion. Therefore, the personal desire for peace and goodwill does not make a person 'Christian by default', but simply a person with good moral values which are, in point of fact, neutral of religious dogma. If we remove the ridiculous items from the Christian Bible we are left with nothing more than a catalogue of plagiarised statements of a moralistic (good or bad moralistic) value from all of the civilisations from history. Statements made by men; not a God or gods.

**Religious ceremonies:**

So what would a Britain without the influence of organised Christianity be like? How bleak to imagine a year with no Christmas and no Easter. What would we do without the wedding ceremony at the Church, or the Christening? How would we say goodbye to our loved ones without a funeral? The perception of christenings, weddings and funerals being a Church invention is nothing more than a trick of time. They have been the domain of the Church for so long that people today see them as inseparable and the brain child of the Church. This is completely wrong. The only claim the Church has to these three life ceremonies is that it hijacked them and re-branded them. These ceremonies have existed since man became a social animal, long before religion crossed his mind; they endured and strengthened through all the pagan beliefs from around the globe and finally became completely absorbed by the Church. There need be no religious overtones to the concept of celebrating the birth of a child, the union of two people in marriage or the celebration of a life upon a person's death. Also, there should be no reason why these events cannot be celebrated without religious rhetoric in the stunning buildings that the oppressive medieval Church forced our ancestors to build, just to please their bigotry. These buildings are only houses of God to those who believe in God; to secular people they are simply stunningly beautiful buildings. There is no reason why churches cannot be used for religious and civil (non religious) life ceremonies. If this sounds absurd, then we should recall that this country once thought William Wilberforce sounded absurd we he suggested abolishing the slave trade. Now it seems absurd that we ever had a slave trade in the first instance.

 With regards to Christmas and Easter, the Church has once again hijacked ceremonies which had existed for millennia prior to the Catholic Church forcing its beliefs onto the world. The Church stole these fantastic solar ceremonies and converted them to suit their own story. Christmas is simply a plagiarism of the winter solstice celebrations, a day celebrated throughout the world by all beliefs and non beliefs for eons. It's original importance and magic has been lost to us today because of the militant nature of the early Church. Its veneration was due to the recognition of the start of a new solar year. The case with Easter is just the same. The Church has simply stolen the spring equinox celebrations. Celebrations originally aimed to demonstrate our pleasure for the return of the growing season and the start of the warmer weather and longer days. This took place when the Sun rose exactly due East. The clue is in the name. So these five ceremonies are not Christian ceremonies at all, they are simply ceremonies that have been, through the passage of time, stolen by Christianity. We can steal them back if we want to!

**Closing thoughts:**

Our only hope of getting the children of today, and therefore the adults of tomorrow, to live together in harmony is to drop the concept of tribal cultures and religious beliefs. This is not something that would be an overnight process; or even a process that can be achieved by means of an instruction or legislation. You simply cannot say to a population, *"you will not follow a religion"*, or, *"you will, from now on, live harmoniously with the people on the other side of the town"*. All we can do here is to try and break the cycle of religious indoctrination by taking the teaching of religion and culture out of the school curriculum. Children's inherent innocence is our main hope. If you do not tell a young white schoolgirl that she has a different religious belief and cultural background to the Asian girl in the next seat; and you do not tell the Asian girl that her entire belief system and way of life is completely different to the white European girls behind her - who knows, they might actually talk to each other and create a friendship? But while the white European boy's parents continually inform him that *"the Jews killed our saviour"*, and the Asian boy's parents read him scripture like *"Do not make friends with any but your own people" Koran 3:118* we can never hope to see the back of religious sectarianism.

If I were asked to sum up Christianity in a short sentence I would use the following description:

*"A massive, fourth century CE, misinterpretation of ancient allegorical stories that were based on astrological observation; a misinterpretation*

238

*which was then spread over the entire globe by force, at the end of a sword".*

While science has made great advances in tackling the question of how we got here, we have made no progress on the question of why we got here. Indeed, we do not even know if it is a legitimate question; Darwin's studies suggest that the question might be futile and there is no 'Why?' Maybe one-day, we will make a breakthrough discovery and answer many burning questions in this area. However, it might prove to be that we physically lack the ability to bridge this knowledge gap and therefore do not possess the necessary skills or senses that would allow us to obtain this information. We may be consigned to never being able to find out by our own physical and biological constraints. We therefore, at the present time, have absolutely no answers on why we came to be and what happens when we cease to be.

To look at a problem and say 'we do not yet know the answer' is admirable and full of human spirit. To fill that knowledge-void with the word 'God' is ignorant, arrogant and dogmatic. To enforce this ignorant 'God' stance, ultimately stops humanity from seeking such knowledge. It prevents humanity from pushing the catchall 'God' response aside and pursuing the real answer. Theology still stands in the way of progress today. Science says 'we do not know what caused the Big Bang', theology says, 'no problem, it was God'. Creationism is still taught to children in schools in favour of evolution all over the world. We cannot even begin to guess at how far we might have advanced with humanity and scientific endeavour, had it not been for religion; it would be true to say that today's societies enjoy modern knowledge 'in spite of religion', not because of it.

The logical - though not necessarily correct - I stress, conclusion on the facts we know at the present time is that life is a one-time journey for us all. A precious possession that we obtain, we hold for a short time, and when it is gone, it is gone. So, accept that it is your life, not Abraham's life to influence, or Moses, or Jesus or Muhammad; it is yours. Do with your life what you want, not what others want. Do not live your short precious life by the instructions of three 1,500 to 2,500 year old novels. Live them by what you want to do, achieve, and experience. Always bear in mind that you do not necessarily need to be a part of a hierarchical religious organisation in order to be compassionate and charitable to fellow humans, you just simply need the desire to be so. So be good, considerate and compassionate to fellow humans, stand your ground when you need to, and enjoy your life your way; not the Archbishop's way or the Pope's way or the Imam's way; live your life your way.

# --Bibliography--

Ali, Sameem . "Belonging": John Murray, 2008

Anderson, M D . "History & imagery in British Churches": John Murray, 1971

Armstrong, Karen . "A History Of Jerusalem": Harper Collins, 1996

Bachelard, Michael . "Behind the Exclusive Brethren": Scribe, 2008

Barnstone & Meyer. "The Gnostic Bible": New Seeds, 2006

Bauval & Hancock. "Keeper of Genesis": Arrow Books, 1997

Bicknell, E. J. "The Thirty-nine Articles of the CofE": Longmans, 1919

Blackmore, Susan . "The Meme Machine": Oxford, 1999

Bock, Darrell . "The Missing Gospels": Nelson, 2006

Boyer, Pascal . "Religion Explained": Vintage, 2002

Buckley, Richard . "The World Of Islam": Global Issues 101, 2001

Cartledge, Paul. "The Spartans": Pan, 2003

Catherwood, Christopher . "A Brief History Of The Middle East": Robinson, 2006

Cave, Peter . "Humanism": Oneworld, 2009

Christian, David. "Maps Of Time": California, 2004

Churchill, Major Senton . "General Gordon A Christian Hero": J. Nisbet & Co, 1896

Clark, Mary T. "Augustine": Geoferey Chapman, 1994

Clayton, Peter A. "Chronicle of The Pharaohs": Thames & Hudson, 2001

Comte-Sponville, Andre . "The Book of Atheist Spirituality": Bantam Press, 2007

Copley, Terence . "Indoctrination, Education and God": SPCK, 2005

Dalley, Stephanie . "Myths From Mesopotamia": Oxford, 2000

Darwin, Charles . "The Origin Of Species": Penguin, 1985

Astonishing Credulity

Darwin, Charles . "The Descent of Man": Penguin, 1879

Darwin, Charles . "Autobiographies": Penguin, 1903

Davies, Norman. "The Isles": Papermac, 2000

Dawkins, Richard . "The Selfish Gene": Oxford, 2006

Dawkins, Richard . "The God Delusion": Bantam Press, 2006

Dawood, N J . "The Koran": Penguin, 2003

Dietrich, Thomas . "The Origin of Culture": Turn Key, 2005

Duncan, David Ewing. "The Calendar": 4Th Estate, 1998

Dunkereley, Roderic . "Beyond the Gospels": Pelican, 1957

Ehrman, Bart D. "Lost Christianities": Oxford, 2003

Ehrman, Bart D. "Misquoting Jesus": Harper One, 2005

Ellerbe, Helen . "The Dark Side of Christian History": Morningstar &Lark, 1995

Ferguson, Niall . "Empire": Penguin, 2004

Finkelstein & Silberman. "The Bible Unearthed": Touchstone, 2002

Forbes, Clarence . "Firmicus Maternus-The Error of the Pagan Religions": Newman, 1970

Fox, Robin Lane . "Pagans & Christians": Penguin, 1985

Freke & Gandy. "The Jesus Mysteries": Elemant, 2003

Gardner Cairns & Lawton. "Faith Schools": Routledge, 2006

Gill, Debbie . "World Religions": Collins, 2003

Goodman, Martin . "Rome & Jerusalem": Penguin, 2007

Government, H M . "Racial And Religious Hatred Act": HMSO, 2006

Grant, Michael. "The Roman Emperors": Phoenix Press, 1998

Grant, Michael. "The Fall of the Roman Empire": Phoenix Press, 2003

Grant, Michael . "Tacitus, The Annals Of Imperial Rome": Penguin, 1996

Graves, Robert. " Greek Gods and Heros": Laurel leaf books, 1960

Greenberg, Gary . "101 Myths of the Bible": Sourcebooks Inc, 2000

Halliday, F E . "England A Concise History": Thames & Hudson, 2000

Hancock, Graham . "Heaven's Mirror": Michael Joseph, 1998

Hancock, Graham . "Underworld": Penguin, 2002

242

# Bibliography

Hancock, Graham . "Fingerprint Of The Gods": Century, 2001

Hard, Robin Lane. "Apollodorus: The Library of Greek Mythology": Oxford, 1997

Harris, Sam . "The End Of Faith": Free Press, 2006

Harris, Sam . "Letter to a Christian Nation": Bantam Press, 2007

Hawking, Stephen . "A Brief History of Time": Bantam Press, 1996

Hawking, Stephen . "The Universe In A Nutshell": Bantam Press, 2001

Hazelton, Fran . "Stories From Ancient Iraq": The Enheduanna Society, 2006

Hibbert, Christopher . "Agincourt": Phoenix Press, 2003

Hilliam, David . "Kings, Queens, Bones and Bastards": Sutton Publishing, 2001

Hindley, Geoffrey . "A Brief History of The Crusades": Robinson, 2003

Hines, John . "The Anglo-Saxons": Boydell, 1997

Hitchins, Christopher . "God Is Not Great": Atlantic Books, 2007

Kleme and Cahn. "The Meaning of Life" Oxford, 2008

Kriwaczekod, Paul. "Babylon" Atlantic Books, 2010

Lane, Melissa . "Plato – The Republic": Penguin, 2007

Law, Stephen . "The War for Children's Minds": Routledge, 2007

Lawson-Tancred, H . "Aristotle – De Anima (On The Soul)": Penguin, 1986

Levy, David. "Sky watching": Time Life Books, 1995

Levy, Thomas . "Archaeology of Society In The Holy Land": Leicester , 1998

Lewis, Bernard . "The Middle East": Phoenix Press, 2000

Lightfoot, Joseph B. "Clement Of Rome 2 Epistles": Elibron Classics, 2007

Mackail, J. W. "Virgil – The Aeneid 19 BCE": Collectors Library, 2004

Mack, Burton. "The Christian Myth": Continuum, 2003

Marcion. "Gospel of Marcion": Internet Source, c 150 CE

Marcus, Amy Dockser . "Rewriting the Bible": Little Brown, 2000

Martyr, Justyn. "2nd apology": internet source, c 150 CE

Martyr, Justyn. "Dialogue with Trypho": internet source, c 150 CE

Martyr, Justyn . "1st apology": internet source, c 150 CE

Mason, Eugene . "Arthurian Chr. 1160 CE (Wade & Laymon)": Dent Dutton, 1966

Matyszak, Philip. "Chronicle of the Roman Republic": Thames & Hudson, 2003

Meier, Christian. "Caesar": Fontana Press, 1996

Miller, Kenneth R . "Finding Darwin's God": Harper Perennial, 2000

Millet, Martin. "Roman Britain": Batsford, 2000

Mitchell, Stephen . "Gilgamesh": Profile Books, 2005

Mithen, Steven. "After The Ice": Phoenix Press, 2003

Mojsov, Bojana . "Osiris; Death and Afterlife Of A God": Blackwell, 2005

Morison, Frank . "Who Moved the Stone": Faber & Faber, 1930

Nabarz, Payam . "The Mysteries of Mithras": Inner Traditions, 2005

Origen. "Origen Against Celsus V1 to V8": Kessinger Publishing, c 248 CE

Pagels, Elaine . "The Gnostic Gospels": Phoenix Press, 1979

Parker-Jenkins, Hatras & Irving. "In Good Faith": Ashgate, 2005

Phillips, Melanie . "Londonistan": Gibson Square, 2007

Pliny, the Younger. "The Letters of Pliny the Younger": Penguin, c 100 CE

Ratzinger, Joseph. "Jesus of Nazareth": Bloomsbury, 2007

Roberts, Alice . "The Incredible Human Journey": Bloomsbury, 2009

Robinson, Cyril E . "A History of Greece": Methuen, 1929

Russell, Bertrand. "An Outline of Philosophy" Routledge, 1927

Saunders, E P . "The Historical Figure Of Jesus": Penguin, 1993

Scott, Eugenie C . "Evolution Vs Creationism": California, 1945

Scullard, H H. "Early Christian Ethics in the West": Williams & Norgate, 1907

Shelley, Percy Bysshe. "The Necessity of Atheism": Prometheus Books, 1811

Shelley, Percy Bysshe. "On Life": Prometheus Books, 1811

Shelley, Percy Bysshe. "On a Future State": Prometheus Books, 1811

Shelley, Percy Bysshe. "A Refutation of Deism": Prometheus Books, 1811

Shelley, Percy Bysshe. "Essay on Christianity": Prometheus Books, 1811

Smith, Andrew P . "The Gnostics": Watkins, 2008

Sophocles. "The Theban Plays": Penguin, c 496 BCE

Stainforth, Maxwell. "Ignatius 7 Epistles": Penguin, 1968

Stainforth, Maxwell. "Polycarp The Philippians": Penguin, 1968

Stainforth, Maxwell. "The Martyrdom of Polycarp": Penguin, 1968

# Bibliography

Stainforth, Maxwell. "Marcion To Diognetus": Penguin, 1968

Stainforth, Maxwell. "Epistle of Barnabas": Penguin, 1968

Stainforth, Maxwell. "The Didache ": Penguin, 1968

Stephenson, Paul . "Constantine": Quercus, 2009

Suetonius. "Lives of the Twelve Caesars": Suetonius, c 100 CE

Swanton, Michael . "The Anglo-Saxon Chronicles": Phoenix Press, 2003

Tertullian. "The Apology": Kessinger Publishing.

Tertullian. "On The Resurrection Of The Flesh": Kessinger Publishing ,

Tertullian. "An Answer To The Jews": Kessinger Publishing,

Tout, T F . "The Empire and the Papacy": Rivingtons, 1932

Tredennick &Tarrant. "Plato – The Last Days of Socrates": Penguin, 2003

Ulansey, David . "The Origins of the Mithraic Mysteries": Oxford Press, 1989

Vermes, Geza . "The Complete Dead Sea Scrolls In English": Penguin, 2004

Vernant, Jean-Pierre. "The Universe, the Gods, and Mortals": Profile Books, 2002

Waterfield, Robin Lane. "Herodotus The Histories": Oxford Classics, c 430 BCE

Wellesy, Kenneth. "Tacitus, The Histories": Penguin, 1995

Whiston, William. "Josephus, The Complete Works": Nelson, 1998

Williamson, G. A. . "Eusebius: The History of the Church": Penguin, 1989

Wilson, Ian . "Jesus the Evidence": Book Club Asc., 1984

Wolffe, John. "Religion In History": Open University, 2004

Wood, Michael. "In Search of the Dark Ages": BBC Books, 1981

Yonge, C D. "The Works Of Philo": Hendrikson, 2006

Zeitlin, Irving M . "The Historical Muhammad": Zenith, 2007

65 — Wells, G.A., "Who was Jesus "—